THE SOHO BIBLIOGRAPHIES

XIX

E. M. FORSTER

THE SOHO BIBLIOGRAPHIES

E. M. Forster, 1950

A BIBLIOGRAPHY OF
E. M. FORSTER

B. J. KIRKPATRICK

With a Foreword by

E. M. FORSTER

RUPERT HART-DAVIS

SOHO SQUARE LONDON

1965

Printed in Great Britain by Richard Clay (The Chaucer Press), Ltd.,
Bungay, Suffolk

CONTENTS

v

ILLUSTRATIONS

FOREWORD

It has been such a pleasure to watch Miss Kirkpatrick at her work and to give her what help I could. Her energy and patience, her accuracy and insight have all impressed me greatly.

Critics have sometimes said—and have sometimes intended it as a compliment—that I have written very little. They must change their tune now. I shall certainly change mine. The longer one lives the less one feels to have done, and I am both surprised and glad to discover from this bibliography that I have written so much.

E. M. FORSTER

PREFACE

The intention of this bibliography is to include all the published work of E. M. Forster, although not all his signed and unsigned contributions to periodicals and newspapers have been traced. Clippings of the following have been seen but the sources not found:

Abbey Theatre—Dublin (under this general heading a review of *Things that are Caesar's*, by Paul Vincent Carroll, performed at the Abbey Theatre, Dublin in August 1932 and at the Arts Theatre, London, the following month; this is a review of the former production. Seen in proof, signed E. M. Forster, and dated 12.9.32; from a periodical)

What Are You Like? The Question that Puzzles Your Friends (based on *Three Plays*, by L. Pirandello published by Dent in October 1923; probably from a periodical)

Review of *Anglo-Indian Studies*, by S. M. Mitra (published by Longmans, Green in August 1913; probably from a periodical)

Review of *Scenes and Portraits*, by Frederick Manning (review of the edition published by Peter Davies in December 1930; from a newspaper)

It is thought that the following appeared in the *Egyptian Mail* between 1916 and 1919:*

Between the Sun and the Moon (*See Pharos and Pharillon*, A9)

* The British Museum's file of the *Egyptian Mail* for the years 1916–19 is incomplete, as is that of the National Library, Cairo; the latter was able to supply on microfilm some of the former's missing numbers.

The Den (there are two articles with this title, the first of
which appeared in the *Egyptian Mail*, 30 December
1917 and was reprinted in *Pharos and Pharillon. See*
A9, C64)

Eliza in Egypt (three articles. *See* A9)

A Little Trip (*See* 'Philo's Little Trip' in *Pharos and
Pharillon*, A9)

Royalty

Shakespeare and Egypt

It is also thought that 'Hymn Before Action' published in
Abinger Harvest, 1936, first appeared in a journal; it is dated
1912, and should, according to the acknowledgments, have
appeared in the *Oxford and Cambridge Review*. Information
on these and any other omissions will be welcomed.* E. M.
Forster has contributed a 'Prefatory Note' to the *Collected
Stories*, by Frank Sargeson due for publication by Blackwood & Janet Paul, Auckland, NZ, in November 1964.

Full bibliographical information is recorded on first
English and American editions in Section A; information
on later editions is much less detailed and in most cases is
very brief. In all these entries blank pages are included in
the total pagination if integral. Where a dust-jacket has not
been seen and where it is reasonably certain that the book
was published with one its assumed presence is noted
merely with 'Dust-jacket'.

Only the first English and American publications of a
contribution to a periodical or newspaper are recorded. Note
has been made of revisions unless they are slight; this ex-

---

* For material on E. M. Forster reference should be made to 'E. M.
Forster: An Annotated Checklist of Writings About Him', compiled
and edited by Helmut E. Gerber, in *English Fiction in Transition*
(*1880–1920*), Spring 1959, Vol. 2, leaves 4–27, published by the
English Department, Purdue University, Indiana, and to 'Criticism of
E. M. Forster: A Selected Checklist', by Martin Beebe and Joseph
Brogunier, in *Modern Fiction Studies*, 1961, Vol. 7, No. 3, pp. 284–292.
Gerber's checklist is being kept up-to-date in later volumes of *English
Fiction in Transition*, now entitled *English Literature in Transition*.

cludes the small variations which usually occurred between an essay published almost simultaneously in an English and American periodical. Essays and short stories later reprinted in anthologies, apart from the author's own collections, have not been included. The contents-notes to these collections do not give the earlier history of the essays and short stories, as this is recorded in Section C; where this information is required, reference should be made to the Index in the first instance. It has not been thought necessary to record pre-publication extracts from E. M. Forster's works in publishers' house journals such as *Everyman* and the *Periodical*.

A few holograph manuscripts are now in libraries; their location, where known, is recorded under the entry for the work concerned. The dates of first stage productions, broadcast and television transmissions of E. M. Forster's works have also been noted under the entry for the work itself.

Works marked with an asterisk have not been seen personally.

This bibliography was to have been compiled originally by Mr O. G. W. Stallybrass. When, at his suggestion, I undertook it he made freely available to me his prepared *Checklist* together with the notes he had already gathered. I am particularly indebted to him for the immense amount of work he did on the periodical and newspaper contributions which has been incorporated in this bibliography, and for his continuous interest, up to the reading of proofs.

My main debt is to Mr Forster for his permission to undertake the bibliography, for his great patience and kindness throughout its preparation, for giving me repeated access to his library, for the loan of material, and for adding so much to my pleasures as a bibliographer.

I also owe a great deal to many individuals and libraries, publishers and printers, a number of whose names I am unable to record. In particular, I wish to thank Mr David H. Stam and Professor Donald Gallup for help with American material, Miss M. E. Holloway for help with proofs, Miss Virginia Warren for supplying descriptions of some dust-jackets, and Mr Leonard Woolf for information on some of the Hogarth Press editions. To Mr John Hayward, I owe a special debt for his much appreciated guidance and criticism.

I am grateful to the following for help in various ways: Miss M. E. Barber, Secretary of the Society of Authors, Mr Paul Cadmus, Mr Paul Vincent Carroll, Mrs Louis Henry Cohn, Mr W. T. Dear, General Manager, Stillwell, Darby & Co. Ltd, Mr Mikhaïlo Djordjevič, Mr Hideo Funado, Miss Joan Greaves, Mr Rupert Hart-Davis, Professor H. W. Häusermann, Mr John Lehmann, Miss Judith Masterman, Secretary to the Keynes Memorial Committee, Mr Genichi Muraoka, Mr Bertram Rota, Dr F. Taylor, Assistant Cultural Attaché, British Embassy, Cairo, Mr Harvey Taylor, Professor Lionel Trilling, Mme Sophia Wadia, Miss Jean Whyte.

Of the many librarians who gave assistance, I must first thank Dr A. N. L. Munby, Fellow and Librarian of King's College, Cambridge, for his unremitting interest and for drawing my attention to items I might otherwise have missed, and Mr Donald Loukes, Assistant Librarian; Mrs Ann Bowden, and her successor as Librarian, Mrs Mary M. Hirth, of the Academic Center, University of Texas; Mr D. G. Neill of the Bodleian Library; Mr R. L. Collison, Librarian of the BBC; Director I. Hatsukade, Division for Interlibrary Services, National Diet Library, Tokyo; Miss Agnes N. Tysse, Reference Librarian, University of Michigan; and the staffs of the Biblioteca Nazionale Centrale, Rome, British Council in Athens and Rio de Janeiro, British Museum, Cambridge University Library, the Houghton Library, Harvard University, Library of Congress, National Library, Cairo, National Central Library, London, New York Public Library, Programme Index, BBC, University of London Library, University of Pennsylvania Library, and Yale University Library.

Publishers have necessarily provided a great deal of information, especially Mr E. A. Hamilton of Edward Arnold (Publishers) Ltd, Miss Margaret Mary McQuillan of Harcourt, Brace & World, Inc., Mr William Holden of William Heinemann Ltd, Miss Anne Davidson of the Hogarth Press, Mr William A. Koshland of Alfred A. Knopf, Inc., Mr H. Summers of Penguin Books Ltd, Mr Walter J. Minton of G. P. Putnam's Sons, Mr J. S. Knapp-Fisher of Sidgwick & Jackson Ltd, and Mr Brian Thynne of Walter & Whitehead Ltd.

Acknowledgments are also made to Miss Hilda M. McGill, Great Hall Librarian, Manchester Public Libraries, and Mr F. B. Singleton, Librarian of the *Guardian*, for help with contributions to the *Manchester Guardian*; and to Mr Jeremy Potter of the *New Statesman* and the Editor of *The Listener*, for permission to identify anonymous contributions.

September 1964   B. J. KIRKPATRICK

A. BOOKS AND PAMPHLETS

B

O Opposite the Volterra gate of Monteriano, outside the city, is a very respectable white washed mud wall, with a coping of red crinkled tiles to keep it from dissolution. It would give an idea of a gentleman's garden, if there was not a large hole in its middle, which grows larger with every rain storm. Through this hole is visible firstly the iron gate that is intended to close it, which has at last become so small that everyone walks round rather than through.

secondly a square piece of ground, which though not quite mud is at the same time not exactly grass: and finally another wall, stone this time, which has a wooden door in the middle, and two wooden shuttered windows each side, apparently forming the facade of a one story house.

This door is always shut, and the door key is a quarter of a yard long. This house is bigger than it looks, for it slides for two stories down the hill behind, and the wooden door, which is always locked, really leads into the attic. The knowing person prefers to follow the presumptuous mule track round the turn of the mud wall, till he can take the edifice in the rear. Then — being now on a level with the cellars — he lifts up his head and shouts. If his voice sounds like something light — a letter for example, or some vegetable, or

Manuscript of *Where Angels Fear to Tread*,
opening paragraphs of Chapter 3.

A1 WHERE ANGELS FEAR TO TREAD 1905

a. First edition:

Where Angels | *Fear to Tread* | BY | E. M. FORSTER | WILLIAM BLACKWOOD AND SONS | EDINBURGH AND LONDON | MCMV | *All Rights reserved*

Crown 8vo. [iv], 320 pp. 7½ × 4⅞ in.

P. [i] half-title; p. [ii] blank; p. [iii] title; p. [iv] blank; pp. [1]–319 text; p. 319 at foot: PRINTED BY WILLIAM BLACKWOOD AND SONS.; p. [320] blank. 32 pp. publisher's advertisements, inserted.

Slate-blue cloth boards; lettered in gold on spine: Where | Angels | fear | to | tread | E. M. | FORSTER | Wᴹ BLACKWOOD & SONS | EDINBURGH & LONDON, and in black on upper cover: [*within a compartment, within a rule:*] Where | Angels | fear | to | tread | E. M. | FORSTER; edges trimmed; ruby end-papers. Dust-jacket.

Published *c.* 4 October 1905; 1050 copies printed. 6*s.*

There was a second impression of 526 copies in January 1906.

The inserted advertisements exist in at least three forms. It is probable that copies containing the first form are those which record in the publisher's advertisements: p. [1] Third Impression of *The Edge of Circumstance*, by Edward Noble announced—p. [3] at foot, *Matriculation Roll of St Andrews University*, edited by J. Maitland Anderson announced as in the press—p. 12 no work by E. M. Forster listed—p. 32 at foot, dated: 5/05. The second form records on these pages: p. [1] entitled Catalogue of Messrs Blackwood & Sons' Publications —p. [3] at foot, *Matriculation Roll of St Andrews University* advertised at 18*s.*—p. 12 *Where Angels Fear to Tread* advertised at 6*s.*—p. 32 at foot, dated 5/05. The third form records information similar to the second form on these pages except for p. 32, which is dated at foot: 10/05. *Points 1874–1930*, by Percy H. Muir, London, Constable, 1931, p. 114 notes two 'issues'.

A copy in red cloth with similar lettering to that noted above is in the library of Mr G. L. Lazarus; it is probably a trial binding. The details noted for the publisher's advertisements, first form, apply to Mr Lazarus's copy.

Dramatized by Elizabeth Hart and first performed at the Arts Theatre, Cambridge, on 28 May 1963 and later at the Arts Theatre, London, on 6 June 1963. Scenes from the London production were televised by the BBC on 29 October 1963. Adapted by Cynthia Pughe and broadcast in the Home Service on 29 August 1964.

The holograph manuscript, entitled *Monteriano*, is in the library of King's College, Cambridge.

b. First American edition. *1920*:

Where Angels Fear | *to Tread* | *By E. M. Forster* | [*publisher's device of a greyhound running on a black ground*, $\frac{5}{8} \times 1$ *in.*] | *New York* | *Alfred · A · Knopf* | *1920*

Crown 8vo. 286 pp. $7\frac{3}{8} \times 5$ in.

P. [1] half-title; p. [2] list of new Borzoi novels; p. [3] title; p. [4] at head: COPYRIGHT, 1920, BY | ALFRED A. KNOPF, INC., at foot: PRINTED IN THE UNITED STATES OF AMERICA; p. [5] fly-title; p. [6] blank; pp. 7–283 text; pp. [284–286] blank, integral.

Orange cloth boards; lettered in black on spine: [*double rule, thick, thin across head*] | WHERE | ANGELS | FEAR · TO | · TREAD· | [*rule*] | FORSTER | [*rule*] | [*triangular design*, $\frac{3}{4} \times 1$ *in.*] | ALFRED A · KNOPF, on upper cover: [*long double rule, thick, thin*] | WHERE · ANGELS · FEAR · TO · TREAD | [*long rule*] | E· M· FORSTER | [*short rule*] | [*triangular design*, $1\frac{1}{8} \times 1\frac{3}{8}$ *in.*]; publisher's device on a black ground on lower cover; edges trimmed, top brown; cream end-papers. Dust-jacket.

Published 10 January 1920; 2630 copies printed. $2.

It is possible that sheets were supplied to Arnold in 1920. *See* A1c. There were further printings of 1000 copies in May and October 1943 and July 1944, 1100 in May 1945, 1000 in December 1947, and 1500 in March 1950.

The Sun Dial Library issued a reprint of 10,000 copies in 1929 at $1. It has not been possible to confirm this print figure recorded in the *Publishers' Weekly*, 25 September 1943, pp. 1161–1162.

c. Second English edition (*Uniform Edition*). [*1924*]:

[*within a double rule:*] WHERE ANGELS | FEAR TO TREAD | [*double rule*] | E. M. FORSTER | [*ornament*]

| *[double rule]* | LONDON: EDWARD ARNOLD & CO.

Small crown 8vo. 256 pp. 7¼ × 4¾ in.

Maroon cloth boards; lettered in gold on spine with ornamental design and a triple rule across head and foot; triple rule in blind round upper cover; edges trimmed; white end-papers. Dust-jacket.

Published 1 July 1924 as the *Uniform Edition*; 2000 copies printed. 5s.

The note on p. [4] describes the *Uniform Edition* as available in cloth or leather binding; the publishers have no record of any copies in leather, and no such copies have been seen.

The publication note on p. [7] records '... Reprinted.... 1920 ...'. The first American edition was published in 1920, and it is possible that sheets were supplied to Arnold by Knopf, although neither publisher now has a record of such a transaction. There is no record of any sheets being taken over by Arnold from William Blackwood.

There were further printings of 1000 copies in February 1937, July 1942, and April 1944.

d. Third English edition (Pocket Edition). [*1947*]:

[*title as above; imprint:*] LONDON | EDWARD ARNOLD & CO.

Royal 16mo. 208 pp. 6½ × 4 in.

Published 23 October 1947 as the *Pocket Edition*; 10,000 copies printed. 6s.

There were further printings of 6000 copies in April 1953, and 5000 in March 1959.

e. Second American edition (Vintage Books). *1958*:

[*title as above; imprint:*] VINTAGE BOOKS NEW YORK | 1958

Small crown 8vo. [iv], 188 pp. 7¼ × 4¼ in.

Published 3 January 1958 as *Vintage Books*, Vol. K61; 15,000 copies printed. 95 cents.

There were further printings of 7500 copies in October 1959, 2800 in January 1961, 5000 in May 1961, and 6000 in September 1961.

f. Fourth English edition (Penguin Books). [1959]:

Foolscap 8vo. 160 pp. 7 × 4⅜ in.

Published 26 March 1959 as *Penguin Books*, Vol. 1344; 30,000 copies printed. 2s. 6d.

There was a further printing of 30,000 copies in May 1960. There was an additional printing, issued in *Penguin Modern Classics*, of 17,500 copies in August 1962.

A2   THE LONGEST JOURNEY   1907

a. First edition:

The Longest Journey | BY | E. M. FORSTER | AUTHOR OF 'WHERE ANGELS FEAR TO TREAD' | WILLIAM BLACKWOOD AND SONS | EDINBURGH AND LONDON | MCMVII | *All Rights reserved*

Crown 8vo. [viii], 360 pp. 7⅜ × 4⅞ in.

P. [i] half-title; p. [ii] blank; p. [iii] title; p. [iv] blank; p. [v] at centre, dedication: FRATRIBUS.; p. [vi] blank; p. [vii] Contents; p. [viii] blank; pp. [1]–360 text; p. 360 at foot: PRINTED BY WILLIAM BLACKWOOD AND SONS.

Dark green cloth boards; lettered in gold on spine: THE | LONGEST | JOURNEY | [*three ornaments*] | E. M. | FORSTER | W. BLACKWOOD & SONS | EDINBURGH & LONDON, and on upper cover: "The Longest Journey." | [*wavy line*]; edges trimmed; white end-papers. Powder-blue dust-jacket printed in pale navy-blue.

Published 8 April 1907; 1587 copies printed. 6s.

There was a second impression of 525 copies in June 1907.
Dramatized by Lance Sieveking and broadcast in the Home Service on 4 March 1957.

b. First American edition. 1922:

[*in pale orange:*] The Longest Journey | [*in black:*] By E. M. *Forster* | [*in pale orange: publisher's device of a greyhound running,* ⅝ × 1 *in.*] | [*in black:*] New York | Alfred · A · Knopf | *1922*

Crown 8vo. 328 pp. 7⅜ × 5 in.

P. [1] half-title; p. [2] list of works by the author; p. [3] title; p. [4] at head: COPYRIGHT, 1922, BY | ALFRED A. KNOPF, INC. | *Published, March, 1922*, at foot, printer's imprint, paper manufacturer's and binder's names; p. [5] at centre, dedication; p. [6] blank; p. [7] Contents; p. [8] blank; p. [9] section-title; p. [10] blank; pp. 11–167 text; p. [168] blank; p. [169] section-title; p. [170] blank; pp. 171–260 text; p. [261] section-title; p. [262] blank; pp. 263–327 text; p. [328] blank.

Orange cloth boards; lettered in black on spine: [*double rule, thick, thin at head*] | [*ornament*] THE [*ornament*] | LONGEST | JOURNEY | [*rule*] | FORSTER | [*rule*] | [*triangular design*, $\frac{3}{4} \times 1$ *in.*] | ALFRED~A~KNOPF, and on upper cover: [*double rule, thick, thin*] | THE · LONGEST · JOURNEY | [*rule*] | E · M · FORSTER | [*short rule*] | [*triangular ornament* $1\frac{1}{8} \times 1\frac{3}{8}$ *in.*]; publisher's device on a black ground on lower cover; edges trimmed, top dark grey; white end-papers. Dust-jacket.

Published 9 March 1922; 2100 copies printed. $2.50.

The publishers state that their records show that this work was first published by them in 1920. No further evidence for this has been found and it is not recorded in the *Catalogue* [*sic*] *of Copyright Entries* of the Library of Congress. The copyright date on the verso of the title is given as 1922.

It is possible that sheets were supplied to Arnold in 1922. *See* A2c.

There were further printings of 2000 copies in December 1952, and 1500 in June 1961.

The Sun Dial Library issued a reprint of 10,000 copies in 1930 at $1. New Directions also issued a reprint in their *New Classics Series* of 1500 copies in July 1943 at $1. It has not been possible to confirm these print figures recorded in the *Publishers' Weekly*, 25 September 1943, pp. 1161–1162.

c. Second English edition (Uniform Edition). [*1924*]:

[*within a double rule:*] THE LONGEST | JOURNEY | [*double rule*] | E. M. FORSTER | [*ornament*] | [*double rule*] | LONDON: EDWARD ARNOLD & CO.

Small crown 8vo. 320 pp. $7\frac{1}{4} \times 4\frac{3}{4}$ in.

Maroon cloth boards; lettered in gold on spine with ornamental design and a triple rule across head and foot; triple rule in blind round upper cover; edges trimmed; white end-papers. Dust-jacket.

Published 1 July 1924 as the *Uniform Edition*; 2000 copies printed. 5s.

The note on p. [2] describes the *Uniform Edition* as obtainable in cloth or leather binding; the publishers have no record of any copies in leather, and no such copies have been seen.

There were further printings of 2000 copies in October 1924, 1000 in April 1929, February 1936, January 1939, March 1942 and October 1943, and 2000 in August 1944.

The publication note on p. [6] records '... Reprinted .... 1922 ...'. The first American edition was published in 1922, and it is possible that sheets were supplied to Arnold by Knopf, although neither publisher now has a record of such a transaction. There is no record of sheets being taken over by Arnold from William Blackwood.

d. Third English edition (Pocket Edition). [1947]:

[*title as above; imprint:*] LONDON | EDWARD ARNOLD & CO.

Royal 16mo. 320 pp. $6\frac{1}{2} \times 4$ in.

Published 23 October 1947 as the *Pocket Edition*; 10,000 copies printed. 6s.

There were further printings of 5700 copies in June 1955, and 5000 in May 1962.

e. Fourth English edition (Penguin Books). [1960]:

Foolscap 8vo. 288 pp. $7 \times 4\frac{3}{8}$ in.

Published 29 September 1960 as *Penguin Books*, Vol. 1470; 30,000 copies printed. 3s. 6d.

There was a further printing of 30,000 copies in November 1960.

f. Fifth English edition (World's Classics). 1960:

[*title as above; imprint:*] LONDON | OXFORD UNIVERSITY PRESS | 1960

Demy 16mo. [2], xiv, 336 pp. $5\frac{3}{4} \times 3\frac{3}{4}$ in.

Published 3 November 1960 as the *World's Classics*, Vol. 578; 10,000 copies printed. 7s. 6d.

Pp. [ix]–xiv Introduction by the author.

g. Second American edition (Vintage Books). [1962]:

[*title as above*; *imprint:*] Vintage Books | A DIVISION OF RANDOM HOUSE | *New York*

Small crown 8vo. [viii], 312 pp. 7¼ × 4½ in.

Published 13 September 1962 as *Vintage Books*, Vol. V40; 12,000 copies printed. $1.65.

A3   A ROOM WITH A VIEW   1908

a. First edition:

A ROOM WITH A VIEW | BY | E. M. FORSTER | AUTHOR OF | "THE LONGEST JOURNEY," "WHERE ANGELS FEAR TO TREAD" | LONDON | EDWARD ARNOLD | 1908 | {*All rights reserved*}

Crown 8vo. viii, 324 pp. 7⅜ × 4⅞ in.

P. [i] half-title; p. [ii] blank; p. [iii] title; p. [iv] blank; p. [v] at centre, dedication: To H.O.M. [*i.e. H. O. Meredith*]; p. [vi] blank; pp. vii–viii Contents; p. [1] section-title; p. [2] blank; pp. [3]–122 text; p. [123] section-title; p. [124] blank; pp. 125–324 text; p. 324 at foot: BILLING AND SONS, LIMITED, PRINTERS, GUILDFORD. 8 pp. publisher's advertisements, inserted.

Dark red cloth boards; lettered in gold on spine: A | ROOM | WITH A | VIEW | E. M. | FORSTER | ARNOLD, and on upper cover: A ROOM WITH A VIEW | E. M. FORSTER; top edges trimmed, others rough trimmed; white end-papers. Dark rose-pink dust-jacket, printed in black.

Published 14 October 1908; 2000 copies printed. 6s.

There was a second impression of 500 copies in January 1909 and probably a third in 1911. Sheets were imported from G. P. Putnam's in 1919. *See* A3c.

Dramatized by Stephen Tait and Kenneth Allott and first performed at the Arts Theatre, Cambridge, on 6 February 1950; it was presented on television by Associated-Rediffusion on 2 July 1958. The play was published in 1951. *See* E9a.

Abridged by Arthur Calder-Marshall and read by Gladys Young in 15 instalments in the Home Service between 20 February and 28 May 1952.

b. First American edition. *1911:*

A Room with a View | By | E. M. Forster | Author of "Howards End," etc. | G. P. Putnam's Sons | New York and London | [*in black letter:*] The Knickerbocker Press | 1911

Crown 8vo. [4], viii, 368 pp. $7\frac{1}{2} \times 5$ in.

Pp. [1–3] blank; p. [4] list of works by the author; p. [i] title; p. [ii] at foot: [*in black letter:*] The Knickerbocker Press, New York; p. [iii] at centre, dedication: [*in black letter:*] To | [*in roman:*] H.O.M.; p. [iv] blank; pp. v–vi Contents; p. [vii] fly-title; p. [viii] blank; p. 1 section-title; p. [2] blank; pp. 3–135 text; p. [136] blank; p. 137 section-title; p. [138] blank; pp. 139–364 text; p. [365] publisher's section-title to advertisements; p. [366] blank; pp. [367–368] publisher's advertisements. 4 pp. inserted; pp. [1–2] publisher's advertisements; pp. [3–4] blank.

Brown-pink cloth boards; lettered in gold on spine: A ROOM | WITH A | VIEW | [*short rule*] | FORSTER | PUTNAM, and on upper cover: [*within a rule, within a compartment:*] A ROOM | WITH A | VIEW | [*ornament*] | E. M. | FORSTER; edges trimmed; white end-papers. Dust-jacket.

Published 6 May 1911; 2027 copies printed. $1.35.

The plates were destroyed in February 1916. Two hundred sheets were supplied to Arnold in July 1919. *See A3c.*

c. First American edition—English issue. *1919:*

A Room with a View | By | E. M. Forster | Author of "Howards End," etc. | NEW EDITION | LONDON | EDWARD ARNOLD | 1919 | (*All rights reserved*)

Small crown 8vo. [iv], 366 pp. $7\frac{3}{8} \times 4\frac{3}{4}$ in.

Dull rose cloth boards; lettered in black on spine and on upper cover; edges trimmed; white end-papers. Dust-jacket.

Issued December 1919; 200 copies bound. 6*s.*

The sheets were supplied by G. P. Putnam's.

d. Second American edition. 1923:

[*in orange:*] A Room with a | View | [*in black:*] By E. M.
Forster | [*in orange: publisher's device*] | [*in black:*] New York
| Alfred · A · Knopf | *1923*

Crown 8vo. 320 pp. 7⅜ × 5 in.

Orange cloth boards; lettered in black on spine with triangular design
and rules, and on upper cover; publisher's device on a black ground
on lower cover; edges trimmed, top dark grey; pale cream end-
papers printed in violet and orange. Dust-jacket.

Published 25 January 1923; 2000 copies printed. $2.50.

There were further printings of 1050 copies in April 1923, 2500 in
December 1952, and 1200 in May 1959. Two further printings of
2500 copies in October and December 1925 were issued as *Borzoi
Pocket Books*, Vol. 27 at $1.50.

The Sun Dial Library issued a reprint of 10,000 copies in 1930 at $1.
New Directions also issued a reprint in their *New Classics Series* of
1500 copies in July 1943 at $1.50. It has not been possible to confirm
these print figures recorded in the *Publishers' Weekly*, 25 September
1943, pp. 1161–1162. *See also* 16 October 1943, p. 1518.

e. Second English edition (Uniform Edition). [1924]:

[*title as above; imprint:*] LONDON: EDWARD
ARNOLD & CO.

Small crown 8vo. 256 pp. 7¼ × 4¾ in.

Published 1 July 1924 as the *Uniform Edition*; 2000 copies printed. 5s.

The note on p. [2] describes the *Uniform Edition* as available in cloth
or leather binding; the publishers have no record of copies in leather,
and no such copies have been seen.

There were further printings of 950 copies in April 1928, and 1000 in
April 1931, September 1936, May 1940, January and November 1943,
and June 1944.

f. Third English edition (Services Edition). [1944]:

[*title as above; imprint:*] Published for | THE BRITISH
PUBLISHERS GUILD | by Edward Arnold & Co.,
London

Crown 8vo. 168 pp. 7 × 5¼ in.

Published 5 May 1944 as *Guild Books*, Vol. S117; 15,000 copies printed. No price available.

g. Fourth English edition (Services Edition). [*1945*]:

[*title as above; imprint:*] Published for | THE BRITISH PUBLISHERS GUILD | *by Edward Arnold & Co., London*

Small crown 8vo. 160 pp. 7 × 4¼ in.

Published 19 September 1945 as *Guild Books*, Vol. S117; 30,000 copies printed. No price available.

h. Fifth English Edition (Pocket Edition). [*1947*]:

[*title as above; imprint:*] LONDON | EDWARD ARNOLD & CO.

Royal 16mo. 256 pp. 6⅝ × 4⅛ in.

Published 23 October 1947 as the *Pocket Edition*; 10,000 copies printed. 6s.

There were further printings of 5000 copies in August 1952, June 1958, and May 1962.

i. Sixth English edition (Penguin Books). [*1955*]:

Foolscap 8vo. 224 pp. 7⅛ × 4⅜ in.

Published 26 May 1955 as *Penguin Books*, Vol. 1059; 40,000 copies printed. 2s. 6d.

There was a further printing of 30,000 copies in July 1958. There were additional printings, issued in *Penguin Modern Classics*, of 30,000 copies in May 1961, and 20,000 in October 1962.

j. Third American edition (Vintage Books). [*1960*]:

[*title as above; imprint:*] Vintage Books | A DIVISION OF RANDOM HOUSE | *New York*

Small crown 8vo. [viii], 248 pp. 7⅜ × 4½ in.

Published 12 December 1960 as *Vintage Books*, Vol. V187; 15,000 copies printed. $1.25.

There was a further printing of 5000 copies in November 1961.

A4 HOWARDS END 1910

a. First edition:

HOWARDS END | BY | E. M. FORSTER | *"Only connect..."* | LONDON | EDWARD ARNOLD | 1910 | ⟨*All rights reserved*⟩

Crown 8vo. [iv], 348 pp. $7\frac{1}{2} \times 4\frac{7}{8}$ in.

P. [i] half-title; p. [ii] list of works by the author; p. [iii] title; p. [iv] blank; pp. [1]–343 text; p. 343 at foot: BILLING AND SONS, LTD., PRINTERS, GUILDFORD.; p. [344] blank; pp. [345–348] publisher's advertisements, integral.

Dull red cloth boards; lettered in gold on spine: HOWARDS | END | E. M. | FORSTER | ARNOLD, and on upper cover: HOWARDS END | E. M. FORSTER; top edges trimmed, others rough trimmed or trimmed; white end-papers. Dust-jacket.

Published 18 October 1910; 2500 copies printed. 6s.

There were two issues of the first impression. This, probably the first issue, records on p. [348] *A Stepson of the Soil*, by Mary J. H. Skrine which was published on 7 March 1910. The second issue contains 8 pp. of publisher's advertisements inserted; p. 3 of the advertisements lists the second impression of *A Stepson of the Soil* which was issued in June 1910; the first impression is also noted on p. [348].

There were further impressions of 1000, 3000, and 2500 copies in November 1910, and 1000 in December 1910 (issued in 1911). The publication note on p. [iv] of the November 1924 printing records: '... Reprinted three times .. 1911 ...'. It is, therefore, possible that there were two more printings in 1911; the publisher has no record now of these printings. Sheets were imported from G. P. Putnam's in 1919 and 1922. *See* A4c. There were further printings, issued in the *Uniform Edition*, of 2000 copies in November 1924, 1000 in April 1929, February 1936, January 1939, March 1942 and October 1943, and 2000 in August 1944. The note on the *Uniform Edition* on p. [ii] of the November 1924 printing describes the *Uniform Edition* as available in cloth or leather; the publishers have no record of copies in leather, and no such copies have been seen. There were additional printings, all issued in the *Kingfisher Library*, of 5000 copies in June 1932, 2750 in May 1945, and 5000 in May 1946.

Dramatized by Lance Sieveking and broadcast in 13 instalments in the Home Service between 14 June and 6 September 1964.

b. First American edition. 1910 [i.e. 1911]:

HOWARDS END | BY | E. M. FORSTER |
AUTHOR OF "A ROOM WITH A VIEW," ETC.
| *"Only connect..."* | G. P. PUTNAM'S SONS
| NEW YORK AND LONDON | [*in black letter:*] The
Knickerbocker Press | 1910

Crown 8vo. [2], vi, 424 pp. $7\frac{1}{2} \times 5$ in.

Pp. [1–2] blank; p. [i] title; p. [ii] at centre: COPYRIGHT, 1910 | BY|
G. P. PUTNAM'S SONS, at foot: [*in black letter:*] The Knickerbocker
Press, New York; pp. iii–v Contents; p. [vi] blank; pp. 1–422 text;
pp. [423–424] publisher's advertisements, integral. 6 pp. inserted;
p. [1] publisher's advertisement; pp. [2–6] blank.

Maroon cloth boards; lettered in gold on spine: HOWARDS | END |
[*short rule*] | FORSTER | PUTNAM; edges trimmed; white end-papers.
Dust-jacket.

Published January 1911; 1500 copies printed. $1.35.

There were further printings of 1004 copies in January, 1020 in
February, and 998 in March 1911. Six hundred and fifty copies,
probably of the fourth printing, were supplied to Arnold. *See*
A4c.

There were at least two issues of the first impression. The first is
recorded above. The second issue contains 10 pp. following p. 422:
p. [1] publisher's section-title to advertisements; p. [2] blank; pp.
[3–5] publisher's advertisements; pp. [6–10] blank; of these pp. [5–6,
i.e. pp. 423–424 and leaf 27₄] are integral, pp. [1–4], [7–10] inserted.
The second issue is also lettered in gold on upper cover: [*within a
rule, within a compartment:*] HOWARDS | END | [*ornament*] | E. M. |
FORSTER. Both issues collate: [1]⁴, 1–26⁸, 27⁴, with 2 leaves [*i.e.*
pp. 1–4] of the publisher's advertisements tipped-in between 27₃ and
27₄ in the second issue. Single copies only of these two issues have
been seen, the first in the Library of Congress and the second in the
Bodleian Library.

Putnam's, without the author's approval, supplied titles to all the
chapters and made some alterations to the text. As a result of his
objections, the chapter titles and the chapter running heads were
deleted. Mr Walter J. Minton, President, G. P. Putnam's, writes that
their records show that bills for additional composition were received
in December 1910 and in March 1911 and that from the amount of
composing time, 24 hours, 'it looks as though some alterations were

made to the plates'. It is probable that the contents-pages, chapter titles, and chapter running heads were deleted at the second printing, of which a copy has not been seen; they were deleted by the third printing in February 1911. The bill received in March 1911 probably relates to additional advertisements inserted in the third printing. No textual alterations were made.

The alterations to the text, apart from minor alterations and corrections, are:

(a) Arnold, p. 38, lines 3–6:, "I do hope that you'll come in and have some tea." "I do hope that you'll come in and have some tea. We should be so glad . . ."
Putnam's, p. 47, lines 17–18:, "I do hope that you'll come in and have some tea. We should be so glad . . ."

(b) Arnold, p. 46, line 16: . . .: through it was a bedroom.
Putnam's, p. 57, line 12: . . .; beyond it was a bedroom.

(c) Arnold, p. 55, lines 35–36: ". . . I never knew that the woman who laced too tightly's name was Matheson."
Putnam's, p. 69, lines 25–26: ". . . I never knew that the name of the woman who laced too tightly was Matheson."

(d) Arnold, p. 61, line 5: . . . listened to the talk of Helen and her husband, . . .
Putnam's, p. 76, lines 5–6: . . . listened to the talk of her husband and Helen, . . .

(e) Arnold, p. 62, line 31: . . ., to eat Elvas plums.
Putnam's, p. 78, line 9: . . ., to eat plums.

(f) Arnold, p. 114, lines 12–13: But Tibby, himself a repartee, was unsympathetic, . . .
Putnam's, pp. 142–143, line 33 and line 1: But Tibbie [sic] was unsympathetic, . . .

(g) Arnold, p. 146, lines 12–13: . . . in the house sentiment gathered, a sentiment that was at times personal, . . .
Putnam's, p. 182, lines 14–15: . . . in the house gathered a sentiment that was at times personal, . . .

(h) Arnold, p. 151, lines 35–36: ". . . do you suppose that he understood of it?"
Putnam's, p. 189, lines 13–14: ". . . how much of it do you suppose he understood?"

(i) Arnold, p. 160, line 37: . . . drawing-room looked thus at Howards End?
Putnam's, p. 199, lines 26–27: . . . drawing-room at Howards End looked thus?

(*j*) Arnold, p. 206, lines 30–31: . . . turned out to be in the wrong part of Shropshire, damn it, and though he never damned his own property aloud, . . .

Putnam's, p. 254, lines 11–12: . . . turned out to be in the wrong part of Shropshire, and though he never ran down his own property to others, . . .

(*k*) Arnold, p. 215, line 28: Charles and Albert Fussell . . .

Putnam's, p. 266, line 9: Charles Wilcox and Albert Fussell . . .

(*l*) Arnold, p. 216, line 1: . . . bathing-dresses.

Putnam's, p. 266, line 11: . . . bathing-suits.

(*m*) Arnold, p. 235, line 19: straight real, . . .

Putnam's, p. 290, line 14: . . . straight and real, . . .

(*n*) Arnold, p. 252, line 27: "I don't care a damn what people think!"

Putnam's, p. 311, line 29: "I don't care an iota what people think!"

(*o*) Arnold, p. 270, lines 2–3: Light flooded the drawing-room and the drawing-room furniture . . .

Putnam's, p. 332, lines 18–19: Light flooded the drawing-room furniture . . .

(*p*) Arnold, p. 317, line 15: . . . oozing grease on the gravel rubbish on a pretentious band.

Putnam's, p. 389, lines 26–27: . . . oozing grease on the gravel, a pretentious band.

(*q*) Arnold, p. 335, line 2: . . ., but the law, being made in his image, . . .

Putnam's, p. 412, lines 12–13: . . ., but the law, notwithstanding, . . .

Forster thinks that he may have published a 'disclaimer' in the American Press in connection with this, but it has not been traced. He made reference to the matter in his evidence before the Select Committee on Obscene Publications, *see* the *Report* (E4*a*), p. 18.

The copyright date is 1910. It is possible that Putnam's intended to publish the book in December 1910 and that publication was postponed when Forster's complaint had been received. Putnam's records show that 1500 copies were 'off the press on December 22nd, 1910. And bound stock was delivered before the end of December 1910.' Mr Minton thinks it unlikely that any copies of the first impression were withdrawn; it is, therefore, probable that 1500 copies bearing the unauthorized chapter titles were sold.

c. First American edition—fourth printing—English issue. 1919:

HOWARDS END | BY | E. M. FORSTER |
AUTHOR OF "A ROOM WITH A VIEW," ETC.
| *"Only connect..."* | NEW EDITION | LONDON
| EDWARD ARNOLD | 1919 | (*All rights reserved*)

Small crown 8vo. [iv], 422 pp. $7\frac{3}{8} \times 4\frac{3}{4}$ in.

Dull rose cloth boards; lettered in black on spine and on upper cover; edges trimmed; white end-papers. Dust-jacket.

Issued December 1919; 500 copies bound. *6s.*

The sheets were supplied by G. P. Putnam's; a further 150 sheets were supplied in August 1922 and issued in October 1922.

d. Second American edition. 1921:

[*in orange:*] *Howards End* | [*in black:*] *By E. M. Forster* |
"Only connect..." | [*publisher's device of a greyhound running on a dark orange ground,* $\frac{5}{8} \times 1$ *in.*] | *New York* | *Alfred · A · Knopf* | *1921*

Crown 8vo. [iv], 396 pp. $7\frac{1}{2} \times 5$ in.

Orange cloth boards; lettered in black on spine with triangular design, ornaments and rules, and on upper cover; publisher's device on a black ground on lower cover; edges trimmed, top dark grey; cream end-papers. Dust-jacket.

Published 25 January 1921; 2100 copies printed. $2.50.

There were further printings of 1000 copies in May and October 1943, 1500 in May 1944, 1100 in May 1945, and 2000 in June 1946, August 1948, and March 1951.

The Sun Dial Library issued a reprint of 10,000 copies in 1929 at $1. It has not been possible to confirm this print figure recorded in the *Publishers' Weekly*, 25 September 1943, pp. 1161–1162.

The alterations to the text in the first American edition were corrected in this edition and follow the first English edition with the exception of p. 363, lines 19–20: 'motor-cars oozing grease on the gravel, rubbish on a pretentious band.' where a comma has been inserted after gravel. *See* Arnold, p. 317, line 15 noted in A4*b*.

e. Second English edition (Penguin Books). [1941]:

Foolscap 8vo. 288 pp. 7⅛ × 4⅜ in.

Published 7 February 1941 as *Penguin Books*, Vol. 311; 55,000 copies printed. 6*d*.

There was a further printing of 55,000 copies in October 1941.

f. Third English edition (Penguin Books). 1943*:

Foolscap 8vo. 256 pp. 7⅛ × 4⅜ in.

Published February 1943 as *Penguin Books*, Vol. 311; 60,000 copies printed. 6*d*.

There was a further printing of 85,000 copies in February 1946.

g. Fourth English edition (Pocket Edition). [1947]:

[*title as above; imprint:*] LONDON | EDWARD ARNOLD & CO.

Royal 16mo. [iv], 364 pp. 6½ × 4 in.

Published 23 October 1947 as the *Pocket Edition*; 10,000 copies printed. 6*s*.

There were further printings of 5000 copies in March 1951, 5645 in April 1956, and 5000 in May 1960.

h. Fifth English edition (Penguin Books). [1950]:

[*title:*] Howard's | End

Foolscap 8vo. 304 pp. 7⅛ × 4⅜ in.

Published 19 May 1950 as *Penguin Books*, Vol. 311; 40,000 copies printed. 1*s*. 6*d*.

There were further printings of 50,000 copies in March 1953, 40,000 in April 1957, and 30,000 in April 1960. There was an additional printing, issued in the *Penguin Modern Classics*, of 30,000 copies in September 1961.

i. Third American edition (Vintage Books). 1954:

[*title as above; imprint:*] VINTAGE BOOKS NEW YORK | 1954

Small crown 8vo. [vi], 346 pp. 7¼ × 4¼ in.

Published 22 June 1954 as *Vintage Books*, Vol. K7; 16,000 copies printed. 95 cents.

There were further printings of 7500 copies in November 1954, 7600 in September 1955, 10,000 in March 1956, 8000 in January 1958, 10,000 in February 1958 and October 1959, 9500 in November 1960, 10,000 in January 1961, 11,000 in September 1961, and 8000 in September 1962.

A5   THE CELESTIAL OMNIBUS   1911

a. First edition:

The Celestial Omnibus | and other Stories: by E. M. Forster | London: Sidgwick & Jackson Ltd. | Adam Street, Adelphi, W.C. 1911.

Crown 8vo. [viii], 168 pp. $7\frac{3}{8} \times 5\frac{1}{4}$ in.

P. [i] half-title; p. [ii] list of works by the author; p. [iii] title; p. [iv] at centre: *All rights reserved*; p. [v] at centre, dedication: TO THE MEMORY OF THE | INDEPENDENT REVIEW; p. [vi] acknowledgments; p. [vii] Contents; p. [viii] blank; pp. 1–[164] text; p. [164] at foot: CHISWICK PRESS: PRINTED BY CHARLES WHITTINGHAM AND CO. | TOOKS COURT, CHANCERY LANE, LONDON.; p. [165] publisher's monogram, at foot: [*square bracket*] P.T.O.; pp. [166–168] publisher's advertisements, integral.

Pale brown cloth boards; lettered in gold on spine: [*triple rule across head*] | THE | CELESTIAL | OMNIBUS | E. M. | FORSTER | SIDGWICK | & JACKSON | [*triple rule across foot*], and on upper cover: [*within an overall ornamental design in gold, $7\frac{1}{8} \times 4\frac{7}{8}$ in.:*] THE | CELESTIAL | OMNIBUS | E. M. FORSTER; publisher's device of a building in blind on lower cover; edges trimmed, top gilt; pale grey pictorial end-papers, printed in darker grey, designed by Roger Fry, entitled: Practical Culture Imperial Culture.

Published 11 May 1911; 1000 copies printed. 3s. 6d.

There was a second impression of either 1000 or 1500 copies in 1912; lettered in black on spine and on upper cover, top edges trimmed, others rough trimmed. There were two further printings from stereotype of probably 4300 copies in August 1923, 2000 of which were supplied to Knopf, and 2000 copies in 1927, 500 of which were supplied to Knopf. *See* A5*b*.

These short stories were republished with those in *The Eternal Moment* as *The Collected Tales* in 1947. *See* A13, A26.

Contents: The Story of a Panic—The Other Side of the Hedge—The Celestial Omnibus—Other Kingdom—The Curate's Friend—The Road from Colonus.

b. First edition—third printing—American issue. 1923:

The Celestial Omnibus | and other Stories: by E. M. Forster | [*publisher's device of a greyhound running, $\frac{5}{8} \times 1$ in.*] | New York: Alfred A. Knopf 1923

Crown 8vo. [viii], 164 pp. $7\frac{3}{8} \times 5$ in.

P. [i] half-title; p. [ii] list of works by the author; p. [iii] title; p. [iv] MADE AND PRINTED IN GREAT BRITAIN; p. [v] dedication; p. [vi] acknowledgments; p. [vii] Contents; p. [viii] blank; pp. 1–[164] text.

Orange cloth boards; lettered in black on spine: [*double rule, thick, thin at head*] | +THE+ | CELESTIAL | OMNIBUS | [*rule*] | FORSTER | [*rule*] | [*triangular design*] | ALFRED A · KNOPF, and on upper cover: [*long double rule, thick, thin*] | THE · CELESTIAL · OMNIBUS | [*long rule*] | E · M · FORSTER | [*short rule*] | [*triangular design*]; publisher's device on a black ground on lower cover; edges trimmed, top dark grey; cream end-papers printed in deep cream, pale orange and purple in a leaf design. Dust-jacket.

Issued 11 July 1923; 1000 or 1040 copies bound. $2.

The sheets were supplied by Sidgwick & Jackson, who supplied a further 500 sheets in August and November 1923, and June 1927.

A6   THE STORY OF THE SIREN   1920

First edition:

THE STORY OF | THE SIREN | BY | E. M. FORSTER | [*illustration of three leaves, $\frac{3}{8} \times \frac{3}{8}$ in.*] | *Printed by Leonard & Virginia Woolf at* | *The Hogarth Press, Paradise Road, Richmond* | 1920

Small royal 8vo. 16 pp. $9\frac{1}{4} \times 5\frac{5}{8}$ in. Wrappers $9\frac{1}{2} \times 5\frac{3}{4}$ in. There is a variation of $\frac{1}{8}$ in. both ways in these two measurements.

Pp. [1–2] blank; p. [3] title; p. [4] blank; pp. 5–14 text; p. [15] publisher's advertisement; p. [16] blank.

White thin paper wrappers marbled either in bright blue or in green, pale grey and orange with edges turned under; white printed paper label on upper cover; fore edges rough trimmed, top uncut, bottom trimmed; wrappers lined with paper to form paste-down end-papers; gummed, single staple at centre.

Published *c.* 2 July 1920; 500 copies printed. *2s. 6d.*

The white printed paper label on the upper wrapper appears in at least three states: (1) label edged in dull gold, $1\frac{7}{8} \times 4\frac{1}{8}$ in., printed in black: [*within a triple frame in gold:*] THE STORY OF THE | SIREN | E. M. FORSTER —(2) label edged in dull gold, $1\frac{7}{8} \times 4\frac{1}{8}$ in., printed in black: [*within a triple frame in gold:*] THE STORY | OF THE SIREN | E. M. FORSTER—(3) plain label, $1–1\frac{5}{8} \times 2\frac{3}{4}$ in. or $1 \times 3\frac{3}{4}$ in., printed in black: THE STORY OF THE SIREN | E. M. FORSTER. Mr Leonard Woolf states that copies with the label noted as (1) above are probably the first state and that no significance should be attached to the two colours of the wrappers, though there were probably more blue than green. There is some variation in the shade of blue.

The story was not published separately in the United States. It was reprinted in the *Atlantic Monthly*, October 1923, Vol. 132, pp. 455–459, in *The Eternal Moment* and in *The Collected Tales*. *See* A13, A26.

Adapted and broadcast in the Third Programme on 13 August 1947.

A7   EGYPT   [1920]

First edition:

[*title on upper wrapper within a rule:*] THE GOVERN-MENT OF EGYPT | *Recommendations by a Committee of the* | *International Section of the Labour* | *Research Department, with Notes on* | E G Y P T *by* E. M. F O R S T E R | Published by the Labour Research Department, | 39, Eccleston Square, S.W.1. Price 6d.

Large 8vo. 12 pp. $8\frac{3}{4} \times 6$ in.

Pp. [1]–2 Recommendations on the Government of Egypt; pp. 3–12 text; p. 12 at foot: Co-operative Printing Society Limited, Tudor Street, New Bridge Street, London, E.C.4.

Pale blue-grey stiff paper wrappers; white paper label on upper wrapper, $2\frac{1}{2} \times 4\frac{1}{8}$ in., printed as above; edges cut flush; stapled.

Published between 2 July and 6 August 1920; not less than 1000 copies printed, probably about 5000. *6d.*

Professor Lionel Trilling in his *E. M. Forster*, London, Hogarth Press, [1944], p. 120, records in a footnote: 'The 1921 edition of the pamphlet bears the imprint, "The Fabian Research Department."' Professor Trilling has confirmed that the imprints and date of the two copies he is likely to have used do not, in fact, vary from that recorded above.

A8   ALEXANDRIA   1922

a. First edition:

ALEXANDRIA: | A HISTORY AND A GUIDE | *By* | E. M. FORSTER, M.A. CANTAB. | [*four line quotation from Ibn Dukmak, two line quotation from Plotinus*] | ALEXANDRIA: | WHITEHEAD MORRIS LIMITED | [*short rule*] | 1922.

Small crown 8vo. [6], x, 228 pp. maps, plans; folding plan facing p. 144; folding maps facing p. 98 and in pocket at end. $7\frac{1}{4} \times 4\frac{3}{4}$ in.

P. [1] half-title; p. [2] list of works by the author; p. [3] at centre, dedication: *G.H.L.* [*i.e. G. H. Ludolf*]; p. [4] map; p. [5] title; p. [6] blank; pp. [i]–ii Preface; pp. iii–vi Authorities; pp. vii–x Contents; pp. [5]–11 text; pp. 12–13 genealogical table; pp. 14–37 text; pp. 38–39 maps; pp. 40–42 text; pp. 44–57 text; pp. 60–78 text; pp. 80–82 text; p. 83 plan; p. 84 text; pp. 86–98 text; pp. 102–107 text; p. 108 plan; pp. 109–121 text; pp. 124–126 text; p. 127 plan; pp. 128–130 text; p. 131 plan; pp. 132–133 text; pp. 134–135 plans; pp. 136–140 text; pp. 142–148 text; p. 149 plan; pp. 150–152 text; pp. 154–157 text; pp. 160–167 text; pp. 170–172 text; p. 174 map; pp. 175–177 text; p. 178 map; pp. 179–188 text; pp. 190–192 text; p. 193 map; pp. 194–195 text; pp. 196–197 plans; pp. 198–201 text; pp. 202–203 plans; pp. 204–209 text; pp. 211–218 appendices; pp. [219]–227 Index of Main References. Blank pages and section-titles are omitted in this entry and in A8*c*.

Buff paper boards; printed in pale navy-blue up the spine: ALEXANDRIA: A HISTORY AND A GUIDE.—FORSTER., and on upper cover: ALEXANDRIA: | A HISTORY AND A GUIDE | FORSTER.; edges trimmed; white end-papers.

Published 1922; no record of the number of copies printed. *7s. 6d.*

In some copies the plan facing p. 144 is incorrectly placed to face p. 44.

Messrs Walter & Whitehead Ltd write '. . . a very large proportion of the original edition was destroyed by fire in our warehouse . . . Also unfortunately all our London records were destroyed in the blitz and the Egyptian branch was sold at the end of the war . . .'

The guide was obtainable in England from Whitehead Morris Ltd, 9–10 Fenchurch Street, London, E.C., and at Francis Birrell and David Garnett's bookshop, 30 Gerrard Street, London, W.1.

b. Second English edition. 1938:

[*title as above; imprint:*] ALEXANDRIA: | WHITE-HEAD MORRIS LIMITED | [*short rule*] | 1938

Large crown 8vo. [8*], xii, 220 pp. maps, plans; 2 folding plans facing pp. 136, 154; 2 maps, facing p. 90 and tipped-in inside lower cover; 7 plates facing pp. 15, 42, 96, 99, 112, 144 and between pp. 60 and 61. 8 × 5¼ in.

Published 1938; no record of the number of copies printed. *7s. 6d.*

P. [5*] dedication: *To C.P.C.* [*i.e. C. P. Cavafy*]; pp. [iii–iv] Preface to the Second Edition.

The text is revised. Mr Bertram Rota has a note of a copy, at one time in his stock, carrying a certificate of limitation indicating that 250 copies were signed by the author for the Royal Archaeological Society of Alexandria.

c. First American edition (Anchor Books). 1961:

ALEXANDRIA: | A HISTORY AND A GUIDE | BY | E. M. FORSTER | [*four line quotation from Ibn Dukmak, two line quotation from Plotinus*] | Anchor Books | Doubleday & Company, Inc. | Garden City, New York | 1961

Foolscap 8vo. xxvi, 254 pp. maps, plans. 7⅛ × 4¼ in.

P. [i] half-title; p. [ii] note on the author; p. [iii] list of works by the author; p. [iv] map; p. [v] title; p. [vi] cover designer's name, typographer's name, Library of Congress number, copyright and printer's notes; p. [vii] dedication: To G.H.L.; p. [viii] blank; pp. ix–xiii Contents; p. [xiv] blank; pp. [xv]–xviii Introduction; pp. [xix]–xxi Preface; p. [xxii] blank; pp. [xxiii]–xxvi Authorities; pp. [2–3] plan; pp. [5]–13 text; pp. [14–15] genealogical table; pp. 16–41 text; pp.

[42–43] maps; pp. 44–88 text; p. [89] plan; pp. 90–104 text; pp. [106–107] map; pp. [109]–115 text; p. [116] plan; pp. 117–137 text; p. [138] plan; pp. 139–142 text; p. [143] plan; pp. 144–147 text; pp. [148–149] plans; pp. 150–157 text; pp. [158–159] plans; pp. 160–163 text; p. [164] plan; pp. 165–[186] text; p. [187] map; p. 188 text; p. [189] map; pp. 190–207 text; p. [208] map; pp. 209–211 text; pp. [212–213] plans; pp. 214–217 text; pp. [218–219] plans; pp. 220–226 text; pp. [227]–236 appendices; pp. [237]–243 Index; pp. [245–254] publisher's advertisements, integral.

White stiff paper pictorial wrappers printed in black, yellow, pale bronze-green and sky-blue; edges cut flush; gummed.

Published 20 January 1961 as *Anchor Books*, Vol. 231; 20,000 copies printed. 95 cents.

There was a second printing of 20,000 copies in July 1961.

The text follows the first edition; the Introduction is new.

Distributed in England first by the Mayflower Publishing Co. Ltd at 8s. and later by TABS, (Transatlantic Book Service Ltd) and W. H. Allen at 7s. 6d.

A9   PHAROS AND PHARILLON   1923

a. First edition:

PHAROS AND | PHARILLON | E. M. FORSTER | PRINTED AND PUBLISHED BY LEONARD | AND VIRGINIA WOOLF AT THE HOGARTH | PRESS HOGARTH HOUSE PARADISE ROAD | RICHMOND SURREY 1923

Small demy 8vo. 80 pp. $8\frac{1}{2} \times 5\frac{1}{2}$ in. There is a variation of $\frac{1}{8}-\frac{1}{4}$ in. in these measurements.

P. [1] title; p. [2] blank; p. [3] dedication: Ἑρμῇ ψυχοπομπῷ; p. 4 acknowledgments; p. 5 Contents; p. [6] blank; pp. 7–8 Introduction; p. [9] section-title; p. [10] blank; pp. 11–45 text; p. 46 poem by C. P. Cavafy; p. [47] section-title; p. [48] blank; pp. 49–80 text.

White paper boards printed in Cambridge-blue shot through with royal-blue, with bright blue cloth spine; white printed paper label, $1\frac{5}{8} \times \frac{3}{4}$ in. (there is a variation of $\frac{1}{4}-\frac{5}{8}$ in. in these measurements) on spine: [*rule*] | PHAROS | AND | PHARILLON | [*ornament*] | E. M. | FORSTER | [*rule*]; edges trimmed, or top trimmed, fore and bottom edges rough trimmed; white end-papers, upper free end-paper, verso, list of works by the author, lower free end-paper, recto, publisher's advertisements. Probably no dust-jacket.

Published 15 May 1923; c. 900 copies printed. 5s.

The paper-covered boards appear in two states, Cambridge-blue shot through with the royal-blue: (1) running vertically, top edges trimmed, fore and bottom edges rough trimmed; cloth spine overlaps c. ½ in.—(2) running horizontally, edges trimmed; cloth spine overlaps c. 1 in. Mr Leonard Woolf states that no priority should be assigned to these two states.

Contents: Pharos: Pharos—The Return from Siwa—Epiphany—Philo's Little Trip—Clement of Alexandria—St. Athanasius—Timothy the Cat & Timothy Whitebonnet—The God Abandons Antony, by C. P. Cavafy. Pharillon: Eliza in Egypt—Cotton from the Outside—The Den—The Solitary Place—Between the Sun and the Moon—The Poetry of C. P. Cavafy. Conclusion.

b. Second edition. 1923:

PHAROS AND | PHARILLON | E. M. FORSTER | *Second Edition* | PUBLISHED BY LEONARD AND VIRGINIA | WOOLF AT THE HOGARTH PRESS HOGARTH | HOUSE PARADISE ROAD RICHMOND SURREY | 1923

Small crown 8vo. 100 pp. 7⅜ × 4⅞ in.

P. [4] printer's imprint: *Printed in Great Britain by* R. & R. CLARK, LIMITED, *Edinburgh*.

Powder-blue stiff paper wrappers; printed in black on upper wrapper within a frame; edges cut flush; white end-papers; sewn and gummed.

Published June 1923; 1000 copies printed. 3s.

There was a further printing of 1500 copies in March 1926. Four hundred of these were issued with a cancel-title as the 'Third Edition' and dated 1926 in stiff powder-blue wrappers. The remainder, 1100 copies, were issued with a cancel-title as the 'Third Edition' with no date on the title-page in November 1943, in black cloth boards with a turquoise-blue dust-jacket printed in navy-blue.

The contents are similar to the first edition. 'Between the Sun and the Moon' precedes 'The Solitary Place' in this edition.

c. First American edition. 1923:

[*in pale orange:*] Pharos and Pharillon | [*in black:*] By E. M. Forster | [*in pale orange: publisher's device of a greyhound running,* $\frac{5}{8} \times 1$ *in.*] | [*in black:*] New York | Alfred · A · Knopf | *1923*

Crown 8vo. [ii], 126 pp. $7\frac{3}{8} \times 5$ in.

Pp. [i–ii] blank; p. [1] half-title; p. [2] list of works by the author; p. [3] title; p. [4] at head: COPYRIGHT, 1923, BY E. M. FORSTER | *Published July, 1923*, towards foot: *Set up and printed by the Vail-Ballou Co., Binghamton, N.Y.*, paper manufacturer's and binder's names; p. [5] acknowledgments; p. [6] at centre, dedication; p. [7] Contents; p. [8] blank; pp. 9–11 Introduction; p. [12] blank; p. [13] section-title; p. [14] blank; pp. 15–66 text; p. 67 poem by C. P. Cavafy; p. [68] blank; p. [69] section-title; p. [70] blank; pp. 71–119 text; pp. [120–126] blank, integral.

Orange cloth boards; lettered in black on spine: [*double rule, thick, thin across head*] | + PHAROS + | AND | PHARILLON | [*rule*] | FORSTER | [*rule*] | [*triangular design,* $\frac{3}{4} \times \frac{3}{4}$ *in.*] | ALFRED A · | KNOPF, and on upper cover: [*long double rule, thick, thin*] | PHAROS · AND · PHARILLON | [*long rule*] | E · M · FORSTER | [*short rule*] | [*triangular design,* $1\frac{1}{8} \times 1\frac{3}{8}$ *in.*]; publisher's device on a black ground on lower cover; edges trimmed, top dark grey; cream end-papers printed in deep cream, pale orange, and purple in a leaf design. Dust-jacket.

Published 30 July 1923; 1500 copies printed. $1.50.

d. Third English edition. 1961:

[*title as above; imprint:*] THE HOGARTH PRESS | LONDON

Crown 8vo. 100 pp. $7\frac{7}{8} \times 5\frac{1}{8}$ in.

P. [100] printer's imprint: ... T. and A. CONSTABLE LTD. | Printers to the University of Edinburgh.

Published 13 July 1961; 3500 copies printed. 8s. 6d.

e. Third English edition—American issue. 1961 [*i.e. 1962*]*:

PHAROS AND | PHARILLON | [*ornament*] | E. M. FORSTER | [*publisher's device*] | NEW YORK: ALFRED · A · KNOPF | 1961

Crown 8vo. 100 pp. 8 × 5⅛ in.

Reddish-brown paper boards printed in an aqua and tan design; lettered on spine in reddish-brown; edges untrimmed; white end-papers.

Issued 26 February 1962; 1500 copies bound. $2.95.

The sheets were supplied by the Hogarth Press. There was a further printing by photo-litho offset of 6750 copies in October 1962, of which 4500 copies were sold to the Reader's Subscription Book Club.

English Fiction in Transition, 1961, Vol. 4, No. 3, leaves 41–42, incorrectly records that *Pharos and Pharillon* was 'reissued' by the Mayflower Publishing Co. Ltd in 1961.

A10   A PASSAGE TO INDIA   1924

a. First edition:

A PASSAGE TO | INDIA | BY | E. M. FORSTER | Author of "Howards End," "A Room | with a View," etc. | LONDON | EDWARD ARNOLD & CO. | 1924 | ⟨*All rights reserved*⟩

Crown 8vo. 328 pp. 7½ × 4⅞ in.

P. [1] title; p. [2] at centre, list of works by the author, at foot: *Made and Printed in Great Britain by* | Butler & Tanner Ltd., *Frome and London* | Copyright in U.S.A.; p. [3] at centre, dedication: TO | SYED ROSS MASOOD | AND TO THE SEVENTEEN YEARS OF OUR FRIENDSHIP; p. [4] blank; pp. 5–121 text; p. [122] blank; pp. 123–325 text; pp. [326–328] publisher's advertisements, integral.

Dark red cloth boards; lettered in black on spine: A | PASSAGE | TO | INDIA | E. M. | FORSTER | ARNOLD, and on upper cover: A PASSAGE TO INDIA | E. M. FORSTER; top and fore edges trimmed, bottom rough trimmed; white end-papers. Champagne dust-jacket printed in rose.

Published 4 June 1924; 5000 copies printed. 7s. 6d.

Two hundred copies were issued as a 'limited edition' at £2 2s. in fawn paper boards, donkey-brown cloth spine, rule in blind down edge of spine at juncture of cloth and paper on upper and lower covers; pale grey paper label on spine, 2⅝ × 1¾ in., printed in black: [*within a rule:*] A | PASSAGE | TO | INDIA | [*short rule*] | E. M. | FORSTER; white end-papers; top edges gilt, others untrimmed; grey slip-in case, pale grey printed label on spine. Fifty copies were supplied to Harcourt, Brace.

There were further printings of 3000 copies in June and July 1924, 2000 in August, October and December 1924, and 1000 in May 1925. There were additional printings, issued in the *Uniform Edition*, of 2000 copies in October 1926, 1000 in April 1929, 2000 in February 1931, and 1000 in July 1931, January and November 1943 and June 1944. There were two further printings, issued in the *Kingfisher Library*, of 5000 copies in October 1932 and 6650 in October 1944.

The first chapter was reprinted as 'Chandrapore, City of Change' in *Senior Scholastic, Teachers Edition*, 14 January 1946, Vol. 47, p. [16].

Dramatized by Lance Sieveking and broadcast in the Home Service on 24 October 1955.

Dramatized by Santha Rama Rau and first performed at the Playhouse, Oxford, on 19 January 1960; the play was published in 1960. *See* E9*b–d*. *See also* B36.

The holograph manuscript, over 500 leaves, including 'earlier draft material, notes and . . . two fragments of what Mr Forster has identified as incomplete short stories . . .,' was presented by the author and sold for £6500 on behalf of the London Library, where he had been on the Committee for over fifteen years, at the sale at Christie, Manson & Woods, London, on 22 June 1960. *See* 'The Wobblings of E. M. Forster,' by O. G. W. Stallybrass, *Guardian*, 20 June 1960, p. 5. This material is now in the Academic Center, University of Texas.

b. First American edition. [*1924*]:

A PASSAGE TO | INDIA | *By* | E. M. FORSTER | *Author of "Howards End," "A Room* | *with a View," etc.* | [*publisher's monogram*] | *New York* | *Harcourt, Brace and Company*

Crown 8vo. 324 pp. $7\frac{1}{2} \times 5\frac{1}{8}$ in.

P. [1] half-title; p. [2] list of works by the author; p. [3] title; p. [4] at centre: COPYRIGHT, 1924, BY | HARCOURT, BRACE and COMPANY, INC., at foot: PRINTED IN THE U.S.A. BY | THE QUINN & BODEN COMPANY | RAHWAY, N.J.; p. [5] dedication; p. [6] blank; pp. 7–322 text; pp. [323–324] blank, integral.

Black cloth boards; lettered in pale primrose on spine: [*rule across head*] |*A* | *PASSAGE* | *TO* | *INDIA* | *E. M.* | *FORSTER* | HARCOURT | BRACE & CO. | [*rule across foot*], and on upper cover: *A PASSAGE* | *TO INDIA* | *E. M.* *FORSTER,* top edges trimmed, fore and bottom edges rough trimmed; white end-papers. Pale green dust-jacket printed in black, terra-cotta, and green.

Published 14 August 1924; 4000 copies printed. $2.50.

The fount '*f*' in *Author of* on the title-page is broken.

There were further printings in 1924 of 2625 copies in August, 2500 and 3000 in September, 3000 and 4275 in October, 5000 in November, 3000, 2000 and 5325 in December, in 1925 of 2500 and 5000 in February and 2000 in July, in 1937 of 500 in February, and in 1944 of 2500 in May and 3000 in November. There were additional printings, issued as *Harbrace Modern Classics*, of 4000 copies in November 1958, 6000 in December 1961, 22,000 in April 1962, and 7000 in November 1962. There were also seventeen printings, issued as '*Text Editions*' by the School and College Departments, between 1950 and 1963 totalling 136,775 copies.

Grosset & Dunlap issued a reprint in 1924 at $1; sales amounted to 20,137 copies.

The Modern Library of the World's Best Books also issued a reprint in 1940 at 95 cents; sales amounted to 48,110 copies.

c. Second English edition (Penguin Books). [1936]:

Foolscap 8vo. 288 pp. $7\frac{1}{8} \times 4\frac{1}{4}$ in.

Published 12 June 1936 as *Penguin Books*, Vol. 48; 50,000 copies printed. 6*d.*

There were further printings of 25,000 copies in October 1936, 15,000 in April 1937, 50,000 in October 1937, 25,000 in December 1939 and December 1940, 55,000 in October 1941, and 50,000 in July 1943.

Modern Age Books, Inc. issued a reprint in 1937 at 25 cents; sales amounted to 10,002 copies.

d. Third English edition (Everyman's Library). [1942]:

[*title as above; imprint:*] LONDON: J. M. DENT & SONS LTD.

Royal 16mo. xxxii, 284, 4 pp. $6\frac{5}{8} \times 4\frac{1}{8}$ in.

Published *c.* 8 October 1942 as *Everyman's Library*, Vol. 972; number of copies printed not disclosed. 3*s.*

P. [vii] dedication: The original edition was dedicated 'To Syed | Ross Masood and to the seventeen years of | our friendship.' I desire in this edition to | join with his name that of His Highness Sir | Tukoji Rao Puar III, K.C.S.I., Maharajah of | Dewas State Senior . . .; p. [x] foreword by the author; pp. [xi]–xxviii Introduction by Peter Burra;

pp. xxviii–xxix A List of E. M. Forster's Writings; pp. xxxi–xxxii Author's Notes.

There were further printings. In the 1957 printing the dedication was omitted and the foreword by the author, 'A List of E. M. Forster's Writings' and the 'Author's Notes' were revised.

e. Second American edition (Penguin Books, Inc.). [*1946*]:

Small crown 8vo. [viii], 304 pp. $7\frac{1}{4} \times 4\frac{1}{4}$ in.

Published February 1946 as *Penguin Books*, Vol. 574; 201,335 copies printed. 25 cents.

f. Fourth English edition (Pocket Edition). [*1947*]:

[*title as above; imprint:*] LONDON | EDWARD ARNOLD & CO.

Royal 16mo. 336 pp. $6\frac{1}{2} \times 4$ in.

Published 23 October 1947 as the *Pocket Edition*; 10,000 copies printed. 6s.

There were further printings of 5000 copies in March 1949, 4385 in August 1953, 5000 in February 1957 and October 1959, and 7500 in February 1961.

g. Fifth English edition (Penguin Books). [*1950*]*:

Foolscap 8vo. 320 pp. $7\frac{1}{4} \times 4\frac{3}{8}$ in.

Published 25 August 1950 as *Penguin Books*, Vol. 48; 40,000 copies printed. 2s.

There were further printings of 40,000 copies in 1952 issued in February 1953, 50,000 in August 1954, and 40,000 in February 1957, May 1959 and December 1960. There were additional printings, issued in *Penguin Modern Classics*, of 40,000 copies in November 1961, and 30,000 in October 1962.

A11   ANONYMITY   1925

First separate edition:

ANONYMITY | An Enquiry | E. M. FORSTER | Published by | Leonard & Virginia Woolf at the Hogarth Press, | 52 Tavistock Square, London, W.C. | 1925

Foolscap 4to. [iv], 28 pp. 8½ × 5½ in.

P. [i] at centre: LEFT PASTE DOWN.; p. [ii] blank; pp. [i–ii] form paste-down end-paper; pp. [iii–iv] blank; p. [1] half-title; p. [2] list of *Hogarth Essays*; p. [3] title; p. [4] at foot: Printed by | LOXLEY BROS., LTD., LONDON.; p. [5] at centre, dedication: To L.H.C.S. [*i.e. Laurence Shuttleworth*], at right foot: A.; p. [6] blank; pp. 7–23 text; p. [24] blank; pp. [25–28] blank, integral; pp. [27–28] form paste-down end-paper.

Pale green paper boards; printed in black on upper cover: *ANONYMITY* | *An Enquiry* | E. M. FORSTER | THE HOGARTH PRESS; illustration on upper cover of a vase of flowers, designed by Vanessa Bell; edges cut flush.

Published 1 December 1925 as the *Hogarth Essays*, Vol. 12; 2000 copies printed. 2*s*.

The covers appear in at least two states: (1) as recorded above—(2) in pale green paper wrappers without boards; these copies lack pp. [i–iv], [27–28]. Mr Leonard Woolf states that no priority should be assigned to these two states.

The essay was not published separately in the United States. It was first published in the *Calendar of Modern Letters*, November 1925 and reprinted in *Two Cheers for Democracy*. *See* A28, C191.

A12   ASPECTS OF THE NOVEL   1927

a. First edition:

ASPECTS | OF THE NOVEL | BY | E. M. FORSTER | *Fellow of King's College, Cambridge* | LONDON | EDWARD ARNOLD & CO. | 1927 | {*All rights reserved*}

Crown 8vo. 224 pp. 7⅜ × 4⅞ in.

P. [1] half-title; p. [2] list of works by the author; p. [3] title; p. [4] at foot: Made and Printed in Great Britain by | Butler & Tanner Ltd., Frome and London; p. [5] at centre, dedication: To | CHARLES MAURON; p. [6] blank; p. 7 Note: 'These are some lectures (the Clark lectures) which were delivered under the auspices of Trinity College, Cambridge, in the spring of 1927 . . .'; p. [8] blank; p. 9 Contents; p. [10] blank; pp. 11–221 text; p. [222] blank; pp. 223–224 Index of Main References.

Crimson cloth boards; lettered in gold on spine: [*rule across head*] |

47

Aspects | of the | Novel | · | E. M. | Forster | Arnold | [*rule across foot*], and on upper cover: *Aspects of the Novel | E. M. Forster |* [*ornament*]; rule in blind round upper cover; edges trimmed; white end-papers. Champagne dust-jacket printed in dark green.

Published 20 October 1927; 2000 copies printed. *7s. 6d.*

There were further printings of 1000 copies in January and July 1927 and November 1936, 950 in March 1941, 1000 in July 1943, and 3650 in February 1945.

b. First American edition. [*1927*]:

ASPECTS OF THE NOVEL | *by* | E. M. FORSTER | FELLOW OF KING'S COLLEGE, CAMBRIDGE | [*publisher's monogram*] | NEW YORK | HARCOURT, BRACE & COMPANY

Crown 8vo. 256 pp. $7\frac{1}{2} \times 5\frac{1}{8}$ in.

P. [1] half-title; p. [2] list of works by the author; p. [3] title; p. [4] at centre: COPYRIGHT, 1927, BY | HARCOURT, BRACE AND COMPANY, INC., at foot: PRINTED IN THE U.S.A. BY | QUINN & BODEN COMPANY, INC. | RAHWAY, N.J.; p. [5] dedication; p. [6] blank; p. [7] Note; p. [8] blank; p. [9] Contents; p. [10] blank; p. [11] fly-title; p. [12] blank; pp. 13–247 text; p. [248] blank; pp. 249–250 Index of Main References; pp. [251–256] blank, integral.

Maroon cloth boards; lettered in pale green on spine: ASPECTS | OF THE | NOVEL | [*ornament*] | E. M. FORSTER | HARCOURT, BRACE | AND COMPANY; publisher's monogram in blind on upper cover; top edges trimmed, fore edges untrimmed, bottom rough trimmed; white end-papers. Dust-jacket.

Published 20 October 1927; 1680 copies printed. $3.50.

There were further printings of 1000 copies in April 1928 and October 1929, 500 in February 1937 and December 1940, 1500 in January, April, June and December 1947 and November 1948, 2500 in August 1949 and April 1950, both issued as *Harbrace Modern Classics*, 2000 in January 1954, 1000 in October 1958 and January 1961, and 2000 in September 1962.

c. Second English edition (Pocket Edition). [*1949*]:

[*title as above; imprint:*] LONDON | EDWARD ARNOLD & CO.

Royal 16mo. 160 pp. 6½ × 4 in.

Published 26 May 1949 as the *Pocket Edition*; 10,000 copies printed. 6s.

There were further printings of 10,000 copies in September 1953, 5000 in July 1958 and May 1960, and 6000 in August 1961.

d. Second American edition (Harvest Books). [1956]:

[*title as above; imprint:*] A HARVEST BOOK | Harcourt, Brace and Company | New York

Small crown 8vo. [xii], 180 pp. 7⅜ × 4⅜ in.

Published 14 September 1956 as *Harvest Books*, Vol. 19; 10,000 copies printed. $1.15.

The copyright renewal date is given as 1954 on the verso of the title.

There were further printings of 3000 copies in January 1958, 192 in May 1958, 3000 in September 1958, 156 in November 1958, 5000 in August 1959, 3000 in May 1960, 4000 in August 1960 and January 1961, and 4120 in July 1961.

e. Third English edition (Penguin Books). [1962]:

Foolscap 8vo. 176 pp. 7¼ × 4⅜ in.

Published 28 June 1962 as *Pelican Books*, Vol. A557; 25,000 copies printed. 3s. 6d.

There was a further printing of 25,000 copies in April 1963.

A13   THE ETERNAL MOMENT   1928

a. First edition:

The Eternal Moment | and other Stories: by E. M. Forster | London: Sidgwick & Jackson, Ltd. | Museum Street, London, W.C. 1928

Crown 8vo. [viii], 188 pp. 7¼ × 5¼ in.

P. [i] half-title; p. [ii] list of works by the author; p. [iii] title; p. [iv] at centre: *First Impression of this Collection, March* 1928, at foot: *Made and Printed in Great Britain | by Turnbull & Spears, Edinburgh*; p. [v] at centre, dedication: To T. E. [*i.e. T. E. Lawrence*] | IN THE ABSENCE OF ANYTHING ELSE; p. [vi] note on the first appearance of the stories; p. [vii] Contents; p. [viii] blank; pp. 1–[188] text.

Maroon cloth boards; lettered in gold on spine: [*triple rule across head*] | THE | ETERNAL | MOMENT | E. M. | FORSTER | SIDGWICK | & JACKSON | [*triple rule across foot*], and on upper cover: [*within a triple rule:*] THE | ETERNAL | MOMENT | [*within a separate triple rule:*] E. M. FORSTER; triple rule in gold round upper cover; edges trimmed; white end-papers. Pale grey dust-jacket printed in black.

Published 27 March 1928; *c.* 3720 copies printed. 5*s.*

Thirty-five copies with gilt tops were supplied to the author for his personal use.

These short stories were republished with those in *The Celestial Omnibus* as *The Collected Tales* in 1947. *See* A5, A26.

Contents: The Machine Stops—The Point of It—Mr Andrews—Co-ordination—The Story of the Siren—The Eternal Moment.

b. First American edition. [*1928*]:

THE | ETERNAL MOMENT | and Other Stories | by | E. M. FORSTER | [*publisher's monogram*] | New York | HARCOURT, BRACE & COMPANY

Crown 8vo. 248 pp. 7½ × 5 in.

P. [1] half-title; p. [2] list of works by the author; p. [3] title; p. [4] at centre: COPYRIGHT, 1928, BY | HARCOURT, BRACE AND COMPANY, INC., at foot: PRINTED IN THE U.S.A. BY | QUINN & BODEN COMPANY, INC. | RAHWAY, N.J.; p. [5] dedication; p. [6] blank; p. [7] note on the first appearance of the stories; p. [8] blank; p. [9] Contents; p. [10] blank; p. [11] title of story; p. [12] blank; pp. 13–85 text; p. [86] blank; p. [87] title of story; p. [88] blank; pp. 89–125 text; p. [126] blank; p. [127] title of story; p. [128] blank; pp. 129–138 text; p. [139] title of story; p. [140] blank; pp. 141–155 text; p. [156] blank; p. [157] title of story; p. [158] blank; pp. 159–176 text; p. [177] title of story; p. [178] blank; pp. 179–245 text; pp. [246–248] blank, integral.

Oxford-blue cloth boards; dull yellow printed label on spine, 1⅞ × 1⅛ in.: [*rule*] | THE | ETERNAL | MOMENT | [*ornament*] | E. M. | FORSTER | [*rule*] | HARCOURT, | BRACE & CO. | [*rule*]; dull gold printed label on upper cover, 2⅝ × 2 in.: [*within a rule with a star in each angle:*] THE | ETERNAL | MOMENT | [*ornament*] | E. M. | FORSTER; top edges pale yellow, others rough trimmed; white end-papers. Dust-jacket.

Published 19 April 1928; 2000 copies printed. $2.50.

There was a further printing of 1000 copies in July 1928.

A14   A LETTER TO   1931
           MADAN BLANCHARD

a. First edition:

A LETTER TO | MADAN BLANCHARD | E. M.
FORSTER | [*publisher's device of a wolf's head after a
design by E. McKnight Kauffer*, ½×⅝ *in.*] | *Published by
Leonard & Virginia Woolf at The* | Hogarth Press, 52
Tavistock Square, London, W.C.1 | 1931

Small crown 8vo. 28 pp. illus. (port.). 7⅜ × 4¾ in.

P. [1] half-title; p. [2] list of works by the author; p. [3] title; p. [4]
at head: *First published* 1931, at foot: MADE AND PRINTED IN GREAT
BRITAIN BY | THE GARDEN CITY PRESS LTD., LETCHWORTH.; p. [5] blank;
p. [6] Note; pp. 7–12 text; p. [13] illustration, portrait of Prince Lee
Boo; pp. 14–26 text; p. 27 Note; p. [28] blank.

Pale buff stiff paper wrappers; printed in black on upper wrapper, at
head: A LETTER TO MADAN | BLANCHARD | By | E. M. FORSTER, at foot:
THE HOGARTH LETTERS No. 1.; pictorial upper wrapper, designed by
John Banting, of a writing pad with a hand holding a pencil printed
in black and sky-blue; edges cut flush; sewn.

Published 15 October 1931 as the *Hogarth Letters*, Vol. 1; 5000 copies
printed. 1*s.*

Five hundred copies of the above were bound up in the collection
entitled *The Hogarth Letters* with ten other volumes in the series; it
was issued in 1933.

The essay is based on *An Account of the Pelew Islands*, by George
Keate, 1788, and *A Supplement to the Account of the Pelew Islands*, by
John Pearce Hockin, 1803. It was reprinted in *Two Cheers for
Democracy. See* A28.

b. First American edition. [*1932*]:

[*in script:*] E. M. Forster | [*ornaments*] | [*in roman:*] A
LETTER | TO | MADAN | BLANCHARD |
[*ornaments*] | HARCOURT, BRACE AND COM-
PANY | NEW YORK

Small crown 8vo. 24 pp. illus. (port.). 7⅜ × 4¾ in.

P. [1] half-title; p. [2] list of *Hogarth Letters*; p. [3] title; p. [4] at head, Note, at foot: COPYRIGHT, 1932, BY | HARCOURT, BRACE AND COMPANY, INC. | PRINTED IN THE UNITED STATES OF AMERICA | BY QUINN & BODEN COMPANY, INC., RAHWAY, N.J., typographer's name; pp. 5–10 text; p. [11] illustration, portrait of Prince Lee Boo; p. [12] blank; pp. 13–23 text; p. [24] Note.

Quaker-grey stiff paper wrappers; printed in pale maroon on upper wrapper: A LETTER TO | MADAN BLANCHARD | [*in script:*] E. M. Forster; edges cut flush; sewn.

Published 28 January 1932 as the *Hogarth Letters*, Vol. 1; 1000 copies printed. $1.

A15   SINCLAIR LEWIS   [1932]
INTERPRETS AMERICA

First separate edition:

SINCLAIR LEWIS | [*double rule, thick, thin*] | INTER-PRETS AMERICA | [*double rule, thick, thin*] | *By* | E. M. FORSTER

Royal 16mo. [5] leaves. 6⅛ × 4⅞ in.

L. [1] title; l. [2] at centre: *Of this first edition one hundred copies* | *have been issued by the* HARVARD PRESS | *for private distribution by* HARVEY TAYLOR | [*in ink:*] No..... | Harvey Taylor; ll. [3–5] text. No wrappers; edges cut flush; stapled.

Published Spring 1932, probably March; 100 copies printed. Unpriced.

This extract is the second paragraph of the essay first published as 'Our Photography: Sinclair Lewis' in the *New York Herald Tribune*, 28 April 1929, reprinted as 'A Camera Man' in *Life and Letters*, May 1929 and as 'Sinclair Lewis' in *Abinger Harvest*. See A18, C212.

A16   GOLDSWORTHY LOWES   1934
DICKINSON

a. First edition:

GOLDSWORTHY | LOWES DICKINSON | BY | E. M. FORSTER | LONDON | EDWARD ARNOLD & CO. | 1934

Small demy 8vo. [2], xiv, 280 pp. front. (port.), 7 plates facing pp. [14], 66, 80, 122, 176, 208, [234]. 8¾ × 5½ in.

Pp. [1–2] blank; p. [i] half-title; p. [ii] blank; p. [iii] title; p. [iv] towards head: COPYRIGHT | FIRST PUBLISHED 1934, at foot: PRINTED IN GREAT BRITAIN BY WALTER LEWIS, M.A., | AT THE CAMBRIDGE UNIVERSITY PRESS; p. [v] at centre: FRATRUM SOCIETATI; p. [vi] blank; pp. [vii]–x Preface; p. [xi] Contents; p. [xii] blank; p. [xiii] List of Illustrations; p. [xiv] blank; pp. [1]–241 text; p. [242] blank; p. [243] section-title; p. [244] Note, signed: R.E.B. [*i.e. R. E. Balfour*]; pp. [245]–268 Bibliography, by R. E. Balfour; p. [269] section-title; p. [270] blank; pp. [271]–277 Index; p. 277 at foot: CAMBRIDGE: PRINTED BY W. LEWIS, M.A., AT THE UNIVERSITY PRESS; pp. [278–280] blank, integral.

Oxford-blue cloth boards; lettered in gold on spine: GOLDSWORTHY | LOWES | DICKINSON | E. M. | FORSTER | ARNOLD; edges trimmed, top Oxford-blue; white end-papers. Pale cream pictorial dust-jacket printed in dark brown.

Published 19 April 1934; 2050 copies printed. 10s. 6d.

There were further printings of 1000 copies in May 1934, October 1944 and August 1946. Of the second printing in May 1934, 400 copies were issued as a *Cheap Edition* at 5s. on 22 September 1938 and 500 copies were destroyed in the war. There was an additional printing, issued in the *Pocket Edition*, of 1500 copies in November 1961, issued in 1962.

b. First edition—American photo-offset reprint. [1934]:

GOLDSWORTHY | LOWES DICKINSON | BY | E. M. FORSTER | [*publisher's monogram*] | HAR-COURT, BRACE AND COMPANY | NEW YORK

Demy 8vo. xvi, 280 pp. front. (port.), 7 plates facing pp. [14], 66, 80, 122, 176, 208, [234]. 8⅝ × 5⅝ in.

Navy-blue cloth boards; lettered in gold on spine: GOLDSWORTHY | LOWES | DICKINSON | E. M. | FORSTER | HARCOURT, BRACE | AND COMPANY; edges trimmed, top primrose; white end-papers. Dust-jacket.

Issued 7 June 1934; 1000 copies printed. $3.

This reprint was printed by photo-litho offset in the United States from the text of the first edition.

A17   PAGEANT OF ABINGER   [1934]

First edition:

PAGEANT OF ABINGER | IN AID OF THE PARISH CHURCH PRESERVATION FUND | SATURDAY, JULY 14 | at 3 p.m. | WEDNESDAY, JULY 18 | at 7 p.m. | Programme Notes and Text of Narrators' Speeches by | E. M. FORSTER | Music Composed and Arranged by | R. VAUGHAN WILLIAMS | MUS. DOC. | Narrator | WILFRED GRANTHAM | Scenario by the Pageant Master | TOM HARRISON | [*within a rule:*] THE BAND of the 2nd Battalion West Yorkshire Regiment (Prince | of Wales' Own) by permission of Lt.-Col. Hobbs and Officers.

Crown 4to. 28 pp. 4 illus. $9\frac{3}{4} \times 7\frac{1}{4}$ in., and insert [4] pp. $9\frac{1}{8} \times 7$ in.

P. [1] title; p. [2] advertisements; pp. [3]–4 list of patrons, guarantors, committee members and box office staff; p. [5] portrait of R. Vaughan Williams; p. [6] portrait of E. M. Forster; p. 7 names of producers, etc., acknowledgments; p. [8] advertisements; p. 9 foreword to visitors; p. [10] advertisements; p. 11 prologue; p. [12] advertisements; pp. 13–15 text; p. [16] advertisements; p. 17 text; p. [18] advertisements; p. 19 text; p. [20] advertisements; pp. 21–22 text; p. [23] portrait of Lady Denny; p. [24] portraits of Tom Harrison and Wilfred Grantham; p. 25 text; p. [26] advertisements; pp. 27–28 text. [4] pp. insert laid-in inside upper wrapper; pp. [1–4] names of performers; p. [4] at foot: A. A. TANNER & SON, Printers, 58, South Street, Dorking.

Apple-green paper wrappers; printed in black on upper wrapper: [*within a triple boxed rule:*] THE | PAGEANT | OF | ABINGER; names of advertisers on upper wrapper, verso and lower wrapper, recto and verso; lower wrapper, verso, at foot: Printed by The Athenaeum Press Ltd., 13 Bream's Buildings, London, E.C.4; edges cut flush; stapled.

Published 14 July 1934; no record of the number of copies printed. Price probably included in the admission ticket.

The pageant was not published separately in the United States. It was reprinted as 'Abinger Pageant' in *Abinger Harvest*. See A18.

A18   ABINGER HARVEST   [1936]

a. First edition:

ABINGER HARVEST | *by* | E. M. FORSTER
| [*publisher's circular device of a man reading*, ¾ *in.*] |
LONDON | EDWARD ARNOLD & CO.

Demy 8vo. viii, 352 pp. 8⅝ × 5½ in.

P. [i] half-title; p. [ii] blank; p. [iii] title; p. [iv] at head: COPYRIGHT |
FIRST PUBLISHED 1936, at foot: PRINTED IN GREAT BRITAIN BY |
BUTLER AND TANNER LTD., FROME AND LONDON; pp. v–vi Prefatory
Note; pp. vii–viii Contents; p. 1 section-title; p. [2] blank; pp. 3–68
text; p. [69] section-title; p. [70] blank; pp. 71–159 text; p. [160]
blank; p. [161] section-title; p. [162] blank; pp. 163–244 text; p. [245]
section-title; p. [246] blank; pp. 247–334 text; p. [335] section-title;
p. [336] blank; pp. 337–351 text; p. [352] blank.

Dark blue cloth boards; lettered in gold on spine: ABINGER | HARVEST
| E. M. | FORSTER | ARNOLD; edges trimmed, top dark blue; white end-
papers. Champagne pictorial dust-jacket printed in pale orange and
black.

Published 19 March 1936; 2000 copies printed. 12s. 6d.

The inclusion of 'A Flood in the Office', *see* C107, led to a libel action
(*see The Times*, 19 February, 1937, p. 4). The publishers think that
their unsold copies and those returned by booksellers in mint condi-
tion were re-issued with the offending article, pp. 278–281, removed
and a cancel inserted. It is, therefore, possible that there were two
issues of the first impression. The first is recorded above. In copies
of the second issue pp. 277–282 were cancelled and a cancel leaf
inserted on which the text of p. 277 (*i.e.* the final page of the preceding
article) and the text of p. 282 (*i.e.* the first page of the following article)
were imposed; a note was inserted at the foot of the cancel leaf, recto:
277–281. No copy in this cancelled state has been traced. Gilbert H.
Fabes in the *Bazaar, Exchange & Mart*, 29 September 1936, p. 1
notes '. . . the first edition exists in two forms.'

There was a second impression of 2000 copies in March 1936. Pp.
277–282 were again cancelled and a cancel of two leaves inserted on
which the text of p. 277 and pp. 282–284 (the first three pages of the
following article 'For the Museum's Sake') were imposed; a note at
the foot of the first leaf, recto of the cancel records: 277–281. The
article was, however, still listed in the Contents.

There were further printings of 3000 copies in November 1940, July 1942, and August 1944 (issued in 1945), and 5000 in May 1946. In these later printings 'For the Museum's Sake', the article following the deleted 'A Flood in the Office', was brought forward to p. 278 and the following pages renumbered. 'The Abinger Pageant' was omitted from the printings between 1940 and 1946 and a revised prefatory note included; the former and the original prefatory note were restored in the second English edition. *See* A18c.

Contents: 1, *The Present:* Notes on the English Character—Mrs. Grundy at the Parkers'—'It is Different for Me'—My Wood—Me, Them and You—A Voter's Dilemma—Our Graves in Gallipoli—Happiness!—Roger Fry: An Obituary Note—Our Diversions: 1, The Scallies—2, The Birth of an Empire—3, The Doll Souse—4, Mickey and Minnie—5, Chess at Cracow—6, The Game of Life—7, My Own Centenary—Liberty in England—2, *Books:* A Note on the Way—Forrest Reid—Ibsen the Romantic—T. S. Eliot—Proust—Word-making and Sound-taking—The Early Novels of Virginia Woolf—Ronald Firbank—Howard Overing Sturgis—Sinclair Lewis—Joseph Conrad: A Note—T. E. Lawrence—Jane Austen: 1, The Six Novels—2, Sanditon—3, The Letters—3, *The Past:* The Consolations of History—Macolnia Shops—Cnidus—Gemistus Pletho—Cardan—Voltaire's Laboratory: 1, How They Weighed Fire—2, Troublesome Molluscs—Captain Edward Gibbon—Trooper Silas Tomkyn Comberbacke—Mr. and Mrs. Abbey's Difficulties—Mrs. Hannah More—Battersea Rise—4, *The East:* Salute to the Orient!—The Mosque—Wilfrid Blunt: 1, The Earlier Diaries (1888–1900)—2, The Later Diaries (1900–1914)—A Flood in the Office—For the Museum's Sake—Marco Polo—The Emperor Babur—Adrift in India: 1, The Nine Gems of Ujjain—2, Advance, India!—3, Jodhpur—4, The Suppliant—5, Pan—Hickey's Last Party—Two Books by Tagore: 1, Chitra—2, The Home and the World—The Mind of the Indian Native State—Hymn before Action—5, The Abinger Pageant.

b. First American edition. [*1936*]:

Abinger Harvest | by E. M. Forster | *New York: Harcourt, Brace and Company*

Demy 8vo. x, 374 pp. $8\frac{5}{8} \times 5\frac{3}{4}$ in.

P. [i] half-title; p. [ii] list of works by the author; p. [iii] title; p. [iv]

at head, copyright note, reservation rights, publication note, at foot: *Designed by Robert Josephy* | PRINTED IN THE UNITED STATES OF AMERICA | BY QUINN & BODEN COMPANY, INC., RAHWAY, N.J.; pp. v–vi Prefatory Note; pp. vii–x Contents; p. [1] section-title; p. [2] blank; pp. 3–70 text; p. [71] section-title; p. [72] blank; pp. 73–164 text; p. [165] section-title; p. [166] blank; pp. 167–253 text; p. [254] blank; p. [255] section-title; p. [256] blank; pp. 257–349 text; p. [350] blank; p. [351] section-title; p. [352] blank; pp. 353–367 text; pp. [368–374] blank, integral.

Chocolate cloth boards; lettered in chocolate on spine: [*on two gold panels:*] Abinger | Harvest | E. M. Forster | [*in gold, outside panels:*] HARCOURT, BRACE | AND COMPANY; edges trimmed, top pale yellow; white end-papers. Pale yellow dust-jacket printed in chocolate and orange.

Published 30 April 1936; 1700 copies printed. $3.50.

There was a further printing of 1000 copies in May 1936; 860 copies of this second printing were pulped as a result of the libel action. *See* A18*a*. There was an additional printing of 2500 copies in August 1947 issued in black cloth boards, lettered on a gold panel on spine, with a buff dust-jacket printed in black and maroon; the copyright date 1936 is recorded on the verso of the title; 'A Flood in the Office' was removed, the succeeding article 'For the Museum's Sake' brought forward to p. 290 and the following pages renumbered with the text ending on p. 363.

The Noonday Press issued a reprint in their *Meridian Books* series in 1955; sales amounted to 12,770 copies.

c. Second English edition (Pocket Edition). [*1953*]:

[*title as above; imprint:*] LONDON | EDWARD ARNOLD & CO.

Foolscap 8vo. 400 pp. $6\frac{1}{2} \times 4\frac{1}{8}$ in.

Published 26 November 1953 as the *Pocket Edition*; 5000 copies printed. 6*s*.

There was a further printing of 3000 copies in August 1961 (issued in 1962).

'The Abinger Pageant' and the original prefatory note were restored.

A19   ENGLAND'S PLEASANT LAND   1938

First edition:

THE DORKING AND LEITH HILL DISTRICT | PRESERVATION SOCIETY PRESENT | ENGLAND'S PLEASANT LAND | *A PAGEANT PLAY* | [*swelled rule*] | *Written by* | E. M. FORSTER | *Music directed by* | R. VAUGHAN WILLIAMS | *Composers* | WILLIAM COLE | MARY COUPER | D. MOULE EVANS | JULIAN GARDINER | JOHN TICEHURST | R. VAUGHAN WILLIAMS | PRODUCED BY TOM HARRISON | [*long rule*] | MILTON COURT, WESTCOTT, SURREY | (*By kind permission of Lady Mallaby-Deeley*) | JULY 9TH, 14TH AND 16TH, 1938

Small royal 8vo. [20] pp. 2 plates facing pp. [5], [16]. $9\frac{1}{2} \times 6\frac{1}{4}$ in.

P. [1] title; p. [2] at foot: *In this Programme, the synopsis of the Pageant Play has been compiled by the* | *author, the synopsis of the music by the Musical Director . . .*; p. [3] list of patrons, guarantors and donors; p. [4] acknowledgments; p. [5] pageant committee members; p. [6] Characters; p. [7] note on the period covered etc.; p. [8] Music to the Play; p. [9] The Prologue; pp. [10–14] text; p. [15] The Epilogue; p. [16] blank; pp. [17–20] What Parliament Has Done Already for the preservation of the countryside, acts of parliament, list of preservation societies; p. [20] at foot: LANGLEY AND SONS, LTD., | THE EUSTON PRESS, N.W.1.

Terra-cotta stiff paper wrappers; printed in black on upper wrapper: ENGLAND'S | [*rule across wrapper*] | PLEASANT | [*rule across wrapper*] | LAND; edges cut flush; stapled.

Published 9 July 1938; no record of the number of copies printed. Price probably included in the admission ticket.

The play was published in full in 1940. *See* A22.

A20   WHAT I BELIEVE   1939

First separate edition:

WHAT I BELIEVE | E. M. FORSTER | [*publisher's circular device of a wolf's head after a design by Vanessa Bell,*

$\frac{3}{4}$ in.] | THE HOGARTH PRESS | 52 TAVISTOCK SQUARE, | LONDON, W.C.1 | 1939

Small crown 8vo. 24 pp. $7\frac{1}{4} \times 4\frac{7}{8}$ in.

P. [1] half-title; p. [2] blank; p. [3] title; p. [4] blank; pp. 5–22 text; p. [23] blank; p. [24] towards foot: PRINTED IN GREAT BRITAIN BY THE GARDEN CITY PRESS LTD. | AT LETCHWORTH, HERTFORDSHIRE.

Pale green paper wrappers; printed in dull red on upper wrapper: *E. M. Forster* | WHAT I BELIEVE | *Hogarth Sixpenny Pamphlets* | *Number One*; edges cut flush; sewn.

Published early May 1939 as *Hogarth Sixpenny Pamphlets*, Vol. 1; 5000 copies printed. 6*d.*

The essay was not published separately in the United States. It was first published as 'Two Cheers for Democracy', with some omissions, in *The Nation*, 16 July 1938, reprinted as 'Credo', with additions, in the *London Mercury*, September 1938 and as 'What I Believe' in *Two Cheers for Democracy*. *See* A28, C316.

A21   READING AS USUAL   1939

First separate edition:

[*title on p. [1] in dark brown:*] READING AS USUAL | E. M. FORSTER | TOTTENHAM PUBLIC LIBRARIES | 1939

Small demy 8vo. [4] pp. $8\frac{1}{8} \times 5$ in.

P. [1] title; pp. [2–4] text; p. [4] at foot: *"Reading as Usual" was delivered as a talk by Mr. E. M. Forster* | *in the B.B.C. Home Service programme on Sunday, September 17th, 1939,* | *and is here reprinted from "The Listener" of September 21st, 1939,* | *with the kind permission of Mr. Forster and the B.B.C.*

No wrappers; biscuit coloured pages; edges trimmed.

Published October 1939; 2000 copies printed. Unpriced.

The printers were Crusha and Sons Ltd, Tottenham, London, N.17.

This essay, a talk broadcast in the Home Service on 17 September 1939, was first published in *The Listener*, 21 September 1939. *See* C338.

A22   ENGLAND'S PLEASANT LAND   1940

First edition:

ENGLAND'S | PLEASANT LAND | *A Pageant Play by* | E. M. FORSTER | THE HOGARTH PRESS | 37 MECKLENBURGH SQUARE | LONDON, W.C.1 | 1940

Small crown 8vo. 80 pp. 7¼ × 4¾ in.

P. [1] half-title; p. [2] list of works by the author; p. [3] title; p. [4] at head: FIRST PUBLISHED 1940, at foot: PRINTED IN GREAT BRITAIN BY THE GARDEN CITY PRESS LTD. | AT LETCHWORTH, HERTFORDSHIRE. p. [5] at centre, dedication: To | TOM HARRISON | WITH ADMIRATION AND GRATITUDE; p. [6] blank; pp. 7–9 Introductory Note; p. [10] blank; p. [11] note on the original production, reservation of production rights; p. [12] blank; p. 13 Characters; p. [14] blank; p. 15 note on the setting of the pageant; p. [16] blank; pp. 17–19 Prologue; p. [20] blank; pp. 21–79 text; p. [80] blank.

Pale orange cloth boards; lettered in green up the spine: ENGLAND'S PLEASANT LAND [*ornament*] E. M. Forster; edges trimmed; white endpapers. Canary-yellow dust-jacket printed in bright green.

Published 29 April 1940; 2030 copies printed. 3s. 6d.

A synopsis of the pageant was published in 1938. *See* A19.

A23   NORDIC TWILIGHT   1940

First edition:

NORDIC TWILIGHT | *By* | E. M. FORSTER | [*design of a flower,* 1 × ¾ *in.*] | LONDON | MACMILLAN & CO. LTD | 1940

Small crown 8vo. 32 pp. 7⅛ × 4⅞ in.

P. [1] title; p. [2] two quotations, at foot: COPYRIGHT PRINTED IN GREAT BRITAIN; pp. 3–32 text; p. 32 at foot: PRINTED BY PURNELL AND SONS, LTD., | PAULTON (SOMERSET) AND LONDON.

Orange stiff paper wrappers; printed in dark blue on upper wrapper: [*within an oval frame in dark blue:*] NORDIC | TWILIGHT | E. M. FORSTER | [*rule across wrapper, outside frame*] | [*oval frame in dark blue, pale orange line round the inside of the frame, lettered in pale orange within the frame:*] MACMILLAN | WAR PAMPHLETS | [*outside frame at foot:*] NO 3 3d NET, and on lower wrapper: MACMILLAN | WAR PAMPHLETS | [*swelled rule*] | [*list of eight volumes in the series*]; dark blue band down the spine; edges cut flush; stapled.

Published 10 September 1940 as *Macmillan War Pamphlets*, Vol. 3; 25,000 copies printed. 3*d.*

The essay was not published separately in the United States. It is similar to 'Two Cultures: The Quick and the Dead', *Listener*, 26 September 1940, 'What has Germany done to the Germans?', *Listener*, 3 October 1940 and 'What would Germany do to us?', *Listener*, 10 October 1940. *See* C353–354, 356.

A24   VIRGINIA WOOLF   1942

a. First edition:

VIRGINIA WOOLF | BY | E. M. FORSTER | THE REDE LECTURE | 1941 | CAMBRIDGE | AT THE UNIVERSITY PRESS | 1942

Small crown 8vo. [ii], 30 pp. $7\frac{1}{8} \times 4\frac{7}{8}$ in.

Pp. [i–ii] blank; p. [1] title; p. [2] towards centre: CAMBRIDGE | UNIVERSITY PRESS | LONDON: BENTLEY HOUSE | NEW YORK: TORONTO, BOMBAY | CALCUTTA, MADRAS: MACMILLAN | *All rights reserved* | Copyrighted in the United | States of America by | Harcourt Brace & Co.; p. [3] towards centre, dedication: *To* | LEONARD WOOLF; p. [4] at centre: NOTE | This, with a few additions, is the text of the Rede | Lecture which was delivered in the Senate House, | Cambridge, on May 29, 1941. The lecture was also | given, in a somewhat different form, at the Royal | Institution of Great Britain on March 5, 1942., at foot: PRINTED IN GREAT BRITAIN; pp. 5–[28] text; p. [28] at foot: CAMBRIDGE: PRINTED BY W. LEWIS, M.A., AT THE UNIVERSITY PRESS; pp. [29–30] blank, integral.

Pink-grey stiff paper wrappers; printed in mauve on upper wrapper: [*within a compartment in mauve:*] VIRGINIA | WOOLF | By E. M. FORSTER | [*outside compartment:*] *Cambridge University Press*; edges cut flush; sewn and gummed.

Published 22 May 1942; 5000 copies printed. 1*s.* 6*d.*

There was a second impression of 5000 copies in June 1942.

The essay was reprinted as 'The Art of Virginia Woolf' in the *Atlantic Monthly*, September 1942, Vol. 170, pp. 82–90, and as 'Virginia Woolf' in *Two Cheers for Democracy*. *See* A28. An extract appeared under the title of 'Virginia Woolf's "Enlightened Greediness"' in *Wine and Food*, Spring 1943, No. 37, pp. 60–61.

b. First American edition. [*1942*]:

VIRGINIA WOOLF | *by* | E. M. FORSTER | HARCOURT, BRACE AND COMPANY | NEW YORK

Crown 8vo. [vi], 42 pp. 7⅜ × 5 in.

P. [i] half-title; p. [ii] blank; p. [iii] title; p. [iv] copyright note, reservation rights, publication note, at foot: PRINTED IN THE UNITED STATES OF AMERICA; p. [v] dedication; p. [vi] blank; p. [1] fly-title; p. [2] Note; pp. 3–40 text; pp. [41–42] blank.

Dark green cloth boards; lettered in primrose down the spine: VIRGINIA WOOLF [*ornament*] E. M. FORSTER [*in two lines:*] HARCOURT, BRACE | AND COMPANY, and on upper cover: VIRGINIA WOOLF | E. M. FORSTER; edges trimmed; white end-papers. Champagne dust-jacket printed in black.

Published 24 September 1942; 2000 copies printed. $1.

A25   THE DEVELOPMENT OF   1945
                    ENGLISH PROSE

First edition:

THE DEVELOPMENT OF | ENGLISH PROSE BETWEEN | 1918 AND 1939 | *The fifth W. P. Ker Memorial Lecture delivered* | *in the University of Glasgow* | *27th April,* 1944 | *by* | E. M. FORSTER | M.A. (CANTAB.), LL.D. (ABERDON.), |FORMERLY FELLOW OF KING'S COLLEGE, CAMBRIDGE | [*device of the arms of the University of Glasgow,* 1 × ⅞ *in.*] | GLASGOW | JACKSON, SON & COMPANY | PUBLISHERS TO THE UNIVERSITY | 1945

Small demy 8vo. 24 pp. 8½ × 5½ in.

P. [1] half-title, at head, device of the arms of the University of Glasgow; p. [2] blank; p. [3] title; p. [4] acknowledgments; pp. [5]–23 text; p. [24] at centre: PRINTED IN GREAT BRITAIN BY ROBERT MACLEHOSE AND CO. LTD. | THE UNIVERSITY PRESS, GLASGOW. FOR JACKSON, SON AND CO. | (BOOKSELLERS), LTD., PUBLISHERS TO THE UNIVERSITY, GLASGOW.

Golden-brown paper wrappers; printed in black on upper wrapper: G.U.P. | LXIII | [*continues as title-page*]; edges cut flush; stapled.

Published 15 December 1945 as *Glasgow University Publications*, Vol. 63; 1000 copies printed. 2s.

There were further printings of 1000 copies in February and March 1946.

The essay was not published separately in the United States. It was reprinted, with some revision, as 'English Prose between 1918 and 1939' in *Two Cheers for Democracy. See* A28. A version of this essay, 'Literature between Two Wars', was read by the author at the First All India Writers' Conference held at Jaipur in 1945; his opening remarks were published in *Indian Writers in Council: Proceedings of the PEN Conference at Jaipur, 1945*, Bombay, International Book House Ltd, 1947, pp. 206–207. *See also* B27.

A26   THE COLLECTED TALES   1947

a. First edition:

THE COLLECTED TALES | OF | E. M. FORSTER | [*publisher's device of a greyhound running*, $\frac{3}{8} \times 1$ *in.*] | [*rule*] | [*ornamental rule*] | ALFRED A. KNOPF *NEW YORK* | 1947

Crown 8vo. x, 310 pp. $7\frac{1}{2} \times 5\frac{1}{4}$ in.

P. [i] half-title; p. [ii] list of works by the author; p. [iii] title; p. [iv] within a frame: THIS IS A BORZOI BOOK, | PUBLISHED BY ALFRED A. KNOPF, INC., outside frame at foot: *Copyright 1928 by Harcourt, Brace and Company, Inc. Copyright 1947 | by Alfred A. Knopf, Inc. All rights reserved* [etc.]; pp. v–[viii] Introduction; p. ix Contents; p. [x] blank; p. [1] fly-title; p. [2] blank; pp. 3–308 text; p. [309] blank; p. [310] note on the type.

Oxford-blue cloth boards; lettered in gold on spine: [*double rule, thick, thin across head*] | [*ornamental design*] | [*double rule*] | THE | COLLECTED | TALES OF | [*in script:*] E. M. | Forster | [*double rule*] | [*ornament*] |

[*quadruple rule*] | Knopf; ornamental design in blind on upper cover; publisher's device of a greyhound running on lower cover; top and bottom edges trimmed, top golden-brown, fore edges rough trimmed; cream end-papers. White dust-jacket printed in black.

Published 10 July 1947; 5500 copies printed. $2.75.

There were further printings of 2500 copies in September 1947, and 1500 in November 1948, January 1952 and August 1959.

The collection incorporates *The Celestial Omnibus* and *The Eternal Moment*. *See* A5, A13.

Contents: The Story of a Panic—The Other Side of the Hedge—The Celestial Omnibus—Other Kingdom—The Curate's Friend—The Road from Colonus—The Machine Stops—The Point of It—Mr Andrews—Co-ordination—The Story of the Siren—The Eternal Moment.

b. First English edition. [*1948*]:

[*within a double rule:*] COLLECTED | SHORT STORIES | OF | E. M. FORSTER | [*ornament*] | SIDGWICK AND JACKSON LIMITED | LONDON

Small crown 8vo. x, 246 pp. $7\frac{1}{4} \times 4\frac{3}{4}$ in.

P. [i] half-title; p. [ii] blank; p. [iii] title; p. [iv] at foot: PRINTED IN GREAT BRITAIN BY ROBERT MACLEHOSE AND CO. LTD. | THE UNIVERSITY PRESS, GLASGOW; pp. v–[viii] Introduction; p. [ix] Contents; p. [x] blank; pp. 1–246 text.

Pale turquoise cloth boards; lettered in gold up the spine: E. M. FORSTER [*in two lines:*] [*ornament*] COLLECTED [*ornament*] | SHORT STORIES; edges trimmed; white end-papers. Cream dust-jacket printed in blue and red.

Published 18 March 1948; 9750 copies printed. 10s. 6d.

There was a further printing of 2500 copies in September 1949. The Readers Union issued a reprint of 7500 copies in September 1949.

The contents are similar to those of the first edition with the exception of the Introduction, which is slightly revised.

c. Second English edition (Penguin Books). [*1954*]:

Foolscap 8vo. 224 pp. $7\frac{1}{4} \times 4\frac{3}{8}$ in.

Published 29 October 1954 as *Penguin Books*, Vol. 1031; 40,000 copies printed. 2s.

There was a further printing of 30,000 copies in December 1956. There were additional printings, issued in *Penguin Modern Classics*, of 29,000 copies in May 1961, and 20,000 in June 1963.

A27   THE NEW DISORDER   1949

First separate edition:

The New Disorder | *E. M. Forster* | NEW YORK 1949 | (*First printing in America*)

Small royal 8vo. 16 pp. front. (port.). 9 × 6 in.

P. [1] half-title; pp. [2–3] blank; p. [4] tipped-in, portrait of the author by Paul Cadmus, $7\frac{3}{4} \times 5\frac{1}{4}$ in., caption: E. M. FORSTER by PAUL CADMUS | Drawn especially for this printing of | THE NEW DISORDER | Edition of 1200 copies, of which 20 numbered copies are signed by both the | author and artist.; p. [5] title; p. [6] blank; pp. 7–14 text; pp. [15–16] blank, integral.

Powder-blue stiff paper wrappers; printed in black on upper wrapper: The New Disorder | *E. M. Forster*; edges cut flush; stapled.

Published 1949; 1200 copies printed. 50 cents (unsigned copies).

Twenty numbered copies are signed by the author and the artist.

Mr Paul Cadmus writes that this work was printed by 'a jobbing printer' in New York City.

The essay was first published in *Horizon*, December 1941; it was largely incorporated in 'Art for Art's Sake' in *Harper's Magazine*, August 1949. *See* C373, 413. Another version was published in *Writers in Freedom*, [1942]. *See* B14.

A28 TWO CHEERS FOR DEMOCRACY [1951]

a. First edition:

TWO CHEERS | FOR | DEMOCRACY | BY | E. M. FORSTER | [*publisher's circular device of a man reading*, $\frac{5}{8}$ *in.*] | LONDON | EDWARD ARNOLD & CO.

Small demy 8vo. 372 pp. $8\frac{1}{2} \times 5\frac{1}{2}$ in.

P. [1] half-title; p. [2] list of works by the author; p. [3] title; p. [4] at head: COPYRIGHT IN ALL COUNTRIES SIGNATORY | TO THE BERNE CONVENTION | FIRST PUBLISHED 1951, at centre: *This book is published in the U.S.A.* | *by Harcourt, Brace & Co.*, at foot: PRINTED IN GREAT BRITAIN BY | BUTLER AND TANNER LTD., FROME AND LONDON; p. [5] at centre, dedication: To | JACK SPROTT | *of the University of Nottingham* | *England* | and to | BILL ROEHRICH | *of Lost Farm Tyringham* | *Massachusetts*; p. [6] blank; pp. 7–8 Prefatory Note; p. 9 Acknowledgments; p. [10] blank; pp. 11–12 Contents; p. [13] section-title; p. [14] blank; pp. 15–74 text; p. [75] section-title; p. [76] blank; pp. 77–85 text; p. [86] blank; pp. 87–143 text; p. [144] blank; pp. 145–371 text; p. [372] blank.

Dark blue cloth boards; lettered in gold on spine: TWO | CHEERS | FOR | DEMOCRACY | E. M. | FORSTER | ARNOLD; edges trimmed, top maroon; white end-papers. White dust-jacket printed in pale brown; portrait of the author by Paul Cadmus.

Published 1 November 1951; 10,000 copies printed. £1 1s.

Contents: Part I, The Second Darkness: The Last Parade—The Menace to Freedom—Jew-consciousness—Our Deputation—Racial Exercise—Post-Munich—Gerald Heard—They Hold their Tongues —Three anti-Nazi Broadcasts: 1, Culture and Freedom—2, What has Germany done to the Germans?—3, What would Germany do to us? —Tolerance—Ronald Kidd—The Tercentenary of the 'Areopagitica' —The Challenge of our Time—George Orwell—Part II, What I Believe: What I Believe—*Art in General:* Anonymity: An Enquiry— Art for Art's Sake—The Duty of Society to the Artist—Does Culture Matter?—The Raison d'Être of Criticism in the Arts—The C Minor of that Life—Not Listening to Music—Not Looking at Pictures—*The Arts in Action:* John Skelton—Julius Caesar—The Stratford Jubilee of 1769—Gibbon and his Autobiography—Voltaire and Frederick the Great—George Crabbe and Peter Grimes—Bishop Jebb's Book —Henry Thornton—William Arnold—'Snow' Wedgwood— William Barnes—Three Stories by Tolstoy—Edward Carpenter— Webb and Webb—A Book that Influenced Me—Our Second Greatest Novel?—Gide and George—Gide's Death—Romain Rolland and the Hero—A Whiff of D'Annunzio—The Complete Poems of C. P. Cavafy—Virginia Woolf—Two Books by T. S. Eliot —The Ascent of F.6 [*sic*]—The Enchafèd Flood—Forrest Reid— English Prose between 1918 and 1939—An Outsider on Poetry— Mohammed Iqbal—Syed Ross Masood—A Duke Remembers—Mrs. Miniver—In my Library—The London Library—*Places:* A Letter to Madan Blanchard—India Again—Luncheon at Pretoria—The United States—Mount Lebanon—Ferney—Clouds Hill—Cambridge —London is a Muddle—The Last of Abinger.

'John Skelton' was first given as a lecture at the Aldeburgh Festival of 1950; a version was later broadcast by the author in the Third Programme on 6 December 1950. 'George Crabbe and Peter Grimes' was also given as a lecture at the Aldeburgh Festival of 1948 and a version was later broadcast by the author in the Third Programme on 24 January 1960. 'Webb and Webb' is a revised version of the broadcast talk on 26 May 1943 in the series 'Some Books' in the Far Eastern Service; no record of prior publication has been traced.

b. First American edition. [*1951*]:

E. M. FORSTER | Two Cheers | for Democracy | New York | Harcourt, Brace and Company

Large crown 8vo. xvi, 368 pp. 8 × 5¼ in.

Pp. [i–ii] blank; p. [iii] half-title; p. [iv] list of works by the author; p. [v] title; p. [vi] copyright note, reservation rights, publication note, at foot: PRINTED IN THE UNITED STATES OF AMERICA; p. [vii] towards centre, dedication: TO | Bill Roerick [*sic*] | of Lost Farm, Tyringham, Massachusetts | AND TO | Jack Sprott | of the University of Nottingham, England; p. [viii] blank; p. [ix] Acknowledgments; p. [x] blank; pp. [xi]–xii Prefatory Note; pp. [xiii]–xvi Contents; p. [1] section-title; p. [2] blank; pp. [3]–63 text; p. [64] blank; p. [65] section-title; p. [66] blank; pp. [67]–363 text; pp. [364–368] blank, integral.

Dark grey cloth boards; lettered in yellow on spine: E. M. Forster | [*short rule*] | TWO | CHEERS | FOR | DEMOC- | RACY | [*short rule*] | Harcourt, Brace | and Company; edges trimmed; white end-papers. White pictorial dust-jacket printed in blue and black.

Published 1 November 1951; 5000 copies printed. $4.

There were further printings of 3000 copies in November 1951 and January 1952. There was an additional printing, issued in the *Harvest Book* series, of 6000 copies in January 1962.

A29   BILLY BUDD   1951

First edition:

BILLY BUDD | OPERA IN FOUR ACTS | *Music by* | BENJAMIN BRITTEN | *Libretto* | *by* | E. M. FORSTER and ERIC CROZIER | *Adapted from the story by* | HERMAN MELVILLE | *Price 2/6 net* | (1951) | Boosey & Hawkes, Ltd. | *London · New York · Toronto · Sydney · Capetown · Buenos Aires · Paris · Bonn*

Large crown 8vo. 64 pp. 8 × 5⅛ in.

P. [1] half-title; p. [2] towards head: Copyright 1951 by Hawkes &
Son (London) Ltd., reservation rights, at foot: PRINTED IN ENGLAND
| FREDK. W. KAHN LTD., LONDON, E.C.1.; p. [3] title; p. [4] blank;
p. 5 Characters; p. 6 Acts; pp. 7–[64] text.

Golden-brown stiff paper wrappers; printed in black on upper wrap-
per: E. M. FORSTER and ERIC CROZIER | BILLY BUDD | *Music by* |
BENJAMIN BRITTEN | BOOSEY & HAWKES, and on lower wrapper within
a frame, publisher's advertisements, dated 11.51; edges cut flush;
stapled.

Published *c.* 5 December 1951; 3000 copies printed. *2s. 6d.*

There was a second printing of 2000 copies in 1952. The third
printing (revised) was issued as the 'revised version 1961' in December
1962; there were alterations to the text and stage directions.

The opera was first performed at Covent Garden Opera House,
London, on 21 April 1952. The revised version was broadcast in the
Third Programme on 13 November 1960 and was performed at
Covent Garden Opera House on 9 January 1964 in honour of Benja-
min Britten's fiftieth birthday. *See also* B40, C422, E10*h*.

A30   DESMOND MACCARTHY   1952

First separate edition:

DESMOND MACCARTHY | *By* E. M. FOSTER
| STANFORD DINGLEY | THE MILL HOUSE
PRESS | MCMLII

Medium 8vo. [16] pp. 9 × 5½—9⅜ × 5⅝ in. Wrappers 10 × 5⅞—
10¼ × 6¼ in.

Pp. [1–2] blank; p. [3] title; p. [4] blank; pp. [5–11] text; p. [12]
blank; p. [13] towards centre: Seventy-two copies of this work have
| been privately printed by Kyrle Leng | and Robert Gathorne-Hardy,
at the | Mill House Press.; pp. [14–16] blank.

Vellum thin paper wrappers; printed in black on upper wrapper:
DESMOND MACCARTHY | *By* E. M. FOSTER; fore and bottom edges
untrimmed, top rough trimmed; sewn with white thread.

Published late summer 1952; 72 copies printed, 64 on mould-made
and 8 on hand-made paper. A few copies were for sale at 7*s. 6d.* and
15*s.* respectively.

P. [13] in the buff hand-made copies continues: Of these, eight | copies have been printed on buff | hand-made paper.; they were published in white thin paper wrappers; sewn with green thread.

There were two issues of this pamphlet: (1) the first as recorded above —(2) with (a) title reprinted to read: DESMOND MACCARTHY | By E. M. FORSTER | [etc.] and (b) white printed cancel slip, $1\frac{1}{2} \times 4$ in. (there is a variation of $\frac{1}{8}-\frac{1}{4}$ in. in these measurements), on upper wrapper: DESMOND MACCARTHY | By E. M. FORSTER, pasted over: DESMOND MACCARTHY | By E. M. FOSTER. Mr Gathorne-Hardy has recorded on p. [1] of the copy in the Bodleian Library: 'The author's name was accidentally printed 'Foster': accordingly the title was reprinted, & the pamphlet re-stitched [.] About 5 or 6 faulty copies, of which this is one, survived. A label with the corrected name was printed to stick on the wrapper.'

This tribute was first published in the *Listener*, 26 June 1952. *See* C434.

A31   THE HILL OF DEVI   [1953]

a. First edition:

THE HILL OF DEVI | *being* | *Letters from Dewas* | *State Senior* | *By* | E. M. FORSTER | [*publisher's circular device of a man reading*, $\frac{3}{4}$ *in.*] | LONDON | EDWARD ARNOLD & CO.

Small demy 8vo. 176 pp. front. (port.), 7 plates facing pp. 20, 50, 80, 92, 116, 138, 170. $8\frac{5}{8} \times 5\frac{1}{2}$ in.

P. [1] blank; p. [2] list of works by the author; p. [3] half-title; p. [4] blank; p. [5] title; p. [6] at head: COPYRIGHT IN ALL COUNTRIES SIGNATORY | TO THE BERNE CONVENTION | FIRST PUBLISHED 1953, at foot: PRINTED IN GREAT BRITAIN BY | BUTLER AND TANNER LTD., FROME AND LONDON; p. [7] at centre, dedication: To | MALCOLM [*i.e.* *Sir Malcolm Darling, K.C.I.E.*]; p. [8] blank; pp. 9–10 Preface; p. 11 Contents; p. [12] blank; p. 13 Illustrations; p. [14] blank; p. [15] section-title; p. [16] blank; pp. 17–34 text; p. [35] section-title; p. [36] blank; pp. 37–155 text; p. [156] blank; p. [157] section-title; p. [158] blank; pp. 159–176 text.

Ash-grey cloth boards; lettered in dull red on spine: THE | HILL | OF | DEVI | E. M. | FORSTER | ARNOLD, and on upper cover: [*monogram:*] EMF; edges trimmed; white end-papers. White pictorial dust-jacket printed in salmon, blue, and red.

Published 15 October 1953; 5155 copies printed. 15*s.*

There was a second impression of 5090 copies in October 1953.

Pp. 108–113 were first published as 'The Birth of Krishna' in the *Observer*, 11 October 1953. *See* C442.

b. First American edition. [*1953*]:

THE HILL OF DEVI | BY E. M. FORSTER | [*ornament*] | HARCOURT, BRACE AND COM-PANY | NEW YORK

Large crown 8vo. [ii], 270 pp. (including plates). $8 \times 5\frac{1}{4}$ in.

Pp. [i–ii] blank; p. [1] half-title; p. [2] list of works by the author; p. [3] title; p. [4] copyright note, reservation rights, Library of Congress note, at foot: PRINTED IN THE UNITED STATES OF AMERICA; p. [5] dedication; p. [6] blank; pp. 7–9 Preface; p. [10] blank; p. [11] Contents; p. [12] blank; p. [13] Plates; p. [14] blank; pp. [15–22] 8 plates; p. [23] section-title; p. [24] blank; pp. 25–52 text; p. [53] section-title; p. [54] blank; pp. 55–76 text; p. [77] section-title; p. [78] blank; pp. 79–238 text; p. [239] section-title; p. [240] blank; pp. 241–267 text; pp. [268–270] blank, integral.

Emerald-green cloth boards; lettered in gold on spine: E. M. Forster | [*triple rule*] | THE | HILL | OF | DEVI | [*ornament*] | Harcourt, Brace | and Company; edges trimmed; white pictorial end-papers printed in pale and royal-blue. White pictorial dust-jacket printed in bright blue, black, and gold.

Published 22 October 1953; 10,700 copies printed. $4.

A32 'I ASSERT THAT THERE IS AN [1955] ALTERNATIVE IN HUMANISM'

First separate edition:

[*title on p.* [*1*]:] 'I ASSERT THAT | THERE IS AN | ALTERNATIVE | IN HUMANISM'

Foolscap 4to. [4] pp. $8\frac{1}{2} \times 5\frac{1}{2}$ in.

Pp. [1–4] text; p. [4] at foot: *Issued by:* | THE ETHICAL UNION, | Stanton Coit House, 13 Prince of Wales Terrace, London, W.8.

No wrappers; edges trimmed.

Published October 1955; 2000 copies printed. Unpriced.

The essay was first published as 'A Letter' in the *Twentieth Century*, February 1955. *See* C453.

A33   BATTERSEA RISE   [1955]

First edition:

E. M. FORSTER | *BATTERSEA RISE* | [*swelled rule, ornament, swelled rule*] | *Harcourt, Brace and Company* | NEW YORK

Small crown 8vo. [iv], 12 pp. plate facing p. 6. $7\frac{5}{8} \times 4\frac{3}{4}$ in.

P. [i] half-title, at head: BATTERSEA RISE | *This first edition has been privately | printed for the friends of the author and | his publishers as a New Year's greeting.*; p. [ii] blank; p. [iii] title; p. [iv] at head: © COPYRIGHT, 1955, BY E. M. FORSTER | *All rights reserved, including | the right to reproduce this book, | or portions thereof, in any form |* "Battersea Rise" *is the first chapter of |* E. M. Forster's forthcoming | *Marianne Thornton: A Domestic Biography* (1797–1887), at foot: PRINTED IN THE UNITED STATES OF AMERICA; p. [1] fly-title; p. [2] blank; pp. 3–11 text; p. [12] blank.

White paper boards printed in a grey and buttercup-yellow design; white paper label printed in grey, $1\frac{7}{8} \times 3\frac{1}{2}$ or $1\frac{7}{8} \times 3$ in., lettered in white: [*within a rule:*] BATTERSEA RISE | BY E. M. FORSTER; edges trimmed; white end-papers. No dust-jacket.

Published 21 December 1955; no record of the number of copies printed. Unpriced.

This, the first chapter of *Marianne Thornton*, slightly condensed, was privately printed for the friends of the author and of the publishers as a New Year's greeting. It was reprinted as 'Daughter Dear' in the *London Magazine*, April 1956. *See* A34, C462.

A34   MARIANNE THORNTON   [1956]

a. First edition:

MARIANNE THORNTON | 1797-1887 | *A Domestic Biography* | *By* | E. M. FORSTER | [*publisher's circular device of a man reading, $\frac{5}{8}$ in.*] | LONDON | EDWARD ARNOLD (PUBLISHERS) LTD.

Demy 8vo. 304 pp. front. (port.), 15 plates facing pp. 18, 22, 26, 32, 76, 85, 104, 142, 144, 150, 176, 202, 230, 265, 270. 8½ × 5½ in.

P. [1] half-title; p. [2] blank; p. [3] title; p. [4] at head: © E. M. Forster 1956 | First published in 1956, list of works by the author, at foot: Printed in Great Britain by | Butler & Tanner Ltd., Frome and London; p. [5] towards head, dedication: *To* | MY MOTHER; p. [6] blank; pp. 7–8 Preface; p. 9 Contents; p. [10] blank; pp. 11–12 Illustrations; p. [13] section-title; p. [14] family tree; pp. 15–72 text; p. [73] section-title etc.; p. [74] blank; pp. 75–198 text; p. [199] section-title etc.; p. [200] blank; pp. 201–245 text; p. [246] blank; p. [247] section-title etc.; p. [248] blank; pp. 249–289 text; p. [290] blank; pp. 291–301 Index; pp. [302–304] blank, integral.

Dark blue cloth boards; lettered in gold on spine: MARIANNE | THORNTON | E. M. | FORSTER | ARNOLD; edges trimmed; white end-papers. White pictorial dust-jacket printed in sky-blue, Oxford-blue, and middle- and sepia-brown.

Published 10 May 1956; 7500 copies printed. £1 1s.

Chapter 1 was first published, slightly condensed, as *Battersea Rise*, 1955, and reprinted as 'Daughter Dear' in the *London Magazine*, April 1956. *See* A33, C462.

b. First American edition. [1956]:

[*within a frame:*] Marianne | Thornton | A DOMESTIC | BIOGRAPHY | 1797-1887 | [*outside frame:*] *by* E. M. FORSTER | HARCOURT, BRACE AND COMPANY · NEW YORK

Large crown 8vo. [2], xii, 338 pp. front. (port.), 15 plates facing pp. 8, 12, 18, 74, 84, 86, 106, 152, 154, 162, 194, 232, 296, 298, 302. 8 × 5¼ in.

Pp. [1–2] blank; p. [i] half-title; p. [ii] list of works by the author; p. [iii] title; p. [iv] copyright note, reservation rights, publication note, Library of Congress note, at foot: PRINTED IN THE UNITED STATES OF AMERICA; p. [v] dedication; p. [vi] blank; pp. vii–viii Preface; p. [ix] Contents; p. [x] blank; pp. xi–xii Illustrations; p. [1] section-title; p. [2] family tree; pp. 3–70 text; p. [71] section-title etc.; p. [72] blank; pp. 73–217 text; p. [218] blank; p. [219] section-title etc.; p. [220] blank; pp. 221–274 text; p. [275] section-title etc.; p. [276] blank; pp. 277–325 text; p. [326] blank; pp. 327–337 Index; p. [338] blank.

Dark apple-green half paper boards, darker green cloth spine; lettered in silver on spine: [*ornament in green*] | E. M. FORSTER | [*rule in green*] | *Marianne* | *Thornton* | A DOMESTIC | BIOGRAPHY | 1797–1887 | [*rule in green*] | HARCOURT, BRACE | AND COMPANY | [*ornament in green*], and in blind on upper cover: [*ornament*] M [*ornament*] T [*ornament*]; edges trimmed; white end-papers. White dust-jacket printed in peacock-green and primrose.

Published 14 May 1956; 8000 copies printed. $5.

A35   TOURISM *V.* THUGGISM   1957

First separate publication:

[*title at head of p. 1:*] *Reprinted from* THE LISTENER, *issue dated January 17, 1957* | Tourism *v.* Thuggism

Royal 4to. An offprint of [2] pp. illus. 12¼ × 9¾ in.

P. [1] text, with illustration, at foot: Printed in England by Waterlow & Sons Limited, London and Dunstable; p. [2] blank.

No wrappers; edges trimmed.

Issued after 17 January 1957; no record of the number of copies printed. Unpriced.

Reprinted from *The Listener*, 17 January 1957. *See* C470.

A36   E. K. BENNETT   [1959]

First separate publication:

[*title at head of p. 123:*] E. K. BENNETT (FRANCIS) (1887–1958)

Small demy 8vo. An offprint of [8] pp. front. (port.). 8½ × 5½ in.

Pp. 123–127 text; p. [128] at centre: Reprinted from the *Caian*, Vol. LV, No. 3; pp. [129–130] blank, integral.

Sky-blue paper wrappers, printed in black on upper wrapper: EDWIN KEPPEL BENNETT; edges cut flush; sewn.

Issued May 1959; 300 copies printed for private distribution. Unpriced.

Reprinted from the *Caian*, Michaelmas Term, 1958. *See* C490.

A37   A PRESIDENTIAL ADDRESS   [1963]

First separate publication:

[*title at head of p. 2:*] A PRESIDENTIAL ADDRESS | [*rule*] | TO THE CAMBRIDGE HUMANISTS— SUMMER 1959 | BY E. M. FORSTER

Imperial 8vo. An offprint of 8 pp. (mimeographed). 10 × 8⅛ in.

P. [1] note on reprint and pagination, at foot: University Humanist Federation: 13, Prince of Wales Terrace, London W.8; pp. 2–8 text. No wrappers; edges trimmed.

Issued April 1963; 50 copies mimeographed for private distribution. Unpriced.

Reprinted from the *University Humanist Bulletin*, Spring 1963. *See* C510. The *University Humanist Bulletin* was published in mimeographed form.

A. BOOKS AND PAMPHLETS

ADDENDA

B. CONTRIBUTIONS TO BOOKS
AND PAMPHLETS

a. Temple Greek and Latin Classics edition:

THE | AENEID OF VIRGIL | *Translated by* E. FAIRFAX TAYLOR | *With an Introduction and Notes* | BY | E. M. FORSTER, B.A. | VOL. ONE | [*VOL. TWO*] | [*publisher's device*] | LONDON: J. M. DENT & CO. | 29 & 30, BEDFORD ST., W.C. | MCMVI

Foolscap 8vo. 2 vols. Vol. 1, pp. [2], xviii, 352; front. (port.) and 2 tables, 2 maps. Vol. 2, pp. [iv], 364; front. and 2 maps. $7 \times 4\frac{1}{4}$ in.

Ruby cloth boards; lettered in gold on spine partly within a rule and with ornaments; top edges gilt, others untrimmed; white end-papers. Dust-jacket.

Published July 1906; number of copies printed not disclosed. 2s. 6d. each.

Vol. 1, pp. vii–xviii Introduction by E. M. Forster; pp. [v], 331–334, 336–340 and 342–350 of Vol. 1 and pp. [ii], 351–353, 355–357 and 359–363 of Vol. 2 Notes by E. M. Forster.

b. First American edition. 1906*:

G. P. Putnam's, New York. 2 vols.

Published 13 October 1906. $2.

It is possible that this is an American issue of the first edition. The publishers write: 'We have no information on the *Aeneid of Virgil* translated by E. Fairfax Taylor with an introduction by E. M. Forster other than confirmation from our catalogue that we published it. There does not seem to be a contract in our files, nor a manufacturing card nor a copy of the book.'

c. Everyman's Library edition. [1957]:

[*title as above; imprint:*] LONDON J. M. DENT & SONS LTD | NEW YORK E. P. DUTTON & CO INC

Small crown 8vo. xviii, 302 pp. $7\frac{1}{8} \times 4\frac{5}{8}$ in.

Published 3 October 1957 as *Everyman's Library*, Vol. 161; number of copies printed not disclosed. 8*s.* 6*d.*

Pp. v–xii Introduction by E. M. Forster. This is a revised version of the introduction to B1*a.*

B2   THE MORAL IDEAL   1907

Second edition:

THE MORAL IDEAL | *A HISTORIC STUDY* | BY | JULIA WEDGWOOD | [*quotation*] | *NEW AND REVISED EDITION* | LONDON | KEGAN PAUL, TRENCH, TRÜBNER & CO. L<u>TD</u> | DRYDEN HOUSE, GERRARD STREET, W. | 1907

Small demy 8vo. xii, 504 pp. $8\frac{1}{2} \times 5\frac{3}{8}$ in.

Dark red cloth boards; lettered in gold on spine with a triple rule across head and foot, and on upper cover; triple rule in blind at head and foot of upper and lower covers; edges trimmed, top gilt; white end-papers. Dust-jacket.

Published *c.* 12 July 1907; no record of number of copies printed, *c.* 250 remained in 1912. 10*s.* 6*d.*

P. xi [*i.e.* p. ix] records: 'I should like to take this opportunity of thanking many helpers . . . the present edition owes more than I can say to two who have put aside their own work to help mine—Edward Morgan Forster and Charles Harold Herford.' E. M. Forster records in *Marianne Thornton*, 1956, p. 223 '. . . for I assisted her in the revised edition . . .' *See* A34. He states that he 'redrafted certain passages with the author's approval'.

B3   ORIGINAL LETTERS FROM INDIA 1925

a. First edition:

ORIGINAL LETTERS | FROM INDIA | (1779-1815) | MRS. ELIZA FAY | WITH INTRODUC-TORY AND TERMINAL NOTES | BY | E. M. FORSTER | PUBLISHED BY LEONARD &

VIRGINIA WOOLF AT THE | HOGARTH PRESS, 52 TAVISTOCK SQUARE, LONDON, W.C. | 1925

Demy 8vo. 288 pp. 1 plate. $8\frac{7}{8} \times 5\frac{5}{8}$ in.

Middle green cloth boards; lettered in gold on spine with publisher's circular device of a wolf's head; edges trimmed; white end-papers. Pale green dust-jacket printed in black.

Published 14 May 1925; probably 1500–2000 copies printed. 15s.

Two hundred and ten copies were pulped in November 1932.

Pp. 7–24 Introductory Notes and pp. 273–285 Terminal Notes by E. M. Forster.

An essay, 'Eliza in Chains', based on these letters was published in the *Cornhill Magazine*, May 1924. *See* C180.

b. First American edition. [1925]:

ORIGINAL LETTERS | FROM INDIA | (1779–1815) | MRS. ELIZA FAY | With Introductory and Terminal Notes | BY | E. M. FORSTER | *Author of "A Passage to India"* | [*publisher's monogram*] | *New York* | HARCOURT, BRACE AND COMPANY

Demy 8vo. 312 pp. 1 plate. $8\frac{3}{4} \times 5\frac{3}{4}$ in.

Dull blue cloth boards; lettered in gold on spine with six rules; publisher's monogram in blind on upper cover, double rule in blind round upper cover; top edges trimmed, dull yellow, others rough trimmed; white end-papers. Pale green dust-jacket printed in black, maroon, and green.

Published 18 June 1925; 2500 copies printed. $4.

Pp. 7–25 Introductory Notes and pp. 289–304 Terminal Notes by E. M. Forster.

B4   FLOWERS AND ELEPHANTS   [1927]

a. First edition:

FLOWERS | AND ELEPHANTS | by | CONSTANCE SITWELL | with a foreword by | E. M. FORSTER | [*publisher's device*] | JONATHAN CAPE 30 BEDFORD SQUARE | LONDON

Crown 8vo. 160 pp. $7\frac{1}{2} \times 4\frac{7}{8}$ in.

Orange cloth boards; white printed label with orange rules and ornament on spine; edges trimmed; white end-papers. Cream dust-jacket printed in black and tan.

Published March 1927; number of copies printed not disclosed. 5s.

One thousand and forty sheets were supplied to Harcourt, Brace. See B4b.

Pp. 7–11 Foreword by E. M. Forster.

b. First edition—American issue. [*1927*]*:

FLOWERS AND ELEPHANTS | by | CON-STANCE SITWELL | with a foreword by | E. M. FORSTER | [*publisher's device*] | New York | Harcourt, Brace & Company

Crown 8vo. 160 pp. $7\frac{1}{2} \times 4\frac{7}{8}$ in.

Tan cloth boards; pale tan label on spine printed in dark tan; edges untrimmed; white end-papers. Dust-jacket.

Issued 18 August 1927; 1040 copies bound. $1.75.

The sheets were supplied by Jonathan Cape.

c. Second English edition. [*1929*]:

[*title as above; imprint:*] LONDON | JONATHAN CAPE 30 BEDFORD SQUARE

Foolscap 8vo. 224 pp. $6\frac{7}{8} \times 4\frac{3}{4}$ in.

Published 9 September 1929 as *The Travellers' Library*, Vol. 115; number of copies printed not disclosed. 3s. 6d.

Pp. 7–11 Foreword by E. M. Forster.

B5   EDWARD CARPENTER   [1931]

First edition:

EDWARD CARPENTER | IN APPRECIATION | Edited by | GILBERT BEITH | *With two portraits* | LONDON | GEORGE ALLEN & UNWIN LTD | MUSEUM STREET

Large crown 8vo. 248 pp. front. (port.) and 1 plate (port.). $7\frac{3}{4} \times 5\frac{1}{4}$ in.

Ginger-brown cloth boards; lettered in gold on spine; edges trimmed; white end-papers. Dust-jacket.

Published 21 April 1931; number of copies printed not disclosed. 7s. 6d.

Pp. 74–81 'Some Memories' by E. M. Forster.

B6   THE LIFE OF GEORGE CRABBE [1933]

World's Classics edition:

THE LIFE OF | GEORGE CRABBE | BY HIS SON | WITH AN INTRODUCTION | BY | E. M. FORSTER | [*publisher's device*] | LONDON | OXFORD UNIVERSITY PRESS | HUMPHREY MILFORD

Demy 16mo. xxiv, 324 pp. $5\frac{7}{8} \times 3\frac{5}{8}$ in.

Navy-blue cloth boards; lettered in gold on spine with five blind rules; blind rule round upper and lower covers, two horizontal and two vertical rules in blind on upper and lower covers, publisher's device in blind on upper cover; edges trimmed, top navy-blue; white end-papers. Dust-jacket.

Published *c.* 23 January 1933 as the *World's Classics*, Vol. 404; 5000 copies printed. 2s.

Pp. [vii]–xix Introduction by E. M. Forster.

B7   TWENTY YEARS A-GROWING   1933

a. First edition:

TWENTY YEARS A-GROWING | *By* | MAURICE O'SULLIVAN | *Rendered from the original Irish* | *by* | *Moya Llewelyn Davies* | *and George Thomson* | *With an Introductory Note* | *by E. M. Forster* | [*long rule*] | CHATTO & WINDUS, LONDON | 1933

Small demy 8vo. xii, 324 pp. end-paper maps. $8\frac{5}{8} \times 5\frac{3}{8}$ in.

Apple-green cloth boards; lettered in gold on spine with a triple wavy rule across head and foot and an ornament; top and fore edges trimmed, top green, bottom rough trimmed; white end-papers. Probably pale cream dust-jacket printed in grass-green.

Published 1 May 1933; 13,000 copies printed. 8s. 6d.

There were further printings of 2100 copies in October 1933, 2000 in September 1934, 2750 in February 1936, and 1500 in November 1941; the third to fifth printing was issued in the *Golden Library* series.

Pp. v–vi Introductory Note by E. M. Forster.

b. First American edition. 1933*:

[*within a double border:*] [*publisher's device*] TWENTY YEARS | A-GROWING | *By* | MAURICE O'SULLIVAN | *With an Introductory Note by* | E. M. FORSTER | MCMXXXIII | THE VIKING PRESS · New York

Large crown 8vo. xii, 304 pp. end-paper maps. $8\frac{1}{8} \times 5\frac{1}{4}$ in.

Tan cloth boards with dark green panel pasted on upper and lower covers and on spine; lettered in tan; edges untrimmed; white end-papers printed in dark green, maps. Dust-jacket.

Published 1 August 1933; 7000 copies printed. $2.50.

Reprinted nine times, the ninth in 1944.

Pp. v–vi Introductory Note by E. M. Forster.

c. Second English edition (Penguin Books). [1938]:

Foolscap 8vo. xii, 13–246, [10] pp. $7\frac{1}{8} \times 4\frac{3}{8}$ in.

Published 1 July 1938 as *Pelican Books*, Vol. 144; 50,000 copies printed. 6d.

There was a further printing of 25,000 copies in January 1939.

Pp. v–vi Introductory Note by E. M. Forster.

d. Third English edition (World's Classics). [1953]:

[*title as above; imprint:*] Geoffrey Cumberlege | OXFORD UNIVERSITY PRESS | *London New York Toronto*

Medium 16mo. [2], xiv, 300 pp. end-paper maps. $5\frac{7}{8} \times 3\frac{5}{8}$ in.

Published 25 June 1953 as the *World's Classics*, Vol. 532; 6000 copies printed. 5s.

There were further printings of 3500 copies in 1955, 3200 in 1957, and 5000 in 1960.

Pp. [v]–vi Introductory Note by E. M. Forster.

B8   UNTOUCHABLE   1935

a. First edition:

UNTOUCHABLE | *A NOVEL* | BY | MULK RAJ ANAND | With a Preface by | E. M. FORSTER | LONDON | WISHART BOOKS LTD. | 1935

Small crown 8vo. 232 pp. $7\frac{1}{4} \times 4\frac{7}{8}$ in.

Pale brown cloth boards; lettered in white on spine; edges trimmed, top pale brown; cream end-papers. Cream pictorial dust-jacket printed in red and brown.

Published early April 1935; probably not more than 1250 copies printed. 7s. 6d.

Pp. 7–11 Preface by E. M. Forster.

Rose Macaulay in her *The Writings of E. M. Forster*, London, Hogarth Press, 1938, p. 302, incorrectly records that *The Coolie*, by Mulk Raj Anand, has an introduction by E. M. Forster. *See* B12.

b. Second English edition (Penguin Books). [1941]:

Foolscap 8vo. viii, 9–160 pp. port. $7 \times 4\frac{3}{8}$ in.

Published 7 February 1941 as *Penguin Books*, Vol. 312; 55,000 copies printed. 6d.

The date of publication is given as 1940 on the verso of the title.

Pp. v–viii Preface by E. M. Forster.

c. Third English edition. 1947:

[*title as above; imprint:*] Hutchinson International Authors | Limited|LONDON:NEW YORK:MELBOURNE: SYDNEY: CAPE TOWN

Small crown 8vo. 128 pp. $7\frac{1}{4} \times 4\frac{3}{4}$ in.

Published 4 December 1947; 7500 copies printed. 6s.

Pp. 5–7 Preface by E. M. Forster.

B9   THE BANNED BOOKS   [1937]
OF ENGLAND

a. First edition:

THE BANNED BOOKS | OF ENGLAND | *by* | ALEC CRAIG | *With a Foreword* | *by* | E. M. FORSTER | LONDON | GEORGE ALLEN & UNWIN LTD | MUSEUM STREET

Large crown 8vo. 208 pp. $7\frac{7}{8} \times 5\frac{1}{8}$ in.

French-grey cloth boards; lettered in gold on spine; edges trimmed, top grey; cream end-papers. Quaker-grey dust-jacket printed in maroon.

Published 8 April 1937; number of copies printed not disclosed. 7s. 6d. Sheets were supplied to the Macmillan Company, New York in June 1937. *See* B9*b*.

Pp. 9–11 Foreword by E. M. Forster.

b. First English edition—American issue. 1937*:

Macmillan Company, New York.

Issued 2 June 1937; number of copies bound not known. $2.90. The sheets were supplied by Allen & Unwin.

B10   T. E. LAWRENCE   [1937]

a. First edition:

T. E. LAWRENCE | BY HIS FRIENDS | EDITED BY | A. W. LAWRENCE | [*publisher's device*] | JONATHAN CAPE | THIRTY BEDFORD SQUARE | LONDON

Medium 8vo. 596 pp. front. (port.) and 7 plates. $8\frac{5}{8} \times 5\frac{3}{4}$ in.

Maroon cloth boards; lettered in gold on spine with publisher's device; top and fore edges trimmed, bottom untrimmed, top maroon; cream end-papers. Pale grey dust-jacket printed in black and powder-blue.

Published 21 May 1937; number of copies printed not disclosed. 15s.

There were further printings in June and September 1937. It was partially reprinted in 1954.

Pp. 282–286 by E. M. Forster in section 'Post-War General Views'. This is reprinted on pp. 235–239 in the 1954 printing.

b. First American edition. 1937:

T. E. Lawrence | BY HIS FRIENDS | EDITED BY A. W. LAWRENCE | [*publisher's device*] | Doubleday, Doran & Company, Inc. | GARDEN CITY 1937 NEW YORK

Medium 8vo. xiv, 538 pp. front. (port.) and 7 plates. 9 × 6 in.

Pale brown cloth boards; lettered in gold on spine with a rule and ornamental design partly on a black ground, and on upper cover, monogram; top edges trimmed, fore and bottom edges rough trimmed, top pale chocolate; pale biscuit end-papers. Dust-jacket.

Published July 1937; no record of the number of copies printed. $4.

Pp. 247–251 by E. M. Forster in section 'Post-War General Views'.

B11   BRITAIN & THE BEAST   [1937]

First edition:

BRITAIN | J. M. KEYNES · H. J. MASSINGHAM | SHEILA KAYE-SMITH · E. M. FORSTER | [*13 lines of contributors' names*] | & THE BEAST

Medium 8vo. xx, 332 pp. front., illus., plan, map and 40 plates. 8⅞ × 5⅝ in.

P. [iv] publisher's imprint: ... *J. M. Dent & Sons Ltd.* ...

Quaker-grey cloth boards; lettered in gold and in blind on spine; edges trimmed, top orange; cream pictorial end-papers printed in sepia-brown. White pictorial dust-jacket printed in poppy, black, and grey.

Published 10 June 1937; number of copies printed not disclosed. 10s. 6d.

The Readers Union issued a reprint in 1938.

Pp. 44–47 'Havoc' by E. M. Forster.

B12   THE WRITINGS OF   1938
                 E. M. FORSTER

a. First edition:

THE WRITINGS OF | E. M. FORSTER | ROSE
MACAULAY | [*publisher's device*] | PUBLISHED BY
LEONARD & VIRGINIA WOOLF AT THE
| HOGARTH PRESS, 52 TAVISTOCK SQUARE,
LONDON, W.C.1 | 1938

Small crown 8vo. 304 pp. $7\frac{1}{4} \times 4\frac{3}{4}$ in.

Bright blue cloth boards; lettered in black on spine; edges trimmed;
white end-papers. Pale pink dust-jacket printed in dark pink.

Published early March 1938; 2250 copies printed. *7s. 6d.*

One thousand and sixty-five sheets were supplied to Harcourt, Brace.
See B12*b.*

Pp. 27–28 extract from an early unpublished novel by E. M.
Forster; p. 128 extract from notes for an unwritten novel by E. M.
Forster.

Extracts from other unpublished novels were published as 'Entrance
to an Unwritten Novel' in *The Listener*, 23 December 1948; as 'A Novel
that "Went Wrong" ', *i.e. Arctic Summer*, in the *Manchester Guardian*,
13 June 1951, in the interview, published in the *Paris Review*, Spring
1953, and in *Tribute to Benjamin Britten*, 1963. *See* B40, C409, 426, 438.
Reference is made to an unpublished play, *The Heart of Bosnia*, in
E. M. Forster, by Lionel Trilling, London, Hogarth Press, [1944],
p. 117, and to an unpublished short story, 'The Rock', by the author
in his Introduction to *The Collected Tales*, 1947, pp. vi–vii. *See* A26.
See also The Letters of T. E. Lawrence, edited by David Garnett,
London, Cape, [1938], pp. 537, 593.

b. First English edition—American issue. 1938*:

Harcourt, Brace, New York.

Issued 11 August 1938; 1065 copies bound. $2.50.

The sheets were supplied by the Hogarth Press.

First edition:

JULIAN BELL | ESSAYS, POEMS AND
LETTERS | EDITED BY QUENTIN BELL |
WITH CONTRIBUTIONS BY | J. M. KEYNES
| DAVID GARNETT | CHARLES MAURON
| C. DAY LEWIS | AND | E. M. FORSTER |
[*publisher's device*] | THE HOGARTH PRESS | 52
TAVISTOCK SQUARE, | LONDON, W.C.1
| 1938

Small demy 8vo. xii, 396 pp. front. (port.) and 5 plates. $8\frac{1}{2} \times 5\frac{3}{8}$ in.
Turquoise cloth boards; lettered in gold on spine; edges trimmed;
cream end-papers. Dust-jacket.

Published 7 November 1938; 1200 copies printed. 12*s.* 6*d.*

Six hundred copies were pulped in May 1941.

Pp. 391–392 'Notes for a Reply' by E. M. Forster to 'War and Peace:
A Letter to E. M. Forster', pp. 335–390.

First edition:

WRITERS IN FREEDOM | *A Symposium* | BASED
ON THE XVII INTERNATIONAL | CON-
GRESS OF THE P.E.N. CLUB HELD | IN
LONDON IN SEPTEMBER, 1941 | *Edited by* |
HERMON OULD | HUTCHINSON & CO.
(Publishers) LTD. | LONDON: NEW YORK:
MELBOURNE

Small crown 8vo. 152 pp. $7\frac{1}{4} \times 4\frac{3}{4}$ in.

Canary-yellow cloth boards; lettered in grass-green on spine and on
upper cover; edges trimmed; white end-papers.

Published 21 May 1942; 1000 copies printed. 8*s.* 6*d.*

Pp. 74–77 'The New Disorder' by E. M. Forster.

Another version of this speech was published in *Horizon*, December 1941; it was also published separately in 1949. *See* A27, C373. It was largely incorporated in 'Art for Art's Sake' in *Harper's Magazine*, August 1949. *See* C413.

B15   TOLSTOY'S WAR AND PEACE [1943]

First edition:

[*title on upper wrapper:*] TOLSTOY'S | *WAR AND PEACE* | *Introduction* | *to the* | *Series of Broadcasts* | THE BRITISH BROADCASTING CORPORA-TION | PRICE SIXPENCE

Small demy 8vo. 24 pp. (including 4 plates). illus. $8\frac{3}{8} \times 5\frac{1}{4}$ in.

Off-white thin paper wrappers; printed in black on upper wrapper, recto and verso, and on lower wrapper, recto at foot: *Published by The British Broadcasting Corporation, The Grammar School, Scarle Road, Wembley.* | *Printed by the Broadwater Press Ltd., Welwyn Garden City, Herts.* | No 1703; edges cut flush; stapled.

Published January 1943; 150,000 copies printed. *6d.*

A second impression was printed by Waterlow & Sons Ltd by photo-litho offset with some of the blocks remade or touched up and the title on the upper wrapper reset; lower wrapper recto: *Published by The British Broadcasting Corporation, The Grammar School, Scarle Road, Wembley.* | *Printed by Waterlow & Sons Limited, London and Dunstable.* | No. 1703. The reprint was probably necessitated by the destruction of some of the first impression; the figure of 150,000 copies probably includes both impressions.

Pp. 7–8, 11 'Tolstoy's "War and Peace"' by E. M. Forster. This essay is similar to the broadcast talk published in *The Listener*, 13 January 1937. *See* C294.

B16   LITERATURE AND   [1943]
AUTHORSHIP IN INDIA

First edition:

P.E.N. BOOKS | *General Editor:* HERMON OULD | [*long rule*] | LITERATURE | AND AUTHOR-SHIP | IN INDIA | *by* | K. R. SRINIVASA

IYENGAR | M.A., D.LITT. | (*Professor of English, Lingaraj College, Belgaum, University of Bombay*) | *With an introduction by* | E. M. FORSTER | LONDON | GEORGE ALLEN & UNWIN LTD

Small crown 8vo. [ii], 50 pp. $7\frac{1}{8} \times 4\frac{3}{4}$ in.

Pink paper boards printed in dark green and black; printed in black on upper cover; edges trimmed; paste-down end-papers formed by pp. [i–ii] and [49–50].

Published July 1943; number of copies printed not disclosed. *2s.*

Pp. 7–8 Introduction by E. M. Forster.

B17   TALKING TO INDIA   [1943]

First edition:

TALKING | TO INDIA | *by* E. M. Forster, | Ritchie Calder, Cedric Dover, | Hsiao Ch'ien and Others | *A Selection of English Language Broadcasts to India* | *edited with an Introduction by* | GEORGE ORWELL | LONDON | George Allen & Unwin Ltd

Small crown 8vo. [iv], 180 pp. 3 plates. $7\frac{1}{4} \times 4\frac{3}{4}$ in.

Rose-pink cloth boards; lettered in white on spine; edges trimmed; end-papers formed by pp. [i–iv] and [177–180]. Dust-jacket.

Published 18 November 1943; number of copies printed not disclosed. *7s. 6d.*

Pp. 11–16 'Edward Gibbon', pp. 117–121 'Tolstoy's Birthday' by E. M. Forster. The former was first published as 'Edward Gibbon, the Historian' in *London Calling*, 30 July 1942. Both essays were reprinted, with alterations, in *Two Cheers for Democracy*, 1951, the former as 'Gibbon and his Autobiography' and the latter as 'Three Stories by Tolstoy.' *See* A28, C376.

B18 NATIONAL GALLERY CONCERTS 1944

First edition:

[*double rule, ornament, double rule*] | NATIONAL GALLERY CONCERTS | *In aid of the Musicians'*

Benevolent Fund | 10th October 1939—10th October 1944 | *[long rule]* | GENERAL COMMITTEE | Dr. R. Vaughan Williams, O.M. | Sir Kenneth Clark, K.C.B. | Sir Henry Piggott, C.B. | Dame Myra Hess, D.B.E. | EXECU-TIVE COMMITTEE | Dame Myra Hess, D.B.E. | Sir Kenneth Clark, K.C.B. | Frank Howes, Esq. | Howard Ferguson, Esq. | W. P. Gibson, Esq. | *[long rule]* | PRINTED FOR THE TRUSTEES | LONDON | 1944 | *[double rule, ornament, double rule]*

Royal 8vo. 76 pp. front. and 4 plates. $9\frac{7}{8} \times 6\frac{1}{4}$ in.

White stiff paper wrappers with upper and lower wrappers printed in elephant-grey with spine white; lettered in beech-brown on upper cover and on spine; edges cut flush; sewn and gummed.

Published 10 October 1944; no record of the number of copies printed.

Pp. 6–7 'From the Audience' by E. M. Forster.

B19 SADLER'S WELLS OPERA BOOKS 1945

First edition:

EDITED BY ERIC CROZIER | SADLER'S WELLS OPERA BOOKS, NO. 3 | *[swelled rule]* | BENJAMIN BRITTEN | Peter Grimes | *essays by* | BENJAMIN BRITTEN | E. M. FORSTER | MONTAGU SLATER | EDWARD SACK-VILLE-WEST | *designs by* | KENNETH GREEN | *published for* | THE GOVERNORS OF SADLER'S WELLS FOUNDATION | *[swelled rule]* | BY JOHN LANE THE BODLEY HEAD | *London 1945*

Small crown 8vo. 56 pp. front. (port.) and 6 plates. $7\frac{1}{4} \times 4\frac{7}{8}$ in.

White thin paper pictorial wrappers printed in blue, pale olive-green, and red; lettered in blue within seven rules on upper and lower wrappers; edges cut flush; white end-papers.

Published 10 July 1954 as *Sadler's Wells Opera Books*, Vol. 3; 10,325 copies printed. 2s. 6d.

There was a second printing of 23,762 copies in February 1946.

Pp. 9–14 'George Crabbe: The Poet and the Man' by E. M. Forster. This is a revised version of the essay first published in *The Listener*, 29 May 1941. *See* C365.

B20   FREEDOM OF EXPRESSION   [1945]

First edition:

Edited By HERMON OULD | [*swelled rule*] | FREE-DOM OF EXPRESSION | A SYMPOSIUM | BASED ON THE CONFERENCE CALLED BY THE LONDON | CENTRE OF THE INTER-NATIONAL P.E.N. TO COMMEMORATE | THE TERCENTENARY OF THE PUBLICA-TION OF MILTON'S | AREOPAGITICA: 22-26TH AUGUST, 1944. | [*publisher's monogram*] | [*swelled rule*] | HUTCHINSON INTERNATIONAL AUTHORS LTD. | LONDON : NEW YORK : MELBOURNE : SYDNEY

Small demy 8vo. [iv], 188 pp. $8\frac{1}{2} \times 5\frac{1}{2}$ in.

Black cloth boards; lettered in black on spine on a silver ground and in silver; rule in blind down upper cover; edges trimmed; end-papers formed by pp. [i–iv] and [185–188]. Dust-jacket.

Published 30 August 1945; 2000 copies printed. 16s.

Pp. 9–14 'Presidential Address' by E. M. Forster. *See also* C391.

B21   LETTERS FROM   [1946]
                JOHN CHINAMAN

Second English edition:

G. LOWES DICKINSON | LETTERS | FROM JOHN CHINAMAN | *and other Essays* | With an Introduction | by | E. M. FORSTER | [*publisher's device*] | London | [*swelled rule*] | GEORGE ALLEN & UNWIN LTD

Small crown 8vo. 216 pp. $7\frac{1}{4} \times 4\frac{7}{8}$ in.

Turquoise cloth boards; lettered in white on spine with swelled rule; edges trimmed, top turquoise; white end-papers. Pale orange dust-jacket printed in green.

Published 21 March 1946; number of copies printed not disclosed. 7s. 6d.

Pp. [7]–8 Introduction, pp. [9]–10 Notes on the Essays by E. M. Forster.

B22 THE CHALLENGE OF OUR TIME 1948

First edition:

The Challenge of | Our Time | A SERIES OF ESSAYS BY | *Arthur Koestler* | *E. L. Woodward* | *J. D. Bernal* | *E. M. Forster* | *Benjamin Farrington* | *Michael Polanyi* | *J. B. S. Haldane* | *V. A. Demant* | *C. H. Waddington* | *A. D. Ritchie* | *Lord Lindsay* | LONDON | *Percival Marshall* | 1948

Small demy 8vo. 80 pp. $8\frac{1}{2} \times 5\frac{1}{2}$ in.

Mustard-yellow cloth boards; lettered in gold on spine; edges trimmed; cream end-papers. Ochre-yellow dust-jacket printed in black and crimson.

Published late November or early December 1948; 3000 copies printed. 7s. 6d.

There is a variant of the binding in portland-stone cloth boards.

Pp. 31–35 'The Point of View of the Creative Artist' by E. M. Forster. This essay was first published in *The Listener*, 11 April 1946, and reprinted as 'The Challenge of our Time' in *Two Cheers for Demo-cracy*, 1951. *See* A28, C395.

B23   HALI   [1950]

First edition:

HALI | *By G. V. Desani* | [*long rule*] | *Foreword by T. S. Eliot & E. M. Forster* | *Frontispiece: Sárika Góth* | THE SATURN PRESS

Large crown 8vo. [xiv], 17–58 pp. front. (port., col.). $8\frac{1}{4} \times 5\frac{3}{8}$ in.

Red half cloth boards, maroon imitation leather spine; lettered in gold on spine and on upper cover with publisher's device; edges trimmed; maroon end-papers. White dust-jacket printed in red and black, with portrait.

Published 10 February 1950; 2500 copies printed. 7s. 6d.

P. [ix] Forewords by T. S. Eliot and E. M. Forster. This book is recorded as B76 in *T. S. Eliot: A Bibliography*, by Donald Gallup, London, Faber, [1952].

B24   MAURA   [1951]

First edition:

Huthi Singh | [swelled rule] | MAURA *| With an Introduction by |* E. M. FORSTER *| [swelled rule] | Constable · London*

Small crown 8vo. [2], viii, 346 pp. $7\frac{1}{4} \times 4\frac{3}{4}$ in.

Azure-blue cloth boards; lettered in pale navy-blue on spine with swelled rule; edges trimmed; white end-papers. White pictorial dust-jacket printed in black and orange.

Published 30 April 1951; number of copies printed not disclosed. 12s. 6d.

Pp. vii–viii Introduction by E. M. Forster.

B25   ZOHRA   [1951]

First edition:

ZOHRA | A NOVEL | ZEENUTH FUTEHALLY | HIND KITABS LTD | PUBLISHERS : : BOMBAY

Small crown 8vo. [xii], 326 pp. $7 \times 4\frac{3}{4}$ in.

Pale buff cloth boards; lettered in green on spine and on upper cover; edges trimmed, pale buff; white end-papers. White dust-jacket printed in Oxford-blue, dark yellow, and silver.

Published December 1951; 2000 copies printed. Rs. 7.50.

There was a second printing issued as a 'cheap edition' at Rs. 4.75.

P. [vii] Foreword by E. M. Forster.

B26   CAMBRIDGE ANTHOLOGY   1952

First edition:

[*within a frame, within a double rule:*] CAMBRIDGE |
ANTHOLOGY | Edited by | PETER TOWNSEND
| Introduction by | E. M. FORSTER | 1952 | THE
HOGARTH PRESS | LONDON

Small crown 8vo. xii, 13–184 pp. 7¼ × 4¾ in.

Powder-blue cloth boards; lettered in gold on spine with ornament;
edges trimmed; white end-papers. Champagne dust-jacket printed in
powder-blue.

Published 19 May 1952; 2000 copies printed. 12s.6d.

Pp. vii–viii Introduction by E. M. Forster.

B27   HERMON OULD   [1952]

First edition:

[*title on p. i:*] *HERMON OULD* | *a tribute*

Demy 8vo. [ii], 14 pp. front. (port.). 8⅜ × 5⅜ in.

P. [14] at foot: *Printed by* | KENION PRESS LTD. | Slough, Buckingham-
shire. 1 leaf laid-in: HERMON OULD MEMORIAL APPEAL. No wrappers;
edges trimmed; stapled.

Published 5 June 1952 by the PEN English Centre, London; 1000
copies printed. Unpriced.

Pp. 6–7 'Indian Recollections' by E. M. Forster. Personal recollections
of a visit with Hermon Ould to the PEN Conference at Jaipur in
1945. *See also* A25.

B28   FORREST REID MEMORIAL   1952

First edition:

[*title on p. [1]:*] FORREST REID MEMORIAL |
[*rule*] | Addresses delivered at the Unveiling | of the Plaque
at 13 Ormiston Crescent | and afterwards at the Luncheon.
| [*rule*] | BELFAST. 10TH OCTOBER 1952.

Small crown 8vo. 12 pp. 7¼ × 4¾ in.

P. [12] at foot: PRINTED AT THE BURLINGTON PRESS, FOXTON, NEAR CAMBRIDGE, ENGLAND.

No wrappers; edges trimmed; stapled.

Published probably during October or November 1952; no record of the number of copies printed.

Pp. 3–6 'Address' by E. M. Forster.

B29   GRANTA AND THE PROCTORS [1953]

First edition:

[*title at head of p.* [*1*].*] GRANTA [*in two lines:*] and the | PROCTORS

Quarto sheet. [4] pp. (mimeographed). 10 × 8 in.

Published May 1953; no record of the number of copies mimeographed. Unpriced.

A protest against the suppression of *Granta* from May to 31 December 1953, the rustication of the editor, and the postponement of his degree.

P. [3] postscript expressing general agreement by E. M. Forster.

B30   TOM BARBER   [1955]

First edition:

FORREST REID | Tom Barber | *Young Tom* | *The Retreat* | *Uncle Stephen* | [*ornament*] | INTRODUCTION BY | E. M. FORSTER | PANTHEON BOOKS | NEW YORK

Small royal 8vo. 576 pp. 9 × 6 in.

Navy-blue cloth boards; lettered in gold on spine within a rule on a black ground with ornament; edges trimmed, top navy-blue; white end-papers. Dust-jacket.

Published 20 September 1955; 4000 copies printed. $5.

Pp. 7–10 'Forrest Reid (1876–1947)' by E. M. Forster.

B31   THE AUTHOR AND THE   [1957]
PUBLIC

First edition:

THE | AUTHOR | AND THE | PUBLIC | [*ornament*]
| *Problems of Communication* | [*publisher's device*] |
HUTCHINSON OF LONDON

Demy 8vo. 202 pp. $8\frac{1}{2} \times 5\frac{1}{2}$ in.

Maroon cloth boards; lettered in gold on spine with ornament and publisher's device; edges trimmed; white end-papers. Dust-jacket.

Published 25 March 1957; 2000 copies printed. 15*s.*

Speeches delivered at the 28th Congress of International PEN in July 1956.

Pp. 106–107 on the art of biography by E. M. Forster.

B32   THE GREEK VIEW OF LIFE   [1957]

a. Fourth edition—second printing:

G. Lowes Dickinson | [*double rule*] | THE GREEK
VIEW | OF LIFE | WITH A PREFACE BY | E. M.
FORSTER | METHUEN & CO LTD | 36 ESSEX
ST · STRAND · LONDON WC2

Small crown 8vo. xvi, 264 pp. $7\frac{1}{4} \times 4\frac{3}{4}$ in.

Beige cloth boards; lettered in ginger-brown on spine; edges trimmed; white end-papers. Pale biscuit dust-jacket printed in terra-cotta.

Issued 28 March 1957; 1500 copies printed. 13*s.* 6*d.*

This printing is incorrectly described as the 'Twenty-third edition' in the publication note on the verso of the title.

Pp. v–ix Preface by E. M. Forster.

*b. Fourth edition—American photo-offset reprint (Ann Arbor
Paperbacks). 1958*:*

University of Michigan Press, Ann Arbor.

Issued 26 September 1958 as *Ann Arbor Paperbacks*, Vol. AA22; 8022 copies printed. $1.75.

There were two further printings totalling 15,024 copies.

c. Fifth edition (University Paperbacks). [1962]:

[*title as above; imprint:*] LONDON : METHUEN & CO LTD

Large crown 8vo. xii, 180 pp. 8¼ × 5⅛ in.

Published 27 September 1962 as *University Paperbacks*, Vol. 49; 5000 copies printed. 9s. 6d.

Pp. v–viii Preface by E. M. Forster.

B33　　　THE FEARFUL CHOICE　　　1958

First edition:

THE FEARFUL CHOICE | A Debate on Nuclear Policy | conducted by | PHILIP TOYNBEE | with | THE ARCHBISHOP OF CANTERBURY | THE BISHOP OF CHICHESTER | KINGSLEY AMIS E. M. FORSTER | PROFESSOR A. J. AYER NOBLE FRANKLAND | ALAN BULLOCK NIGEL GOSLING | [*9 lines of contributors*] | LONDON | VICTOR GOLLANCZ LTD | 1958

Small crown 8vo. 112 pp. 7¼ × 4¾ in.

Pale French-blue cloth boards; lettered in gold on spine; edges trimmed; white end-papers. Canary-yellow dust-jacket printed in black and mauve.

Published 14 July 1958; number of copies printed not disclosed. 8s. 6d. There was a second impression in August 1958.

Pp. 82–83 by E. M. Forster.

B34　　　ELIZABETH OF THE　　　[1958]
　　　　　GERMAN GARDEN

a. First edition:

ELIZABETH | OF THE GERMAN GARDEN | A Biography by | LESLIE DE CHARMS | [*ornament*] | 'Parva sed apta' | [*publisher's device*] | HEINEMANN | LONDON MELBOURNE TORONTO

Demy 8vo. 430 pp. front. (port.) and 6 plates. 8 × 5½ in.

Pale green cloth boards; lettered in gold on spine with ornament; edges trimmed; white end-papers. White pictorial dust-jacket printed in green, blue, yellow, black, and brown.

Published 10 November 1958; 5000 copies printed. £1 5s.

One thousand, five hundred copies were supplied to Doubleday. *See* B34*b*. There were further printings of 2000 copies in December 1958 and February 1960.

Pp. 73, 101–104 reminiscences by E. M. Forster; these were taken from a fuller account which remains in manuscript. Further reminiscences arising out of this book were published as 'Recollections of Nassenheide' in *The Listener*, 1 January 1959. *See* C493.

b. First English edition—American issue. 1959*:

Doubleday, New York.

Issued 22 January 1959: 1500 copies bound. $5.

The sheets were supplied by Heinemann.

B35   SOME LETTERS OF   [1959]
            E. H. W. MEYERSTEIN

First edition:

SOME LETTERS | OF | E. H. W. MEYERSTEIN | *Selected, Edited and Introduced* | *by* | ROWLAND WATSON | [*publisher's device*] | *London* | NEVILLE SPEARMAN

Demy 8vo. [ii], 406 pp. front. (port.) and 1 plate. $8\frac{5}{8} \times 5\frac{1}{2}$ in.

Dove-grey cloth boards; lettered in gold on spine with publisher's device; edges trimmed; white end-papers. White dust-jacket printed in sky-blue, dark brown, and black.

Published May 1959; 1000 copies printed. £1 5s.

P. 298 footnote by E. M. Forster.

B36   A PASSAGE TO INDIA—   1960
            PROGRAMME

First edition:

MEADOW PLAYERS LIMITED | present | A PASSAGE TO | INDIA | by | SANTHA RAMA

RAU | from the novel by | E. M. FORSTER | *FIRST PERFORMED ON TUESDAY, 19TH JANUARY, 1960* | Settings by MICHAEL RICHARDSON | THE PLAY DIRECTED BY FRANK HAUSER

Small demy 8vo. [12] pp. 8¼ × 5½ in.

White thin paper wrappers printed on upper wrapper in pale orange and black and in black on lower wrapper; lettered in black; lower wrapper, verso, at foot: HALL THE PRINTER, LTD., SIX BREWER STREET, OXFORD.; edges cut flush; stapled.

Published 19 January 1960; 10,800 copies printed. *6d.*

Performed at the Playhouse, Oxford.

P. [7] note by E. M. Forster. The same note appeared in the programme at the Comedy Theatre, London, where it was first performed on 20 April 1960; there were two editions of the programme, of which 40,180 and 35,000 copies respectively were printed. The play was also performed at the Royal Court Theatre, Liverpool, on 22 February 1960 and at other provincial theatres; it is likely that the note appeared in all the programmes.

English Fiction in Transition, 1961, Vol. 4, No. 2, leaf 51, incorrectly records that this programme note appears in 'A Passage to India' by Santha Rama Rau, *Life International*, 24 October 1960, pp. 76–77. *See also* A10, E9*b–d*.

B37 THE WARM COUNTRY 1960

a. First edition:

THE WARM | COUNTRY | DONALD WINDHAM | *with an introduction by* | E. M. FORSTER | [*publisher's device*] | RUPERT HART-DAVIS | SOHO SQUARE LONDON | 1960

Crown 8vo. 208 pp. 7⅛ × 5⅛ in.

Mid-brown cloth boards; lettered in silver on spine; edges trimmed; white end-papers. White pictorial dust-jacket printed in pale orange and black.

Published 5 December 1960; 3500 copies printed. *15s.*

Pp. [9–10] Introduction by E. M. Forster.

b. First edition—American photo-offset reprint. 1962:*

Scribner's, New York.

Issued 11 April 1962: 7500 copies printed. $3.50 (cloth), $1.65 (paper).

B38   LORD OF THE FLIES   1962

First American edition—13th printing:

[*across two pages:*] LORD OF THE FLIES | *William Golding* | INTRODUCTION BY E. M. FORSTER | COWARD-McCANN, INC. | New York | 1962 | [*illustration*]

Demy 8vo. xvi, 248 pp. 8⅝ × 5¾ in.
Off-white cloth boards; lettered in red and black on spine and on upper cover with illustration; top and bottom edges trimmed, front edges rough trimmed, top salmon-pink; pale olive-green end-papers. White pictorial dust-jacket printed in mauve, green, French-blue, and pink.
Issued 7 September 1962; 5000 copies printed. $5.
There was a further printing of 7000 copies.
Pp. ix–[xiii] Introduction by E. M. Forster.

B39   TWO STORIES AND A MEMORY   1962

a. First edition:

Two Stories and | *a Memory* | [*swelled rule*] | GIUSEPPE | DI LAMPEDUSA | *Translated from the Italian by* | ARCHIBALD COLQUHOUN | *With an Introduction by* | E. M. FORSTER, C.H. | *Collins and Harvill Press* | LONDON | 1962

Demy 8vo. 128 pp. 6 plates. 8⅝ × 5½ in.
Forget-me-not cloth boards; lettered in gold on spine; edges trimmed; white end-papers, paste-down and free end-papers, recto printed in beige. White pictorial dust-jacket printed in pale brown, cinnamon, maize, green, sky-blue, and black.

Published 1 October 1962; 7500 copies printed. 18s.

Pp. 5–8 Introduction by E. M. Forster.

b. First American edition. [*1962*]*:

TWO STORIES | *and a* MEMORY | *Giuseppe di Lampedusa* | [*ornament*] | *Translated from the Italian by* | ARCHIBALD COLQUHOUN | *With an Introduction by* | E. M. FORSTER | [*publisher's device*] | PANTHEON BOOKS

Large crown 8vo. 192 pp. 6 plates. $8\frac{1}{4} \times 5\frac{1}{2}$ in.

Green-grey paper boards, pale green cloth spine; lettered in gold on spine with ornament, leopard device in gold on upper cover; edges trimmed, top yellow; white end-papers, streaked with blue.

Published 21 November 1962; 7000 copies printed. $3.95.

There was a second printing in January 1963.

Pp. 13–17 Introduction by E. M. Forster.

B40   TRIBUTE TO   [1963]
                    BENJAMIN BRITTEN

First edition:

TRIBUTE TO | BENJAMIN BRITTEN | *on his Fiftieth Birthday* | [*ornament*] | Edited by | ANTHONY GISHFORD | FABER AND FABER | 24 Russell Square | London

Demy 8vo. 196 pp. front., illus. and 8 plates. $8\frac{5}{8} \times 5\frac{1}{2}$ in.

Bright green cloth boards; lettered in gold on spine, partly on a reddish-brown panel; edges trimmed; white end-papers. Pale green dust-jacket printed in black and reddish-brown.

Published 22 November 1963; 2000 copies printed. £2 2s.

Pp. 46–55 *Arctic Summer: Fragment of an Unfinished Novel* by E. M. Forster. Read by the author at the Aldeburgh Festival on 10 June 1951. Extracts were published in the *Manchester Guardian*, 13 June 1951, and in the *Paris Review*, Spring 1953. *See* C426, 438. For other unpublished material *see also* B12, C409.

B. CONTRIBUTIONS TO BOOKS

ADDENDA

C. CONTRIBUTIONS TO PERIODICALS AND NEWSPAPERS

All articles are signed: E. M. Forster, unless stated otherwise.
Reference should be made to the Index for place of publication.

CI   TRAFALGAR. *Prolusiones Praemiis Annuis Dignatae, in Schola Tonbrigiensi*, Tonbrigiae, Quint. A.D. 1897, pp. 5–6. Prize-winning Latin verse.

C2   "THE INFLUENCE OF CLIMATE AND PHYSICAL CONDITIONS UPON NATIONAL CHARACTER." *Prolusiones Praemiis Annuis Dignatae, in Schola Tonbrigiensi*, Tonbrigiae, Quint. A.D. 1897, pp. 12–14. Concluding ten paragraphs of a prize-winning English essay.

1900

C3   ON GRINDS. *Cambridge Review*, 1 February 1900, Vol. 21, p. 185. Signed P[eer]. G[ynt].

C4   ON BICYCLING. *Cambridge Review*, 10 May 1900, Vol. 21, pp. 301–302. Signed P[eer]. -G[ynt].

C5   THE CAMBRIDGE THEOPHRASTUS, BEING A GUIDE FOR THE INEXPERIENCED TO CHARACTERS THAT MAY BE MET WITH IN THE UNIVERSITY WORLD: THE STALL-HOLDER. *Basileona*, 1 June 1900, No. 1, pp. 5–6. Unsigned. *See also* C9.

C6   A LONG DAY. *Basileona*, 1 June 1900, No. 1, p. 13. Unsigned.

C7   A TRAGIC INTERIOR (BEING AN ATTEMPT TO INTERPRET THE INNER MEANING OF THE AGAMEMNON OF AESCHYLUS). *Basileona*, 21 November 1900, No. 2, pp. 19–21. Dialogue. Unsigned. *See also* C11.

C8   THE PACK OF ANCHISES. *Basileona*, 21 November 1900, No. 2, pp. 21–22. Unsigned.

C9   THE CAMBRIDGE THEOPHRASTUS: THE EARLY FATHER. *Basileona*, 21 November 1900, No. 2, pp. 23–24. Unsigned. *See also* C5.

1901

C10   A BRISK WALK. *Basileona*, 21 February 1901, No. 3, pp. 30–31. Unsigned.

C11   A TRAGIC INTERIOR, 2 (BEING A FURTHER ATTEMPT TO ASSIST THE EARNEST STUDENT OF AESCHYLUS, BY MEANS

OF AN INTERPRETATION OF THE CHOEPHORI). *Basileona*,
21 February 1901, No. 3, pp. 32–34. Dialogue. Unsigned.
See also C7.

C12 STRIVINGS AFTER HISTORICAL STYLE (WITH APOLOGIES
TO A CERTAIN SERIES OF OXFORD TEXT-BOOKS). *Basileona*,
June 1901, No. 4, p. 43. Unsigned.

1903

C13 MACOLNIA SHOPS. *Independent Review*, November 1903,
Vol. 1, pp. 311–313.
Reprinted: *Abinger Harvest*, 1936.

C14 ALBERGO EMPEDOCLE. *Temple Bar*, December 1903, Vol.
128, pp. 663–684. First published story.

1904

C15 CNIDUS. *Independent Review*, March 1904, Vol. 2, pp. 278–282.
Reprinted: *Abinger Harvest*, 1936.

C16 A DAY OFF. *Pilot*, 14 May 1904, Vol. 9, pp. 445–446.

C17 THE ROAD FROM COLONUS. *Independent Review*, June 1904,
Vol. 3, pp. 124–134.
Reprinted: *Living Age*, 16 July 1904, Vol. 242, pp. 174–181.
The Celestial Omnibus, 1911. *The Collected Tales*, 1947.

C18 THE STORY OF A PANIC. *Independent Review*, August 1904,
Vol. 3, pp. 453–472.
Reprinted: *The Celestial Omnibus*, 1911. *The Collected Tales*,
1947.

C19 THE OTHER SIDE OF THE HEDGE. *Independent Review*,
November 1904, Vol. 4, pp. 297–301.
Reprinted: *Living Age*, 7 January 1905, Vol. 244, pp. 55–59.
The Celestial Omnibus, 1911. *The Collected Tales*, 1947.
Broadcast in the Home Service on 1 August 1963.

1905

C20 CARDAN. *Independent Review*, April 1905, Vol. 5, pp. 365–374.
Reprinted: *Abinger Harvest*, 1936.

C21 THE ETERNAL MOMENT. *Independent Review*, 1905, Vol. 6,
June, pp. 206–215, July, pp. 86–95, August, pp. 211–223.
Reprinted: *The Eternal Moment*, 1928. *The Collected Tales*,
1947.

Adapted by Alec Macdonald and broadcast in the Home Service on 25 February 1945.

C22 GEMISTUS PLETHO. *Independent Review*, October 1905, Vol. 7, pp. 211–223. Signed Edward Morgan Forster. Reprinted: *Abinger Harvest*, 1936.

1906

C23 ROSTOCK AND WISMAR. *Independent Review*, June 1906, Vol. 9, pp. 332–335.

C24 LITERARY ECCENTRICS: A REVIEW. *Independent Review*, October 1906, Vol. 11, pp. 105–110. Review of *Some Literary Eccentrics*, by John Fyvie.

1907

C25 PESSIMISM IN LITERATURE. *Working Men's College Journal*, January–February 1907, Vol. 10, pp. 6–10, 26–30. Paper opening discussion on 'Is the Pessimism in Modern Literature to be Deplored?' at a meeting of the Old Students' Club, 1 December 1906; summary of discussion pp. 30–33.

C26 THE CURATE'S FRIEND. *Pall Mall Magazine*, October 1907, N.S., Vol. 6, pp. 470–474.

Reprinted: *Putnam's Monthly*, October 1907, Vol. 3, pp. 43–47. *The Celestial Omnibus*, 1911. *The Collected Tales*, 1947.

1908

C27 THE CELESTIAL OMNIBUS. *Albany Review*, January 1908, Vol. 2, pp. 459–475.
Reprinted: *The Celestial Omnibus*, 1911. *The Collected Tales*, 1947.
Adapted and broadcast in 1942. *See also* C377.

C28 DANTE. *Working Men's College Journal*, February–April 1908, Vol. 10, pp. 261–264, 281–286, 301–306. Paper read to the Working Men's College Literary Society, 21 November 1907.

1909

C29 OTHER KINGDOM. *English Review*, July 1909, Vol. 2, pp. 651–672.

Reprinted: *Living Age*, 28 August 1909, Vol. 262, pp. 547–561. *The Celestial Omnibus*, 1911. *The Collected Tales*, 1947.

Adapted and broadcast in the Third Programme on 29 May 1947.

C30 THE MACHINE STOPS. *Oxford and Cambridge Review*, Michaelmas Term 1909, Vol. 8, pp. 83–122.

Reprinted: *The Eternal Moment*, 1928. *The Collected Tales*, 1947.

1911

C31 MR. ANDREWS. *Open Window*, April 1911, Vol. 2, pp. 4–13.

Reprinted: *The Eternal Moment*, 1928. *The Collected Tales*, 1947.

Broadcast by the author on 7 May 1927.

C32 MR. WALSH'S SECRET HISTORY OF THE VICTORIAN MOVEMENT. *Basileon Z* [*i.e.* zeta], June 1911, Vol. 13, pp. 4–7. On *A Manual of Domestic Economy*, by J. H. Walsh.

C33 THE POINT OF IT. *English Review*, November 1911, Vol. 9, pp. 615–630.

Reprinted: *The Eternal Moment*, 1928. *The Collected Tales*, 1947.

The holograph manuscript is in the Academic Center, University of Texas.

1912

C34 AN ALLEGORY (?)*. *Basileon H* [*i.e.* eta], June 1912, Vol. 14, pp. 6–7. Dialogue. '*This contribution was sent in without a title. We have done our best, but feel doubtful—Editors.' Signed E.M.F.

Reprinted as: Back to the Backs, *Granta*, 28 April 1956, Vol. 59, No. 1163, pp. 12–13.

C35 CO-OPERATION. *English Review*, June 1912, Vol. 11, pp. 366–372.

Reprinted as: Co-ordination, with this word and its cognates substituted throughout, *The Eternal Moment*, 1928. *The Collected Tales*, 1947.

Adapted and broadcast as 'Co-ordination' in the Third Programme on 29 May 1947.

C36 INSPIRATION. *Author*, July 1912, Vol. 22, pp. 281–282. Unsigned.

1913

C37   IRON HORSES IN INDIA. *Golden Hynde*, December 1913, [Vol. 1], pp. 35–39. On railway travel in India.

1914

C38   ADRIFT IN INDIA: THE NINE GEMS OF UJJAIN. *New Weekly*, 21 March 1914, Vol. 1, p. 10. The first of a series of four articles. *See also* C40, 42, 47.
Reprinted: *Abinger Harvest*, 1936.

C39   THE INDIAN MIND. *New Weekly*, 28 March 1914, Vol. 1, p. 55. Review of *Reflections on the Problems of India*, by A. S. Wadia.

C40   ADRIFT IN INDIA, 2: ADVANCE, INDIA! *New Weekly*, 11 April 1914, Vol. 1, p. 106.
Reprinted: *Abinger Harvest*, 1936.

C41   THE WEDDING. *New Weekly*, 2 May 1914, Vol. 1, p. 216. Review of *Marriage Ceremonies in Morocco*, by Edward Westermarck.

C42   ADRIFT IN INDIA, 3: IN RAJASTHAN. *New Weekly*, 16 May 1914, Vol. 1, pp. 269–270.
Reprinted (omitting the first paragraph) as: Adrift in India, 3: Jodhpur, *Abinger Harvest*, 1936.

C43   THE GODS OF INDIA. *New Weekly*, 30 May 1914, Vol. 1, p. 338. Review of *The Gods of India*, by E. O. Martin.

C44   CHITRA. *New Weekly*, 13 June 1914, Vol. 1, p. 403. Review of *Chitra*, by Rabindranath Tagore.
Reprinted as: Two Books by Tagore, 1: Chitra, *Abinger Harvest*, 1936.

C45   THE AGE OF MISERY. *New Weekly*, 27 June 1914, Vol. 2, p. 52. Review of *Ancient India*, by E. J. Rapson.

C46   THE ROSE SHOW. *New Weekly*, 11 July 1914, Vol. 2, p. 119. Review of *The Press and Poetry of Modern Persia*, by E. G. Browne.

C47   ADRIFT IN INDIA, 4: THE SUPPLIANT. *New Weekly*, 25 July 1914, Vol. 2, p. 166.
Reprinted: *Abinger Harvest*, 1936.

C48   TO SIMPLY FEEL. *New Weekly*, 8 August 1914, Vol. 2, pp. 245–246. Review of *Poems of Problems*, by Ella Wheeler Wilcox; and *Love's Legend*, by H. Fielding Hall.

C49   THE ELDER TAGORE. *Daily News and Leader*, 11 November 1914, p. 7. Review of *The Autobiography of Maharshi ('the Saint') Devendranath Tagore*, translated by S. Tagore and I. Devi. Signed E. M. Foster.

1915

C50   THE INDIAN BOOM. *Daily News and Leader*, 2 February 1915, p. 7. Review of *Svarnalata: Scenes from Hindu Village Life in Bengal*, by T. N. Ganguli, translated by D. Roy Macmillan.

C51   THE FUNCTIONS OF LITERATURE IN WAR-TIME. *Working Men's College Journal*, March 1915, Vol. 14, pp. 57–61. Paper read to the Old Students' Club, 13 February 1915; discussion pp. 61–62.

C52   A GREAT ANGLO-INDIAN. *Daily News and Leader*, 29 March 1915, p. 7. Review of *Studies in Literature and History*, by Sir Alfred Lyall.

C53   A NEW NOVELIST. *Daily News and Leader*, 8 April 1915, p. 7. Review of *The Voyage Out*, by Virginia Woolf.

C54   THE MISSION OF HINDUISM. *Daily News and Leader*, 30 April 1915, p. 7. Review of *Footfalls of Indian History*, by Sister Nivedita (Margaret E. Noble); and *Hinduism in Europe and America*, by Elizabeth A. Reed.

C55   TATE VERSUS CHANTREY. *Daily News and Leader*, 26 May 1915, p. 8. Report of the National Gallery Committee on matters connected with the National Arts Collections.

C56   SHORT STORIES FROM RUSSIA. *New Statesman*, 24 July 1915, pp. 373–374. Review of *The Steppe and Other Stories*, by Anton Tchekov, translated by Adeline Lister Kay; *Stories of Russian Life*, by Anton Tchekov, translated by Marian Fell; and *The Old House and Other Tales*, by Feodor Sologub, translated by John Cournos.

C57   RECONSTRUCTION IN THE MARNE AND THE MEUSE. *Westminster Gazette*, 30 August 1915, pp. 1–2.

1917

C58   OUR DIVERSIONS, [1]: DIANA'S DILEMMA. *Egyptian Mail*, 26 August 1917, p. [2]. Signed Pharos.

C59   OUR DIVERSIONS, 2: SUNDAY MUSIC. *Egyptian Mail*, 2 September 1917, p. [2]. Signed Pharos.

C60   A MUSICIAN IN EGYPT. *Egyptian Mail*, 21 October 1917, p. [2]. Signed Pharos. On a symphonic poem, by Enrico Terni, a local composer, performed at San Stefano, Alexandria.

C61   OUR DIVERSIONS, [3]: THE SCALLIES. *Egyptian Mail*, 18 November 1917, p. 2. Signed Pharos.
Reprinted as: Our Diversions, 1: The Scallies, *Abinger Harvest*, 1936.

C62   XXTH CENTURY ALEXANDRIA: THE NEW QUAY. *Egyptian Mail*, 2 December 1917, p. 2. Signed Pharos. *See also* letters in the *Egyptian Mail*, 5 December 1917, p. 2.

C63   GIPPO ENGLISH. *Egyptian Mail*, 16 December 1917, p. 2. Signed Pharos.

C64   THE DEN. *Egyptian Mail*, 30 December 1917, p. 2. Signed Pharos.
Reprinted: *Pharos and Pharillon*, 1923. *See also* p. 12.

1918

C65   ALEXANDRIA VIGNETTES: HANDEL IN EGYPT. *Egyptian Mail*, 6 January 1918, p. 2. Signed Pharos.

C66   ALEXANDRIA VIGNETTES: PHOTOGRAPHIC EGYPT. *Egyptian Mail*, 13 January 1918, p. 2. Signed Pharos.

C67   ALEXANDRIA VIGNETTES: COTTON FROM THE OUTSIDE. *Egyptian Mail*, 3 February 1918, p. 2. Signed Pharos.
Reprinted as: Cotton from the Outside, *Pharos and Pharillon*, 1923.

C68   ALEXANDRIA VIGNETTES: THE SOLITARY PLACE. *Egyptian Mail*, 10 March 1918, p. 2. Signed Pharos.
Reprinted (revised) as: The Solitary Place, *Pharos and Pharillon*, 1923.

C69   ALEXANDRIA VIGNETTES: HIGHER ASPECTS. *Egyptian Mail*, 5 May 1918, p. [2]. Signed Pharos.

C70   ALEXANDRIA VIGNETTES: THE RETURN FROM SIWA (B. C. 331). *Egyptian Mail*, 14 July 1918, p. [2]. Signed Pharos.
Reprinted as: The Return from Siwa, *Pharos and Pharillon*, 1923.

C71   ALEXANDRIA VIGNETTES: LUNCH AT THE BISHOP'S (A.D. 310). *Egyptian Mail*, 31 July 1918, p. [2]. Signed Pharos.
Reprinted as: St. Athanasius [Part 1], *Athenaeum*, 16 May 1919, p. 327. *See* C87. *Pharos and Pharillon*, 1923.

C72 THE MODERN SONS OF THE PHARAOHS: [SECOND NOTICE]. *Egyptian Mail*, 18 August 1918, p. [2]. Review of *Modern Sons of the Pharaohs*, by S. H. Leeder. Signed Pharos. The first review, entitled 'The Copts', unsigned and not by Forster, was published in the issue of 28 July, p. [2].

C73 ALEXANDRIA VIGNETTES: EPIPHANY (B.C. 204). *Egyptian Mail*, 6 October 1918, p. [2]. Signed Pharos. Reprinted as: Epiphany, *Pharos and Pharillon*, 1923.

C74 ALEXANDRIA VIGNETTES: CANOPUS, MENOUTHIS, ABOU-KIR. *Egyptian Mail*, 29 December 1918, p. [2]. Signed Pharos. Review of *Canopus, Menouthis, Aboukir*, by J. Faivre.

1919

C75 ALEXANDRIA VIGNETTES: ARMY ENGLISH. *Egyptian Mail*, 12 January 1919, p. [2]. Signed Pharos.

C76 ALEXANDRIA VIGNETTES: ENGLAND'S HONOUR (BEING EXTRACTS FROM THE DIARY OF MME. KYRIAKIDIS, RAMLEH). *Egyptian Mail*, 26 January 1919, p. [2]. Signed Pharos.

C77 A FIRST FLIGHT. *National Review*, March 1919, Vol. 73, pp. 118–119. Signed M[organ].

C78 A BERESFORD NOVEL. *Daily News*, 19 March 1919, p. 6. Review of *The Jervaise Comedy*, by J. D. Beresford. Unsigned.

C79 THE TROUBLE IN EGYPT: TREATMENT OF THE FELLAHIN. *Manchester Guardian*, 29 March 1919, p. 8. Letter.

C80 THE YOUNG PRETENDER. *Daily News*, 17 April 1919, p. 6. Review of *Mr. Misfortunate*, by Marjorie Bowen. Unsigned.

C81 A POPULAR THEATRE. *Athenaeum*, 18 April 1919, pp. 216–217. Review of *The People's Theatre*; and *Two Plays of the French Revolution*, by Romain Rolland, translated by Barrett H. Clark. Signed E.M.F.

C82 THE FICTION FACTORY (BY A NOVELIST). *Daily News*, 23 April 1919, p. 6. Review of *Materials and Methods of Fiction*, by Clayton Hamilton. Unsigned.

C83 THE POETRY OF C. P. CAVAFY. *Athenaeum*, 25 April 1919, pp. 247–248. Signed E. M. Forster and G. Valassopoulo, who translated the poems. Attention is drawn to a serious blunder by the printers in a letter to the *Athenaeum*, 9 May 1919, p. 311. *See* C86.

Reprinted (corrected and with the poem 'The God Abandons Antony' detached from the essay): *Pharos and Pharillon*, 1923.

C84　FROM GAY TO GRAVE. *Daily News*, 1 May 1919, p. 6. Review of *The Burning Spear*, by A.R.P.-M. [*i.e.* John Galsworthy]; *Our Casualty and Other Stories*, by George Birmingham; and *The Moon and Sixpence*, by W. S. Maugham.

C85　DUAL CONTROL. *Daily News*, 2 May 1919, p. 6. Review of *The Gay-Dombeys*, by Sir Harry Johnston.

C86　THE POETRY OF C. P. CAVAFY. *Athenaeum*, 9 May 1919, p. 311. Letter signed E. M. Forster and G. Valassopoulo. *See* C83.

C87　ST. ATHANASIUS [PART 2]. *Athenaeum*, 23 May 1919, pp. 358–359.
Reprinted: *Pharos and Pharillon*, 1923. Part 1 was first published in the *Egyptian Mail*, 31 July 1918. *See* C71.

C88　EIGHT SNAKES. *Daily Herald*, 21 May 1919, p. 8. Review of *The Price of Things*, by Elinor Glyn.

C89　IDEALS AND REALITIES OF BATTLE. *Daily News*, 24 May 1919, p. 2. Review of *Naked Warriors*, by Herbert Read.

C90　A LITTLE BIT OF ALL RIGHT. *Daily Herald*, 28 May 1919, p. 8. Review of *A London Lot*, by A. Neil Lyons.

C91　HAWKERITIS. *Daily Herald*, 30 May 1919, p. 4. Letter on the publicity given to a recent flying feat.

C92　TWO EGYPTS. *Athenaeum*, 30 May 1919, pp. 393–394. Review of *Recollections and Reflections*, by Coles Pasha; and *Through Egypt in War-time*, by Martin S. Briggs. Signed E.M.F.

C93　BREAKABLE BUTTERFLIES. *Athenaeum*, 6 June 1919, pp. 426–427. Review of *Diminutive Dramas*, by Maurice Baring. Signed E.M.F.

C94　ENTERTAINMENT. *Daily News*, 9 June 1919, p. 6. Review of *The Wife who Came Alive*, by William Caine. Unsigned.

C95　PAINTED REALITY. *Daily News*, 10 June 1919, p. 2. Review of *Java Head*, by Joseph Hergesheimer.

C96　KILL YOUR EAGLE! *Daily News*, 17 June 1919, p. 5. Review of *Prometheus Ill-bound*, by André Gide, translated by Lilian Rothermere.

C97　THE GAME OF LIFE. *Athenaeum*, 27 June 1919, pp. 517–518. Unsigned.
Reprinted as: Our Diversions, 6: The Game of Life, *Abinger Harvest*, 1936.

C98 THE EXTREME CASE. *Athenaeum*, 4 July 1919, pp. 561–562. Review of *Lettres de Paul Gauguin à G.-D. de Monfreid, précédées d'un hommage par V. Segalen*. Signed E.M.F.

C99 A CONCERT OF OLD INSTRUMENTS. *Athenaeum*, 11 July 1919, p. 597. Notice of a concert by Mrs Gordon Woodhouse at Queen Anne's Gate, London. Unsigned.

C100 BEYOND GOG AND MAGOG. *Nation*, London, 19 July 1919, pp. 479–480. Review of *My Diaries, 1888–1900, Part 1*, by W. S. Blunt. Signed E.M.F.
Reprinted as: Wilfrid Blunt, 1: The Earlier Diaries, *Abinger Harvest*, 1936. *See also* C132.

C101 TIMOTHY WHITEBONNET AND TIMOTHY THE CAT. *Athenaeum*, 25 July 1919, pp. 646–647.
Reprinted: *Living Age*, 6 September 1919, Vol. 302, pp. 594–595.
Reprinted as: Timothy the Cat & Timothy Whitebonnet, *Pharos and Pharillon*, 1923.

C102 "AMIS AND AMILES" AT WEYBRIDGE. *Athenaeum*, 25 July 1919, pp. 662–663. Review of the play at the Hall School, Weybridge. Unsigned. *See also* C161.

C103 A MOVING DOCUMENT. *Daily Herald*, 30 July 1919, p. 8. Review of *Mary Olivier: A Life*, by May Sinclair.

C104 VISIONS. *Daily News*, 31 July 1919, p. 2. Review of *The Mark on the Wall*; and *Kew Gardens*, by Virginia Woolf.

C105 TAGORE AS A NOVELIST. *Athenaeum*, 1 August 1919, p. 687. Review of *The Home and the World*, by Rabindranath Tagore. Signed E.M.F.
Reprinted as: Two Books by Tagore, 2: The Home and the World, *Abinger Harvest*, 1936.

C106 CLEMENT OF ALEXANDRIA. *Athenaeum*, 8 August 1919, pp. 713–714. Review of *Clement of Alexandria*, with an English translation by G. W. Butterworth, Loeb Classical Library. Signed E.M.F.
Reprinted: *Pharos and Pharillon*, 1923.

C107 A FLOOD IN THE OFFICE. *Athenaeum*, 8 August 1919, pp. 717–718. Review of *The Nile Projects*, by Sir William Willcocks. Signed E.M.F.
Reprinted: *Abinger Harvest*, 1936. The reprinting of this review led to a libel action and its omission from later reprints and editions. *See* A18a.

C108 MY COUNTRY! *Daily News*, 15 August 1919, p. 6. Review of *An Anthology of Modern Slavonic Literature*, by P. Selver.

C109 GREEN PASTURES AND PICCADILLY. *Athenaeum*, 22 August 1919, p. 790. Review of the play by John Walton at the Ambassadors Theatre, London. Signed P[haros].

C110 A LITTLE JAM. *Daily Herald*, 23 August 1919, p. 8. Review of *My Little Bit*, by Marie Corelli.

C111 ALMOST TOO SAD? *Daily News*, 23 August 1919, p. 2. Review of *The Bishop and Other Stories*, by A[nton] Tchehov, translated by Constance Garnett.

C112 GRIP. *Athenaeum*, 5 September 1919, p. 852. Review of the play *The Voice from the Minaret*, by Robert Hichens at the Globe Theatre, London. Signed P[haros].

C113 MATERNAL LOVE. *Athenaeum*, 19 September 1919, pp. 923–924. Review of *Trimmed in Scarlet*, by William Hurlbut at the Court Theatre, London. Signed P[haros].

C114 THE TEMPLE. *Athenaeum*, 26 September 1919, p. 947. Review of some official Indian archaeological publications. Signed E.M.F.

C115 NOT A NICE GIRL: MR. SWINNER ON'S [*sic*] NEW HEROINE. *Daily Herald*, 7 October 1919, p. 2. Review of *September*, by Frank Swinnerton.

C116 TOLSTOY AT THE ST. JAMES'S. *Athenaeum*, 10 October 1919, p. 1011. Review of the play *Reparation*, by Count Tolstoy at the St James's Theatre, London. Signed P[haros].

C117 THE END OF THE SAMOVAR. *Daily News*, 11 November 1919, p. 5. Review of *An Honest Thief and Other Stories*, by F. Dostoevsky, translated by Constance Garnett.

C118 THE EGYPTIAN LABOUR CORPS. *The Times*, 13 November 1919, p. 8. Letter.

C119 NEWS FROM NORWAY. *Daily Herald*, 26 November 1919, p. 8. Review of *The Face of the World*, by Johan Bojer, translated by J. Muir.

C120 IMPERSONAL INTIMACIES. *Daily News*, 26 November 1919, p. 5. Review of *Impressions that Remained*, by Ethel Smyth.

C121 PHAROS. *Athenaeum*, 28 November, 5 and 12 December 1919, pp. 1250–1251, 1282–1283, 1330–1331. Reprinted: *Pharos and Pharillon*, 1923.

C122 [SAKUNTALA]. *Athenaeum*, 28 November 1919, p. 1267. Review of the play *Sakuntala*, by Kalidasa; English version by Das Gupta and Laurence Binyon at the Winter Garden Theatre, London. Unsigned. *See also* C140.

C. CONTRIBUTIONS TO PERIODICALS

C123 MUSIC IN EDINBURGH: THE REID CONCERTS. *Athenaeum*,
26 December 1919, p. 1406. Held in the McEwan Hall, by
Professor Donald Tovey. Unsigned.

1920

C124 LITERATURE AND HISTORY. *Athenaeum*, 2 January 1920,
pp. 26–27. Review of *Études et Fantaisies historiques*, 2e Série,
by E. Rodocanachi. Signed E.M.F.

C125 FRENCHMEN AND FRANCE. *Daily News*, 3 January 1920, p. 7.
Review of *French Ways and their Meanings*, by Edith Wharton.

C126 THE CONSOLATIONS OF HISTORY. *Athenaeum*, 16 January
1920, pp. 69–70. Signed E.M.F.
Reprinted: *Abinger Harvest*, 1936.

C127 CIVILISATION. *Daily Herald*, 21 January 1920, p. 8. Review
of *Civilisation*, by Georges Duhamel.

C128 L'EXPÉRIENCE DU BONHEUR. *Athenaeum*, 23 January 1920,
pp. 122–123. Review of *Macao et Cosmage*, by E. L. L. Edy-
Legrand. Signed E.M.F.
Reprinted as: Happiness!, *Abinger Harvest*, 1936.

C129 SONGS OF LOVELINESS. *Daily News*, 27 January 1920, p. 5.
Review of *More Translations from the Chinese* and *Japanese
Poetry: The "Uta"*, by Arthur Waley.

C130 COUSIN X—. *Daily News*, 3 February 1920, p. 5. Review of
Mansoul, by C. M. Doughty.

C131 [NOTICE OF sketches by Sir Bartle Frere on view at the Walker
Gallery]. *Athenaeum*, 13 February 1920, p. 215. Unsigned.

C132 WILFRID BLUNT AND THE EAST. *Nation*, London, 21 February 1920, pp. 712, 714. Review of *My Diaries, 1900–14, Part 2*,
by W. S. Blunt. Unsigned.
Reprinted as: Wilfrid Blunt, 2: The Later Diaries, *Abinger
Harvest*, 1936. *See also* C100.

C133 WHERE THERE IS NOTHING. *Athenaeum*, 27 February 1920,
pp. 270–271. Review of *The Strongest*, by Georges Clemenceau.
Signed E.M.F.

C134 THE MOSQUE. *Athenaeum*, 19 March 1920, pp. 367–368.
Review of *Moslem Architecture*, by G. T. Rivoira, translated by
G. McN. Rushworth. Signed E.M.F.
Reprinted: *Abinger Harvest*, 1936.

C. CONTRIBUTIONS TO PERIODICALS

C135 THE WHITE DIVEL AT CAMBRIDGE. *New Statesman*, 20 March 1920, pp. 708–709. Review of the play by John Webster performed by the Marlowe Society.

C136 THE WORK OF FORREST REID. *Nation*, London, 10 April 1920, pp. 47–48. Review of *Pirates of the Spring*, by Forrest Reid. Unsigned.
Reprinted as: Forrest Reid, *Abinger Harvest*, 1936.

C137 LITERARY NOTES. *Daily Herald*, 14 April 1920, p. 8. Signed Pharos. *See also* C146–147.

C138 DUST JACKETS. *Daily Herald*, 5 May 1920, p. 7.

C139 THE OBJECTS. *Athenaeum*, 7 May 1920, pp. 599–600. Review of *By Nile and Tigris*, by Sir Wallis Budge. Signed E.M.F. Reprinted as: For the Museum's Sake, *Abinger Harvest*, 1936.

C140 THE GOLDEN PEAK. *Athenaeum*, 14 May 1920, pp. 631–632. Review of *Sakuntala*, by Kalidasa; a version for the English Stage by Das Gupta and Laurence Binyon, with an introduction by Rabindranath Tagore. Signed E.M.F. *See also* C122.

C141 THE CHURNING OF THE OCEAN. *Athenaeum*, 21 May 1920, pp. 667–668. Review of *The Ideals of Indian Art*, 2nd edition, by E. B. Havell; and *Chatterjee's Picture Albums, Vols. 1–5*. Signed E.M.F.

C142 ADVENTURE. *Daily Herald*, 26 May 1920, p. 7. Review of *Miss Haroun al-Raschid*, by Jessie Douglas Merruish. Unsigned.

C143 THE SCHOOL FEAST. *Daily News*, 28 May 1920, p. 4. Review of *Naturalism in English Poetry*, by Stopford A. Brooke.

C144 JEHOVAH, BUDDHA AND THE GREEKS. *Athenaeum*, 4 June 1920, pp. 730–731. Review of *Hellenism*, by Norman Bentwich; and *Hellenism in Ancient India*, by Gauranga Nath Bannerjee. Signed E.M.F.

C145 THE BOY WHO NEVER GREW UP. *Daily Herald*, 9 June 1920, p. 7. Review of *Letters of Travel*, by Rudyard Kipling.

C146 LITERARY NOTES. *Daily Herald*, 9 June 1920, p. 7. Signed Pharos. *See also* C137, 147.

C147 LITERARY NOTES. *Daily Herald*, 23 June 1920, p. 7. Signed Pharos. *See also* C137, 146.

C148 A GREAT HISTORY. *Athenaeum*, 2 and 9 July 1920, pp. 8–9, 42–43. Review of *The Outline of History, Vol. 1*, by H. G. Wells. Signed E.M.F. For a review of Vol. 2, *see* C158.

C149 BIG STICK AND GREEN LEAF. *Athenaeum*, 16 July 1920, p. 76. Review of *Recreation*, by Viscount Grey of Fallodon. Signed E.M.F.

C150 THE SITTERS. *Nation*, London, 24 July 1920, p. 532. Review of *Adventures in Interviewing*, by Isaac F. Marcosson. Unsigned.

C151 LUSO-INDIA. *Athenaeum*, 27 August 1920, p. 268. Review of *The Book of Duarte Barbosa, Vol. 1*; and *History of the Portuguese in Bengal*, by J. J. A. Campos. Signed E.M.F.

C152 BEYLE AND BYRON. *Athenaeum*, 24 September 1920, p. 419. Letter.

C153 [REVIEW OF] *Dead Towns and Living Men*, by C. Leonard Woolley; and *Discovery in Greek Lands*, by F. H. Marshall. *London Mercury*, October 1920, Vol. 2, pp. 763–764. Unsigned.

C154 A CAUTIONARY TALE. *Nation*, London, 9 October 1920, pp. 47–48. Review of *Europe and the Faith*, by H. Belloc. Unsigned.

C155 MISSIONARIES. *Athenaeum*, 22 October 1920, pp. 545–547. Review of *In Unknown China*, by S. Pollard; *The Rebuke of Islam*, by W. H. T. Gairdner; *Women Workers of the Orient*, by M. E. Burton; and *Character Building in Kashmir*, by C. E. Tyndale-Biscoe. Signed E.M.F.

C156 THE DEDLOCK PAPERS. *Athenaeum*, 29 October 1920, pp. 580–581. Review of *The Mirrors of Downing Street*, by A Gentleman with a Duster [*i.e.* Harold Begbie]. Signed E.M.F.

C157 WELL, WELL! *Athenaeum*, 5 November 1920, p. 612. Review of *The Uses of Diversity*, by G. K. Chesterton. Unsigned.

C158 MR. WELLS' "OUTLINE". *Athenaeum*, 19 November 1920, pp. 690–691. Review of *The Outline of History, Vol. 2*, by H. G. Wells. Signed E.M.F. For a review of Vol. 1, *see* C148.

C159 [REVIEW OF] *The Diary of Ananda Ranga Pillai, Vol. 7*, edited by H. Dodwell. *Athenaeum*, 3 December 1920, p. 761. Unsigned.

C160 THE UNTIDY GENTLEMAN. *Nation*, London, 4 December 1920, pp. 344, 346. Review of *The New Jerusalem*, by G. K. Chesterton. Unsigned.

C161 BREAKING-UP DAY—NEW STYLE. *Manchester Guardian*, 8 December 1920, p. 8. Review of the play *The Ballad of Sir Patrick Spens* at the Hall School, Weybridge. Signed E.M.F. *See also* C102.

C162 THE POETRY OF IQBAL. *Athenaeum*, 10 December 1920, pp. 803–804. Review of *The Secrets of Self*, by Sheikh Muhammed [*sic*] Iqbal, translated from the Persian by R. A. Nicholson.

1921

C163 IN THE TEMPLE OF CRITICISM. *Nation*, London, 8 January 1921, pp. 512, 514. Review of *Aspects of Literature*, by J. Middleton Murry; *Essays on Books*, by A. Clutton-Brock; and *The Art of Letters*, by Robert Lynd. Unsigned.

C164 VICTORIAN WRITERS. *Athenaeum*, 28 January 1921, pp. 93–94. Review of *A Survey of English Literature: 1830–1880*, by Oliver Elton. Signed E.M.F.

C165 PILGRIM'S PROGRESS. *Daily News*, 8 February 1921, p. 6. Review of *The Magic Flute*, by G. Lowes Dickinson.

C166 THE PRIDE OF MR. CONRAD. *Nation and Athenaeum*, 19 March 1921, pp. 881–882. Review of *Notes on Life and Letters*, by Joseph Conrad. Unsigned.
Reprinted as: Joseph Conrad: A Note, *Abinger Harvest*, 1936.

C167 SALUTE TO THE ORIENT! *London Mercury*, July 1921, Vol. 4, pp. 271–281.
Reprinted: *Abinger Harvest*, 1936.

1922

C168 REFLECTIONS IN INDIA, 1: TOO LATE? (BY OUR INDIAN CORRESPONDENT.) *Nation and Athenaeum*, 21 January 1922, pp. 614–615. Unsigned.

C169 REFLECTIONS IN INDIA, 2: THE PRINCE'S PROGRESS (BY OUR INDIAN CORRESPONDENT.) *Nation and Athenaeum*, 28 January 1922, pp. 644–646. Unsigned.

C170 THE EMPEROR BABUR. *Nation and Athenaeum*, 1 April 1922, pp. 21–22. Review of *The Memoirs of Babur*, Leyden and Erskine's translation, annotated and revised by Sir Lucas King. Signed E.M.F.
Reprinted: *Abinger Harvest*, 1936.

C171 THE MIND OF THE INDIAN NATIVE STATE (BY OUR INDIAN CORRESPONDENT.) *Nation and Athenaeum*, 29 April and 13 May 1922, pp. 146–147, 216–217. Unsigned.
Reprinted as: The Mind of the Indian Native State, *Abinger Harvest*, 1936.

C172 MR. AND MRS. ABBEY'S DIFFICULTIES. *London Mercury*, May 1922, Vol. 6, pp. 28–33. On Keats' guardians.
Reprinted: *Abinger Harvest*, 1936.

C173 INDIA AND THE TURK (FROM OUR CORRESPONDENT LATELY IN INDIA.) *Nation and Athenaeum*, 30 September 1922, pp. 844–845. Signed F.

C174 "ANOTHER LITTLE WAR". *Daily News*, 9 October 1922, p. 6. Letter on the same subject as C175.

C175 OUR GRAVES IN GALLIPOLI: A DIALOGUE. *New Leader*, 20 October 1922, p. 8. *See also* C174.
Reprinted as: Our Graves in Gallipoli, *Abinger Harvest*, 1936.

1923

C176 PAN. *Criterion*, July 1923, Vol. 1, pp. 402–408.
Reprinted as: Adrift in India, 5: Pan, *Abinger Harvest*, 1936.

C177 A VOTER'S DILEMMA. *New Leader*, 30 November 1923, p. 8. Verse.
Reprinted: *Abinger Harvest*, 1936. *New Republic*, 19 January 1948, p. 7 (omitting 10 lines in Verse 3).

1924

C178 JANE, HOW SHALL WE EVER RECOLLECT... *Nation and Athenaeum*, 5 January 1924, pp. 512–514. Review of *The Novels of Jane Austen*, edited by R. W. Chapman; and *Jane Austen*, by Léonie Villard, translated by Veronica Lucas.
Reprinted: *New Republic*, 30 January 1924, pp. 260–261. Reprinted (omitting the section on Villard's book) as: Jane Austen, 1: The Six Novels, *Abinger Harvest*, 1936.

C179 THE BIRTH OF AN EMPIRE. *Nation and Athenaeum*, 26 April 1924, pp. 110–111. On the British Empire Exhibition at Wembley.
Reprinted as: Our Diversions, 2: The Birth of an Empire, *Abinger Harvest*, 1936.

C180 ELIZA IN CHAINS. *Cornhill Magazine*, May 1924, N.S., Vol. 56, pp. 598–609. Based on *Original Letters from India (1779–1815)*, by Mrs Eliza Fay. *See* B3.
Reprinted: *Dial*, May 1924, Vol. 76, pp. 391–403.

C181 THE BAD FAIRIES. *Nation and Athenaeum*, 2 August 1924, pp. 562–563. On the Queen's dolls' house at the British Empire Exhibition, Wembley.

Reprinted as: Our Diversions, 3: The Doll Souse, *Abinger Harvest*, 1936.

C182 AN EIGHTEENTH-CENTURY SAILOR. *Nation and Athenaeum*, 4 October 1924, p. 22. Review of *A History of the Indian Wars*, by Clement Downing, edited by William Foster. Signed E.M.F.

C183 A BIRTH IN THE DESERT. *Nation and Athenaeum*, 8 November 1924, pp. 210–211. On Burg el Arab.

1925

C184 SANDITON. *Nation and Athenaeum*, 21 March 1925, p. 860. Review of *Fragment of a Novel*, by Jane Austen.
Reprinted as: Jane Austen, 2: Sanditon, *Abinger Harvest*, 1936.

C185 EDWARD VII. *Calendar of Modern Letters*, April 1925, Vol. 1, pp. 156–159. Review of *King Edward VII: A Biography, Vol. 1*, by Sir Sidney Lee.

C186 THE TRUE JOAN OF ARC: SHAW'S OR FRANCE'S? *New Leader*, 19 June 1925, p. 10. Review of *The Life of Joan of Arc*, by Anatole France.

C187 INDIAN CAVES. *Nation and Athenaeum*, 11 July 1925, p. 462. Review of *My Pilgrimages to Ajanta and Bagh*, by S. M. C. Dey. Signed E.M.F.

C188 PEEPING AT ELIZABETH. *Nation and Athenaeum*, 8 August 1925, pp. 568–569. Review of *The Elizabethan Home*, discovered in two dialogues by Claudius Hollyband and Peter Erondell; edited by M. St Clare Byrne.

C189 POVERTY'S CHALLENGE: THE TERRIBLE TOLSTOY. *New Leader*, 4 September 1925, pp. 11–12. Review of *What then Must We Do?*, by Leo Tolstoy, translated by Aylmer Maude.

C190 LITERATURE OR LIFE? HENRY W. NEVINSON: THE BOY WHO NEVER STUCK. *New Leader*, 2 October 1925, p. 14. Review of *More Changes, More Chances*, by H. W. Nevinson.

C191 ANONYMITY: AN ENQUIRY. *Calendar of Modern Letters*, November 1925, Vol. 2, pp. 145–156.
Reprinted as: Anonymity: An Inquiry, *Atlantic Monthly*, November 1925, Vol. 136, pp. 588–595. Reprinted: Hogarth Press, 1925. *See* A11. *Two Cheers for Democracy*, 1951.

C192 MRS. HANNAH MORE. *New Republic*, 16 December 1925, Vol. 45, pp. 106–109. Review of *The Letters of Hannah More*, selected with an introduction, by R. Brimley Johnson.

Reprinted: *Nation and Athenaeum*, 2 January 1926, pp. 493–494. *Abinger Harvest*, 1936.

C193 [REVIEW OF] *War at Wittenberg*, by A. R. D. Watkins, performed by the Cambridge Amateur Dramatic Society. *Nation and Athenaeum*, 19 December 1925, pp. 435–436.

1926

C194 NOTES ON THE ENGLISH CHARACTER. *Atlantic Monthly*, January 1926, Vol. 137, pp. 30–37. Title on wrapper: An Englishman's Character.
Reprinted: *Abinger Harvest*, 1936.

C195 ME, THEM AND YOU: SARGENT AT THE ROYAL ACADEMY. *New Leader*, 22 January 1926, p. 3.
Reprinted as: Me, Them and You, *Abinger Harvest*, 1936.

C196 HICKEY'S LAST PARTY. *Calendar of Modern Letters*, February 1926, Vol. 2, pp. 437–439. Review of *Memoirs of William Hickey, Vol. 4*.
Reprinted: *Abinger Harvest*, 1936.

C197 THE BOOK OF THE AGE? JAMES JOYCE'S "ULYSSES". *New Leader*, 12 March 1926, pp. 13–14.

C198 THE NOVELS OF VIRGINIA WOOLF. *New Criterion*, April 1926, Vol. 4, pp. 277–286.
Reprinted: *Yale Review*, April 1926, N.S., Vol. 15, pp. 505–514. Reprinted as: The Early Novels of Virginia Woolf, *Abinger Harvest*, 1936.

C199 ESCAPING THE HOUSE OF COMMON-SENSE. *New Leader*, 16 April 1926, p. 11. Review of *The Poetry of Nonsense*, by Emil Cammaerts.

C200 "IT IS DIFFFERENT FOR ME". *New Leader*, 16 July 1926, p. 3. Verse.
Reprinted: *Abinger Harvest*, 1936.

C201 VIRGIL AND TOMMY: THE MYSTERY OF DEAN INGE. *New Leader*, 17 September 1926, p. 11. Review of *England*, by W. R. Inge.

C202 MY WOOD, OR THE EFFECTS OF PROPERTY UPON CHARACTER. *New Leader*, 15 October 1926, p. 3.
Reprinted as: My Wood, *Abinger Harvest*, 1936.

C. CONTRIBUTIONS TO PERIODICALS

1927

C203 MY CENTENARY: OR WHY NOT? *Nation and Athenaeum*, 1 October 1927, pp. 835–836.
Reprinted as: My Own Centenary, *Abinger Harvest*, 1936.

C204 HAKLUYT. *Nation and Athenaeum*, 12 November 1927, pp. 226, 228, 230. Review of *Hakluyt's Voyages*, with an introduction by John Masefield.

1928

C205 IBSEN THE ROMANTIC. *Nation and Athenaeum*, 17 March 1928, pp. 902–903.
Reprinted: *New Republic*, 28 March 1928, pp. 186–188. *Abinger Harvest*, 1936.

C206 LITTLE CREATURES. *Nation and Athenaeum*, 9 June 1928, p. 333. Review of *Words and Poetry*, by G. H. W. Rylands. Signed E.M.F.

C207 OF RAILWAY BRIDGES: AN EXTRACT FROM THE TALK GIVEN ON JULY 16. *Radio Times*, 10 August 1928, p. 238.

C208 THE NEW CENSORSHIP. *Nation and Athenaeum*, 1 September 1928, p. 696. Unsigned. On the suppression of *The Well of Loneliness*, by Radclyffe Hall. *See also* C209.

C209 THE NEW CENSORSHIP. *Nation and Athenaeum*, 8 September 1928, p. 726. Letter signed E. M. Forster and Virginia Woolf, on the suppression of *The Well of Loneliness*, by Radclyffe Hall. *See also* C208. Forster made reference to this letter in his evidence before the Select Committee on Obscene Publications, *see* the *Report* (E4a), p. 18.

1929

C210 THE 'CENSORSHIP' OF BOOKS, 4. *Nineteenth Century and After*, April 1929, Vol. 105, pp. 444–445. Part of a symposium, the other contributors being the Right Hon. Lord Darling, Havelock Ellis, Stephen Foot, Virginia Woolf and Carrol Romer.

C211 OUR CURIOSITY AND DESPAIR. *New York Herald Tribune*, 21 April 1929, Section 11, Books, pp. 1, 6. Review of *A la Recherche du Temps perdu*, 2 vols., by Marcel Proust, translated by C. K. Scott Moncrieff; and *Proust*, by Clive Bell.

Reprinted as: The Epic of Curiosity and Despair, *Nation and Athenaeum*, 27 April and 4 May 1929, pp. 107–108, 158. Proust, *Abinger Harvest*, 1936.

C212 OUR PHOTOGRAPHY: SINCLAIR LEWIS. *New York Herald Tribune*, 28 April 1929, Section 11, Books, pp. 1, 6.
Reprinted as: A Camera Man, *Life and Letters*, May 1929, Vol. 2, pp. 336–343. Sinclair Lewis, *Abinger Harvest*, 1936. See also A15.

C213 OUR BUTTERFLIES AND BEETLES. *New York Herald Tribune*, 5 May 1929, Section 11, Books, pp. 1, 6. Review of *Collected Edition of the Works of Ronald Firbank*, with an introduction by Arthur Waley; and *No Love*, by David Garnett.
Reprinted as: Butterflies and Beetles, *Life and Letters*, July 1929, Vol. 3, pp. 1–9. Reprinted (omitting most of the review of Garnett's book) as: Ronald Firbank, *Abinger Harvest*, 1936.

C214 SOME OF OUR DIFFICULTIES. *New York Herald Tribune*, 12 May 1929, Section 11, Books, pp. 1, 6.
Reprinted as: T. S. Eliot and his Difficulties, *Life and Letters*, June 1929, Vol. 2, pp. 417–425. T. S. Eliot, *Abinger Harvest*, 1936.

1930

C215 MR. D. H. LAWRENCE AND LORD BRENTFORD. *Nation and Athenaeum*, 11 January 1930, pp. 508–509. Review of *Pornography and Obscenity*, by D. H. Lawrence; and *Do We Need a Censor?*, by Viscount Brentford. Signed E.M.F.

C216 D. H. LAWRENCE. *Nation and Athenaeum*, 29 March, p. 888, 12 and 26 April 1930, pp. 45, 109. Letters, the second in reply to T. S. Eliot's in the issue of 5 April, p. 11.

C217 D. H. LAWRENCE. *Listener*, 30 April 1930, pp. 753–754. From a talk broadcast on 16 April.

C218 A BROADCAST DEBATE. *Nation and Athenaeum*, 10 May 1930, p. 191. Review of *Points of View*, with an introduction and summing up by G. Lowes Dickinson.

C219 THE HAT-CASE. *Spectator*, 28 June 1930, p. 1055. Review of *The English Novel*, by Ford Madox Ford; and *The History of the English Novel, Vol. 1*, by Ernest A. Baker. The latter protested about the review in a letter in the issue of 12 July, p. 54 and the Editor quoted E. M. Forster's reply. See C220.

C220 THE HAT-CASE. *Spectator*, 12 July 1930, p. 54. E. M. Forster's reply, quoted by the Editor, to Ernest A. Baker's criticism of his review. *See* C219.

1931

C221 THE FREEDOM OF THE B.B.C. *New Statesman and Nation*, N.S., 4 April 1931, pp. 209–210.

C222 THE CULT OF D. H. LAWRENCE. *Spectator*, 18 April 1931, p. 627. Review of *Son of Woman: The Story of D. H. Lawrence*, by John Middleton Murry.

C223 AN ARTIST'S LIFE. *Spectator*, 25 April 1931, p. 669. Review of *A Life of Gaudier-Brzeska*, by H. S. Ede.

C224 THE CEREMONY OF BEING A GENTLEMAN. *Spectator*, 27 June 1931, p. 1014. Review of *The English: Are They Human?*, by G. J. Renier.

C225 INCONGRUITIES: CAPTAIN GIBBON. *New York Herald Tribune*, 16 August 1931, Section 11, Books, pp. 1, 4.
Reprinted as: Incongruities: Captain Edward Gibbon, *Spectator*, 29 August and 5 September 1931, pp. 264–265, 288–289. Captain Edward Gibbon, *Abinger Harvest*, 1936.

C226 INCONGRUITIES: WEIGHING FIRE. *New York Herald Tribune*, 23 August 1931, Section 11, Books, pp. 1, 4.
Reprinted as: Voltaire's Laboratory, 1: How They Weighed Fire, *Life and Letters*, September 1931, Vol. 7, pp. 157–164. *Abinger Harvest*, 1936.

C227 DEATH OF A POET: BIRTH OF A CRITIC. *Listener*, 26 August 1931, p. 333. Review of *Poems*, by S. T. Coleridge, Oxford University Press.

C228 INCONGRUITIES: VOLTAIRE'S SLUGS. *New York Herald Tribune*, 30 August 1931, Section 11, Books, pp. 1, 4.
Reprinted as: Voltaire's Laboratory, 2: Troublesome Molluscs, *Life and Letters*, September 1931, Vol. 7, pp. 165–173. *Abinger Harvest*, 1936.

C229 INCONGRUITIES: 'COMBERBACKE'. *New York Herald Tribune*, 6 September 1931, Section 11, Books, pp. 1, 4.
Reprinted (revised) as: Incongruities: S.T.C., *Spectator*, 19 and 26 September 1931, pp. 348–349, 381–382. Trooper Silas Tomkyn Comberbacke, *Abinger Harvest*, 1936.

C230 ON A NOVEL THAT STANDS APART. *News Chronicle*, 6 November 1931, p. 4. Review of *Uncle Stephen*, by Forrest Reid.

C231 GHOSTS ANCIENT AND MODERN. *Spectator*, 21 November 1931, p. 672. Review of *The Supernatural Omnibus*, edited with an introduction by Montague Summers; and *Witchcraft, Magic and Alchemy*, by Grillot de Givry, translated by J. Courtenay Locke.

C232 THE MAN BEHIND THE SCENES. *News Chronicle*, 30 November 1931, p. 4. Review of *The Trial of Jeanne d'Arc and Other Plays*, by Edward Garnett.

C233 MARCO POLO. *Spectator*, 12 December 1931, p. 816. Review of *The Travels of Marco Polo*, translated into English from the text of L. F. Benedetto by Aldo Ricci.
Reprinted as: Marco Polo's New Life, *New York Herald Tribune*, 13 December 1931, Section 11, Books, pp. 1, 6. Marco Polo, *Abinger Harvest*, 1936.

C234 ARE THE B.B.C. TOO CAUTIOUS? *Spectator*, 19 December 1931, p. 848. Letter.

1932

C235 NAPOLEON. *New Statesman and Nation*, N.S., 16 January 1932, p. 68. Review of *Bonaparte's Adventure in Egypt*, by P. G. Elgood.

C236 WILLIAM COWPER, AN ENGLISHMAN. *Spectator*, 16 January 1932, p. 75. On the bicentenary of his birth.
Reprinted as: The Stricken Deer, *New York Herald Tribune*, 17 January 1932, Section 11, Books, pp. 1, 6.

C237 THE NEXT WAR. *New Statesman and Nation*, N.S., 23 January 1932, p. 90. Letter.

C238 GEORGE CRABBE. *Spectator*, 20 February 1932, pp. 243–245. Reprinted (omitting 'Crabbe on Smugglers') as: Crabbe, A Worm with an Immortal Soul, *New York Herald Tribune*, 13 March 1932, Section 11, Books, p. 6.

C239 [REVIEW OF] *Hamlet*, performed by the Marlowe Society at Cambridge. *Spectator*, 12 March 1932, p. 366. Signed E.M.F.

C240 THE "OSTERLEY PARK" BALLADS. *Spectator*, 19 March 1932, p. 420. Review of *The "Osterley Park" Ballads*, with an introduction and notes by F. Burlington Fawcett. Signed E.M.F.

C241 AN APPROACH TO BLAKE. *Spectator*, 2 April 1932, p. 474. Review of *Poems of Blake*, chosen and edited by Laurence Binyon. Reprinted as: Prophet and Artist, *New York Herald Tribune*, 21 August 1932, Section 10, Books, pp. 1, 4.

C242 THE STRATFORD JUBILEE OF 1769. *Spectator*, 23 April 1932,
p. 586.
Reprinted: *Two Cheers for Democracy*, 1951.

C243 [REVIEW OF] *The Bride of Dionysus*, poem by R. C. Trevelyan,
music by D. F. Tovey, at the King's Theatre, Edinburgh.
Spectator, 7 May 1932, pp. 659–660. Signed E.M.F.

C244 WRITERS AT BAY. *Spectator*, 21 May 1932, p. 724.

C245 THE EYES OF SIBIU. *Spectator*, 25 June 1932, p. 894. On
Sibiu, formerly Hermannstadt, in Transylvania.

C246 HAS "IT" BROKEN DOWN? *New Statesman and Nation*,
N.S., 25 June 1932, p. 822. Letter, from Bucharest, on currency
restrictions.

C247 AFFABLE HAWK. *Spectator*, 23 July 1932, p. 125. Review of
Criticism, by Desmond MacCarthy who, as literary editor of
the *New Statesman and Nation*, signed his weekly article
'Affable Hawk'.

C248 MR. G. LOWES DICKINSON. *The Times*, 6 August 1932, p. 10.
Personal tribute.

C249 G. L. DICKINSON: A TRIBUTE. *Spectator*, 13 August 1932,
pp. 199–200.
Reprinted: *Living Age*, October 1932, Vol. 343, pp. 141–143.

C250 CHESS AT CRACOW. *Time and Tide*, 13 August 1932, pp. 885–
886.
Reprinted as: Our Diversions, 5: Chess at Cracow, *Abinger
Harvest*, 1936.

C251 COLERIDGE IN HIS LETTERS. *Spectator*, 10 September 1932,
pp. 309–310. Review of *Unpublished Letters of S. T. Coleridge*,
edited by E. L. Griggs.

C252 MRS. GRUNDY AT THE PARKERS'. *New Statesman and Nation*, N.S., 10 September 1932, pp. 284–285.
Reprinted: *Abinger Harvest*, 1936.

C253 BOOKS OF THE WEEK. *Listener*, 12 October 1932, pp. 536–537.
Review of *Wordsworth*, by Herbert Read; *An Outline of English
Literature*, compiled by L. A. G. Strong and Monica Redlich;
and *The Pleasures of Poetry, Third Series: The Victorian Age*, by
Edith Sitwell. First of a series of seven broadcast talks on books.
For the other talks *see* C255–256, 259–262.

C254 D.O.R.A. *New Statesman and Nation*, N.S., 15 October 1932,
p. 442. Letter on Defence of Rights and Amusements.

C255 LOWES DICKINSON. *Listener*, 19 October 1932, pp. 572–573. Second in a series of seven talks on books.

C256 BOOKS OF THE WEEK. *Listener*, 2 November 1932, p. 644. Review of *My World as in my Time*, by Sir Henry Newbolt; *Memories of a Misspent Youth*, by Grant Richards; *As We Are*, by E. F. Benson; and *Theatre and Friendship*, by Elizabeth Robins. Third in a series of seven talks on books.

C257 MISS AUSTEN AND JANE AUSTEN. *Times Literary Supplement*, 10 November 1932, pp. 821–822. Review of *Jane Austen's Letters*, collected and edited by R. W. Chapman. Unsigned. Reprinted as: Jane Austen, 3: The Letters, *Abinger Harvest*, 1936.

C258 MR. LOWES DICKINSON. *Times Literary Supplement*, 10 November 1932, p. 839. Letter requesting the loan of letters. Reprinted as: Lowes Dickinson, *New Statesman and Nation*, N.S., 12 November 1932, p. 575.

C259 BOOKS OF THE WEEK. *Listener*, 16 November 1932, pp. 721–722. Review of *The 'Egypt's' Gold*, by David Scott; *A Man's a Man*, by Francis Anthony; *Bowsprit Ashore*, by Alexander Bone; *The Din of a Smithy*, by J. A. R. Stevenson; *The Common Earth*, by E. L. Grant Watson; and *Memories of the Months, Third Series*, by Sir Herbert Maxwell. Fourth in a series of seven talks on books.

C260 SIDE DISHES. *Listener*, 30 November 1932, pp. 799–800. Review of *The Letters of Jane Austen*, edited by R. W. Chapman; *A Fitzgerald Friendship: Letters from Edward Fitzgerald to W. B. Donne*; *Macaulay*, by Arthur Bryant; *Texts and Pretexts*, by Aldous Huxley; and *Words and Names*, by Ernest Weekley. Fifth in a series of seven talks on books.

C261 TALES OF UNREST. *Listener*, 14 December 1932, pp. 869–870. Review of *Mask and Man*, by F. Chaliapin; *History of the Russian Revolution*, by Leon Trotsky; *Low's Russian Sketch-Book*, text by Kingsley Martin; *The Journals of Arnold Bennett: 1911–1921*; *Just the Other Day*, by John Collier and Iain Lang; and *Escapers All*, published by the Bodley Head. Sixth in a series of seven talks on books.

C262 NOT NEW BOOKS. *Listener*, 28 December 1932, pp. 951–952. Seven books by Lytton Strachey and eight other authors reviewed. Last in a series of seven talks on books. Discussed in leading article on p. 924. *See also* C263.

C. CONTRIBUTIONS TO PERIODICALS

1933

C263 THE FUTURE OF BOOKS. *Listener*, 18 January 1933, p. 105. Letter in reply to leading article in issue of 28 December 1932. *See* C262.

C264 THE UNIVERSITY AND THE UNIVERSE. *Spectator*, 17 March 1933, pp. 368–369.

C265 THE ENGLISH ECCENTRICS. *Spectator*, 19 May 1933, p. 716. Review of *The English Eccentrics*, by Edith Sitwell.

C266 THE BARN DOOR. *New Statesman and Nation*, N.S., 27 May 1933, pp. 690, 692. Review of *Looking Back: An Autobiographical Excursion*, by Norman Douglas.

C267 BREAKING UP. *Spectator*, 28 July 1933, p. 119. On school speech-days.

C268 MUS IN URBE. *Spectator*, 17 November 1933, pp. 746, 748. In English.

1934

C269 MICKEY AND MINNIE. *Spectator*, 19 January 1934, pp. 81–82. Reprinted as: Our Diversions, 4: Mickey and Minnie, *Abinger Harvest*, 1936.

C270 'SEVEN DAYS' HARD'. *Listener*, 14 March 1934, p. 452. Broadcast on 10 March.

C271 NOTES ON THE WAY. *Time and Tide*, 2, 9, 16 and 23 June 1934, pp. 694–696, 723–724, 765–767, 796–797. *See also* editorial article 'Investment for Peace—or War', in the issue of 16 June, pp. 761–762; cartoon by Arthur Wragg "In the Name of Charity", 16 June, p. 763; and letters, 9 June, pp. 729–730, 16 June, p. 771, 23 June, pp. 799–800, 30 June, p. 829, 7 July, p. 855. For E. M. Forster's reply to letters *see* C274. *See also* C287, 329. Second contribution reprinted (omitting the last two paragraphs) as: A Note on the Way, *Abinger Harvest*, 1936.

C272 OUR GREATEST BENEFACTOR, 4. *Spectator*, 15 June 1934, p. 914. On Sir James Simpson, fourth in a series of articles, the other contributors being Sir C. G. Robertson, H. W. Nevinson, André Maurois, Lord Eustace Percy and Sir Arnold Wilson. *See also* letters in the issue of 22 June, p. 970.

C273 GOOD SOCIETY. *New Statesman and Nation*, N.S., 23 June 1934, pp. 950, 952. Review of *A Backward Glance*, by Edith Wharton.

C274 MR. E. M. FORSTER REPLIES. *Time and Tide*, 30 June 1934, p. 829. Letter in reply to letters arising out of his series of 'Notes on the Way'. *See* C271.

C275 PAGEANT OF TREES. *The Times*, 18 July 1934, p. 10. Letter on the Abinger Pageant. *See* A17.

C276 THE OLD SCHOOL. *Spectator*, 27 July 1934, p. 136. Review of *The Old School*, edited by Graham Greene. Partly in the form of a conversation between Herbert and Agnes Pembroke, characters in *The Longest Journey*. *See* A2.

C277 ROGER FRY. *London Mercury*, October 1934, Vol. 30, pp. 495–496.
Reprinted as: Roger Fry: An Obituary Note, *Abinger Harvest*, 1936.

C278 STILL THE SEDITION BILL! *Time and Tide*, 27 October 1934, p. 1340. The last word, 'respectively', appears to be a misprint for 'retrospectively'.

C279 ENGLISH FREEDOM. *Spectator*, 23 November 1934, pp. 791–792.
Partially incorporated in: Liberty in England, *London Mercury*, August 1935, Vol. 32, pp. 327–331. *Abinger Harvest*, 1936. *See also* C286.

C280 THE INVADERS. *Now and Then*, Winter 1934, No. 49, pp. 15–16. Review of *The Invaders*, by William Plomer.

1935

C281 BATTERSEA RISE. *London Mercury*, January 1935, Vol. 31, pp. 243–246. Review of *Battersea Rise*, by Dorothy Pym. Reprinted: *Abinger Harvest*, 1936.

C282 WORD-MAKING AND SOUND-TAKING. *New Statesman and Nation*, N.S., 9 March 1935, p. 321.
Reprinted: *Abinger Harvest*, 1936.

C283 HOWARD OVERING STURGIS. *London Mercury*, May 1935, Vol. 32, pp. 42–47. Review of *Belchamber*, by H. O. Sturgis, introduction by Gerard Hopkins.
Reprinted: *Abinger Harvest*, 1936.

C284 INTERNATIONAL CONGRESS OF WRITERS. *New Statesman and Nation*, N.S., 6 July 1935, p. 9.
Reprinted as: Writers *in* Paris, *Living Age*, September 1935, Vol. 349, pp. 63–65. *See also* C286.

C285 T.E. *Listener*, 31 July 1935, pp. 211–212. Review of *Seven Pillars of Wisdom*, by T. E. Lawrence.
Reprinted as: T. E. Lawrence, *Abinger Harvest*, 1936.

C286 LIBERTY IN ENGLAND: AN ADDRESS DELIVERED AT THE CONGRÈS INTERNATIONAL DES ECRIVAINS AT PARIS ON JUNE 21ST. *London Mercury*, August 1935, Vol. 32, pp. 327–331.
Reprinted as: Liberty in England, *Abinger Harvest*, 1936. *See also* C279, C284.

C287 NOTES ON THE WAY. *Time and Tide*, 2, 9, 16 and 23 November 1935, pp. 1571–1572, 1607–1608, 1657–1658, 1703–1704.
Third contribution reprinted (revised and omitting last paragraph) as: Does Culture Matter? [first half], *Two Cheers for Democracy*, 1951. *See also* C271, 329, 355.

C288 THE MENACE TO FREEDOM. *Spectator*, 22 November 1935, pp. 861–862. One of a series of articles entitled 'Aspects of Freedom', the other contributors being the Warden of All Souls College, Oxford (Professor W. G. S. Adams), Henry W. Nevinson, W. R. Inge, J. A. Spender, P. Carnegie Simpson, C. E. M. Joad, Walter Greenwood and Rose Macaulay.
Reprinted: *Two Cheers for Democracy*, 1951.

1936

C289 THE PSYCHOLOGY OF MONARCHY. *New Statesman and Nation*, N.S., 22 February 1936, p. 260. Letter.

C290 HACKNEY MARSHES. *New Statesman and Nation*, N.S., 25 April 1936, p. 629. Letter.

C291 ENGLISH HOTELS. *New Statesman and Nation*, N.S., 29 August 1936, pp. 286–287. Letter.

C292 CHORMOPULODA. *Listener*, 14 October 1936, Supplement, p. vii. Review of *The Ascent of F6*, by W. H. Auden and Christopher Isherwood.
Reprinted as: The Ascent of F.6 [*sic*], *Two Cheers for Democracy*, 1951.

C293 ANCIENT AND MODERN. *Listener*, 11 November 1936, pp. 921–922. Review of *More Poems*, by A. E. Housman; and *A. E. Housman*, by A. S. F. Gow.

1937

C294 TOLSTOY'S 'WAR AND PEACE'. *Listener*, 13 January 1937, p. 87.
Broadcast talk to sixth forms in the Schools Programme. This talk is similar to B15.

C295 CHURCH, COMMUNITY AND STATE. *Listener*, 27 January 1937, p. 177. Letter on a talk by Arnold Toynbee on 'Post-war Paganism versus Christianity' in the issue of 20 January, pp. 123–124.

C296 THAT JOB'S DONE. *Listener*, 10 March 1937, Supplement, No. 33, pp. iii–iv. Review of *Something of Myself*, by Rudyard Kipling.

C297 RECOLLECTIONISM. *New Statesman and Nation*, N.S., 13 March 1937, pp. 405–406.

C298 CORONATION NIGHTMARE. *Spectator*, 19 March 1937, pp. 509–510.
Reprinted: *Daily Herald*, 23 March 1937, p. 10. *Living Age*, May 1937, Vol. 352, pp. 258–260. *See also* letters in the *Spectator*, 26 March, p. 586, and 2 April 1937, p. 622.

C299 ROYALTY AND LOYALTY. *New Statesman and Nation*, N.S., 24 April 1937, p. 680. Review of *The Magic of Monarchy*, by Kingsley Martin.

C300 E. M. FORSTER LOOKS AT LONDON, THE... [*sic*] CITY OF ODD SURPRISES. *Reynolds News*, 9 May 1937, p. 8.
Reprinted as: London is a Muddle, *Two Cheers for Democracy*, 1951.

C301 A SMACK FOR RUSSIA? *Listener*, 12 May 1937, p. 943. Review of *Back from the U.S.S.R.*, by André Gide, translated by Dorothy Bussy.

C302 ECCENTRIC ENGLISHWOMEN, 7: LUCKIE BUCHAN. *Spectator*, 28 May 1937, pp. 986–987. Based on *The Buchanites from First to Last*, by Joseph Train, Blackwood, 1846. One of a series of articles by various authors.

C303 SELFRIDGE'S DECORATIONS. *New Statesman and Nation*, N.S., 5 June 1937, p. 920. Letter.

C304 A CONVERSATION. *Spectator*, 13 August 1937, pp. 269–270.
Reprinted as: Entretien in Paris, *Living Age*, October 1937, Vol. 353, pp. 171–173.

C305 MORE BROWNING LETTERS. *Listener*, 13 October 1937, Supplement, No. 36, p. xv. Review of *Robert Browning and Julia Wedgwood*, edited by Richard Curle.
Reprinted as: 'Snow' Wedgwood, *Two Cheers for Democracy*, 1951.

C306 [LETTER TO the Editor and appreciation of Sir Syed Ross Masood]. *Urdu*, October 1937, Vol. 17, pp. 853–860. In English; appreciation also translated into Urdu.
Reprinted (omitting the letter) as: Syed Ross Masood, *Two Cheers for Democracy*, 1951.

C307 THE LAST PARADE. *New Writing*, Autumn 1937, No. 4, pp. 1–5. Published in November. On the Paris exhibition.
Reprinted: *Two Cheers for Democracy*, 1951.

C308 DUCAL REMINISCENCES. *Listener*, 8 December 1937, Supplement, No. 38, p. xix. Review of *Men, Women and Things*, by the Duke of Portland.
Reprinted as: A Duke Remembers, *Two Cheers for Democracy*, 1951.

C309 SIR TUKOJI RAO PUAR. *The Times*, 28 December 1937, p. 14. Personal tribute.

1938

C310 BOOKS OF THE YEAR: FROM A TALK BROADCAST ... ON DECEMBER 30. *Listener*, 5 January 1938, pp. 41–42.

C311 GENERAL KNOWLEDGE. *New Statesman and Nation*, N.S., 15 January 1938, pp. 78–79. Letter in reply to one from Lancelot Hogben in the issue of 1 January, p. 11, which had criticized the *New Statesman's* general knowledge paper for over-emphasis on the arts.

C312 EFFICIENCY AND LIBERTY—GREAT BRITAIN: DISCUSSION BETWEEN E. M. FORSTER AND CAPTAIN A. M. LUDOVICI, WITH WILSON HARRIS IN THE CHAIR. *Listener*, 9 March 1938, pp. 497–498, 530–531. Broadcast.

C313 THE REV. JAMES GATLIFF. *New Statesman and Nation*, N.S., 9 April 1938, pp. 620, 622. Review of *Stations, Gentlemen: The Autobiography of James Gatliff*.

C314 A MEDITERRANEAN PROBLEM. *Spectator*, 22 April 1938, pp. 701–702. Review of *D'Annunzio*, by Tom Antongini.
Reprinted as: A Whiff of D'Annunzio, *Two Cheers for Democracy*, 1951.

C315 TREES—AND PEACE. *Manchester Evening News*, 15 July 1938, p. 12.

C316 TWO CHEERS FOR DEMOCRACY. *Nation*, New York, 16 July 1938, pp. 65–68. The first essay in a series by various authors entitled 'Living Philosophies'.
Reprinted (with additions) as: Credo, *London Mercury*, September 1938, Vol. 38, pp. 397–404. *What I Believe*, Hogarth Press, 1939. What I Believe, *Two Cheers for Democracy*, 1951.

C317 THE FEAST OF TONGUES. *Spectator*, 29 July 1938, pp. 194–195. Review of *Oscar Wilde*, by Frank Harris, with a preface by Bernard Shaw.

C318 INDIANS IN ENGLAND. *New Statesman and Nation*, N.S., 27 August 1938, pp. 311–312. Letter.

C319 CLOUDS HILL. *Listener*, 1 September 1938, pp. 426–427. Broadcast talk on the home of T. E. Lawrence.
Reprinted: *Two Cheers for Democracy*, 1951.

C320 THE DUTY OF AN EDITOR. *Listener*, 20 October 1938, p. 850. Letter.

C321 [REVIEW OF] *Victorian Peepshow: An Autobiography*, by Martin Armstrong. *Listener*, 24 November 1938, p. 1142. Unsigned.

C322 THE IVORY TOWER. *London Mercury*, December 1938, Vol. 39, pp. 119–130.
Reprinted: *Atlantic Monthly*, January 1939, Vol. 163, pp. 51-58.

C323 THE LONG RUN. *New Statesman and Nation*, N.S., 10 December 1938, pp. 971–972. Review of *Studies in a Dying Culture*, by Christopher Caudwell.

C324 THE BOOKS OF 1938: REVIEWED BY E. M. FORSTER AT THE MICROPHONE ON DECEMBER 26. *Listener*, 29 December 1938, pp. 1422–1423.

1939

C325 HERE'S WISHING! MESSAGES BROADCAST ON DECEMBER 26, 1: E. M. FORSTER. *Listener*, 5 January 1939, p. 18. The other speakers were James Stephens, Walter de la Mare and John Masefield.

C326 COMMENT AND DREAM: JEW-CONSCIOUSNESS. *New Statesman and Nation*, N.S., 7 January 1939, pp. 7–8.
Reprinted as: Jew-consciousness, *Two Cheers for Democracy*, 1951.

C327 COMMENT AND DREAM: ON A DEPUTATION. *New Statesman and Nation*, N.S., 14 January 1939, pp. 43–44.
Reprinted as: Our Deputation, *Two Cheers for Democracy*, 1951.

C328 HOW I LISTEN TO MUSIC, I: BY E. M. FORSTER. *Listener*, 19 January 1939, p. 173. First of a series of broadcasts, the other speakers being R. H. Wilenski, P. de Lande Long, Robert Nichols and M. D. Calvocoressi.
Reprinted as: Not Listening to Music, *Two Cheers for Democracy*, 1951.

C329 NOTES ON THE WAY. *Time and Tide*, 18 March 1939, pp. 335–336.
Reprinted (omitting the last paragraph on a performance of the Antigone at Cambridge) as: Racial Exercise, *Two Cheers for Democracy*, 1951. *See also* C271, 287.

C330 PORRIDGE OR PRUNES, SIR? *Wine and Food*, Spring 1939, No. 22, pp. 111–112.

C331 HENRY THORNTON (1760–1815). *New Statesman and Nation*, N.S., 1 April 1939, pp. 491–492.
Reprinted as: Henry Thornton, *Two Cheers for Democracy*, 1951.

C332 WOODLANDERS ON DEVI. *New Statesman and Nation*, N.S., 6 May 1939, pp. 679–680.

C333 FREEDOM FOR WHAT? *Listener*, 1 June 1939, p. 1177. Review of *A Handbook of Freedom*, edited by Jack Lindsay and Edgell Rickword.

C334 THE 1939 STATE. *New Statesman and Nation*, N.S., 10 June 1939, pp. 888–889.
Reprinted as: Post-Munich, *Two Cheers for Democracy*, 1951.

C335 NOT LOOKING AT ART. *New Statesman and Nation*, N.S., 15 July 1939, pp. 82–83.
Reprinted as: Not Looking at Pictures, *Two Cheers for Democracy*, 1951.

C336 BOOKS IN GENERAL. *New Statesman and Nation*, N.S., 19 August 1939, pp. 282–283. *See also* C385.

C337 THE TRIGGER. *Listener*, 14 September 1939, p. 542. Review of *Pain, Sex and Time*, by Gerald Heard.
Reprinted as: Gerald Heard, *Two Cheers for Democracy*, 1951.

C338 READING AS USUAL. *Listener*, 21 September 1939, pp. 586–587. Broadcast talk.
Reprinted: Tottenham Public Libraries, 1939. *See* A21.

C339 THEY HOLD THEIR TONGUES. *New Statesman and Nation*, N.S., 30 September 1939, p. 453.
Reprinted: *Two Cheers for Democracy*, 1951.

C340 'MY POULTRY ARE NOT OFFICERS'. *Listener*, 26 October 1939, Supplement No. 46, p. iii. Review of *The Complete Works of Lewis Carroll*, with an introduction by Alexander Woolcott.

C341 THE TOP DRAWER BUT ONE. *New Statesman and Nation*, N.S., 4 November 1939, p. 648. Review of *Mrs. Miniver*, by Jan Struther.
Reprinted as: Mrs. Miniver, *Two Cheers for Democracy*, 1951.

C342 HOMAGE TO WILLIAM BARNES. *New Statesman and Nation*, N.S., 9 December 1939, pp. 819–820.
Reprinted as: William Barnes, *Two Cheers for Democracy*, 1951.

1940

C343 LUNCHEON AT PRETORIA. *Abinger Chronicle*, January 1940, Vol. 1, pp. 15–18.
Reprinted: *Two Cheers for Democracy*, 1951.

C344 BOOKS IN 1939. *Listener*, 11 January 1940, pp. 85–86. Broadcast talk.

C345 THE FREEDOM OF THE ARTIST: A DISCUSSION BETWEEN E. M. FORSTER AND H. V. HODSON. *Listener*, 28 March 1940, pp. 636–637. Tenth in a series of broadcasts entitled 'This Freedom'.

C346 NAZISM AND MORALS: DANGERS OF "GESTAPO" METHODS. *Daily Telegraph and Morning Post*, 16 April 1940, p. 6. Letter.

C347 BLIND OAK GATE. *Abinger Chronicle*, June 1940, Vol. 1, pp. 63–65. Incorporated (with omissions) in: The Last of Abinger, *Two Cheers for Democracy*, 1951.

C348 [REVIEW OF] *Diamonds to Sit On*, by Ilya Ilf and Eugene Petrov, translated by Elizabeth Hill and Doris Mudie, Labour Book Service, 1940. *Labour Book Service Bulletin*, July 1940, No. 6, p. 3. *E. M. Forster*, by Rex Warner, revised by John Morris, Longmans, Green, 1960, p. 35, records that this edition of *Diamonds to Sit On* contains an introduction by E. M. Forster; there is no introduction to this edition or to that published by Methuen in 1930.

C349 THESE "LOST LEADERS". *Spectator*, 5 July 1940, p. 12. Letter. *See also* C350.

C350 "ENGLISH QUISLINGS". *Spectator*, 19 July 1940, p. 63. Reply to letter by F. Yeats-Brown, in the issue of 12 July, p. 37, commenting on E. M. Forster's previous letter. *See* C349.

C351 OMEGA AND ALPHA. *New Statesman and Nation*, N.S., 10 August 1940, pp. 140–141. Review of *Roger Fry*, by Virginia Woolf.

C352 LORD HALIFAX'S BROADCAST. *Listener*, 15 August 1940, p. 244. Letter criticizing Lord Halifax for having called the war a 'crusade for Christianity' in the issue of 25 July, p. 115.

C353 TWO CULTURES: THE QUICK AND THE DEAD. *Listener*, 26 September 1940, pp. 446–447.
Reprinted as: Two Cultures: The Quick and the Dead, The Nazi Blind Alley, *Vital Speeches of the Day*, 15 October 1940, Vol. 7, pp. 28–30. Reprinted as: Three anti-Nazi Broadcasts, 1: Culture and Freedom, *Two Cheers for Democracy*, 1951.
This and the other two talks, C354, 356, are similar to *Nordic Twilight*. *See* A23.

C354 WHAT HAS GERMANY DONE TO THE GERMANS? *Listener*, 3 October 1940, pp. 477–478.
Reprinted as: Three anti-Nazi Broadcasts, 2: What has Germany done to the Germans?, *Two Cheers for Democracy*, 1951. *See also* C353, 356.

C355 DOES CULTURE MATTER? *Spectator*, 4 October 1940, pp. 337–338.
Reprinted: Does Culture Matter? [second half], *Two Cheers for Democracy*, 1951. *See also* C287.

C356 WHAT WOULD GERMANY DO TO US? *Listener*, 10 October 1940, pp. 515–516
Reprinted (revised) as: What would Germany do to Britain if she won?, *London Calling*, 10 October 1940, No. 57, p. 2. Reprinted as: Three anti-Nazi Broadcasts, 3: What would Germany do to us?, *Two Cheers for Democracy*, 1951. *See also* C353–354.

C357 A NOTE ON CAPTUREDISM. *Mermaid*, October 1940, Vol. 11, No. 1, p. 15.

C358 HAPPY ENDING. *New Statesman and Nation*, N.S., 2 November 1940, p. 442. On Voltaire's Geneva home.
Reprinted as: Ferney, *Two Cheers for Democracy*, 1951.

C359 A BEDSIDE BOOK. *Listener*, 7 November 1940, p. 675. Review of *Friends of a Lifetime: Letters to S. C. Cockerell;* edited by Viola Meynell.

C360 THE INDIVIDUAL AND HIS GOD. *Listener*, 5 December 1940, pp. 801–802. Extract from a broadcast talk in the Overseas Service on 22 November on the photographic exhibition of Indian art at the Warburg Institute, London.

C361 THE BLESSED BISHOP'S BOOK. *New Statesman and Nation*, N.S., 7 December 1940, pp. 563–564.
Reprinted as: Bishop Jebb's Book, *Two Cheers for Democracy*, 1951.

1941

C362 'BUT . . .'. *Listener*, 23 January 1941, pp. 120–121. Broadcast talk.
Reprinted (revised) as: When Voltaire Met Frederick the Great, *London Calling*, 30 January 1941, No. 73, pp. 2, 4. Reprinted as: Voltaire and Frederick the Great, *Two Cheers for Democracy*, 1951.

C363 CAMBRIDGE. *New Statesman and Nation*, N.S., 29 March 1941, pp. 328, 330. Review of *Cambridge*, by John Steegman.
Reprinted: *Two Cheers for Democracy*, 1951.

C364 THE CENTENARY OF THE LONDON LIBRARY. *New Statesman and Nation*. N.S., 10 May 1941, p. 481.
Reprinted as: The London Library, *Two Cheers for Democracy*, 1951.

C365 GEORGE CRABBE: THE POET AND THE MAN. *Listener*, 29 May 1941, pp. 769–770. Broadcast talk in the Overseas Service.
Reprinted (revised): John Lane, 1945. *See* B19.

C366 THE C MINOR OF THAT LIFE. *Abinger Chronicle*, June 1941, Vol. 2, pp. 35–39.
Reprinted: *Two Cheers for Democracy*, 1951.

C367 THE NATIONAL COUNCIL FOR CIVIL LIBERTIES. *Time and Tide*, 28 June and 5 July 1941, pp. 540, 561. Letters arising out of E8*d*. *See also* letter and the leader in the issue of 28 June, pp. 539–540, 536 and further letters and editorial comment in the issue of 5 July, pp. 560–561.

C368 BOOKS IN 1941. *Listener*, 10 July 1941, p. 63. Broadcast talk in the Home Service.

C369 THE UNSUNG VIRTUE OF TOLERANCE. *Listener*, 31 July 1941, pp. 160–166. Broadcast talk in the Overseas Service.
Reprinted as: The Unsung Virtue of Tolerance: It is very easy to see fanaticism in other people, *Vital Speeches of the Day*, 15

October 1941, Vol. 8, pp. 12–14. Tolerance, *Two Cheers for Democracy*, 1951.

C370 INDIAN BROADCASTING. *New Statesman and Nation*, N.S., 2 and 16 August 1941, pp. 112, 160. Letters.

C371 THE WOMAN AND THE ONION. *Listener*, 27 November 1941, p. 720. Extract from a broadcast talk in the Indian Service. On a story from *The Brothers Karamazov*, by F. Dostoevsky. *See also The Hill of Devi*, 1951 (A31), p. 75.

C372 YOU SAUSAGE! *Wine and Food*, Winter 1941, No. 32, pp. 162–164.

C373 THE NEW DISORDER. *Horizon*, December 1941, Vol. 4, pp. 379–384. 'The substance of a speech made this autumn at the seventeenth International Congress of the P.E.N. Club' with additional concluding remarks.
Reprinted: New York, 1949. *See* A27. Another version of this speech was published in *Writers in Freedom*, edited by Hermon Ould, 1942; it was largely incorporated in 'Art for Art's Sake.' *See* B14, C413.

1942

C374 THE DUTY OF SOCIETY TO THE ARTIST. *Listener*, 30 April 1942, pp. 565–566. Broadcast talk in the Overseas Service.
Reprinted: *Two Cheers for Democracy*, 1951.

C375 RONALD KIDD. *New Statesman and Nation*, N.S., 23 May 1942, p. 336. Address delivered at Kidd's funeral on 16 May.
Reprinted: *Two Cheers for Democracy*, 1951.

C376 EDWARD GIBBON, THE HISTORIAN. *London Calling*, 30 July 1942, No. 151, pp. 14–15. Broadcast talk in the Overseas Service.
Reprinted as: Edward Gibbon, *Talking to India*, Allen and Unwin, 1943. *See* B17. Reprinted (revised) as: Gibbon and his Autobiography, *Two Cheers for Democracy*, 1951.

C377 'THE CELESTIAL OMNIBUS'. *Listener*, 17 September 1942, p. 374. Letter in defence of the broadcast version. *See* C27.

C378 AN INDIAN ON W. B. YEATS. *Listener*, 24 December 1942, p. 824. Review, broadcast in the Indian Service, of *The Development of William Butler Yeats*, by V. K. Narayana Menon; and *Little Gidding*, by T. S. Eliot.

1943

C379 WHY 'JULIUS CAESAR' LIVES. *Listener*, 7 January 1943, p. 21. First 'of a series of talks to India, covering some of the set books in the B.A. course in English literature at Calcutta University.' Reprinted as: Julius Caesar, *Two Cheers for Democracy*, 1951.

C380 THE SECOND GREATEST NOVEL? *Listener*, 15 April 1943, pp. 454–455. Broadcast talk on Proust in the Indian Service. Reprinted as: Our Second Greatest Novel?, *Two Cheers for Democracy*, 1951.

C381 MON CAMARADE EST ANGLAIS. *Abinger Chronicle*, April/May 1943, Vol. 4, pp. 14–17. In English.

C382 HUMANIST AND AUTHORITARIAN. *Listener*, 26 August 1943, pp. 242–243. Broadcast talk in the Indian Service. Reprinted as: Gide and George, *Two Cheers for Democracy*, 1951. The holograph manuscript entitled 'Gide' in the Academic Center, University of Texas, is a version of this talk.

C383 THE CLAIMS OF ART. *Listener*, 30 December 1943, pp. 742–743. One of a series of broadcast talks entitled 'The World We Want'.

1944

C384 A CLASH OF AUTHORITY. *Listener*, 22 June 1944, pp. 685–686. Extract from a review, broadcast in the Eastern Service, of *The Road to Serfdom*, by F. A. Hayek; and *Faith, Reason and Civilisation*, by Harold Laski.

C385 BOOKS IN GENERAL. *New Statesman and Nation*, N.S., 15 July 1944, p. 43. On *Erewhon*, by Samuel Butler. Shortened version of a script for a series of broadcast talks entitled 'Books that Influenced Me'. Reprinted (shortened again) as: A Book that Influenced Me, *Two Cheers for Democracy*, 1951. *See also* C336.

C386 THREE COURSES AND A DESSERT: BEING A NEW AND GASTRONOMIC VERSION OF THE GAME OF 'CONSEQUEN-CES', 2: THE SECOND COURSE. *Wine and Food*, Summer 1944, No. 42, pp. 83–90. Short story. 'The First Course', by Christopher Dilke, was published in the issue for Spring 1944, No. 41, pp. 15–27, and 'The Third Course', by A. E. Coppard, in Autumn 1944, No. 43, pp. 149–155.

C387 EDWARD CARPENTER: A CENTENARY NOTE. *Tribune*, 22
September 1944, pp. 12–13.
Reprinted as: Edward Carpenter, *Two Cheers for Democracy*,
1951.

C388 ABINGER NOTES. *Abinger Chronicle*, September 1944, Vol. 5,
pp. 2–5.
Incorporated in: The Last of Abinger, *Two Cheers for Democracy*,
1951.

C389 AN ARNOLD IN INDIA. *Listener*, 12 October 1944, pp. 410–
411. Broadcast talk in the Eastern Service.
Reprinted as: William Arnold, *Two Cheers for Democracy*, 1951.

C390 CORRESPONDENCE RE "IDOLATRY AND CONFUSION".
Message from Nowhere, Message de Nulle Part, November
1944, pp. 20–21. Letter on receiving the pamphlet *Idolatry and
Confusion*, by Jacques B. Brunius and E. L. T. Mesens; other
contributors to the correspondence include Sir Osbert Sitwell
and Herbert Read.

C391 A TERCENTENARY OF FREEDOM. *Listener*, 7 December 1944,
pp. 633–634. Broadcast talk in the Home Service. *See also* B20.
Reprinted as: The Tercentenary of the 'Areopagitica', *Two
Cheers for Democracy*, 1951.

1945

C392 ROMAIN ROLLAND AND THE HERO. *Listener*, 8 March 1945,
pp. 269–270. Broadcast talk in the Eastern Service.
Reprinted: *Two Cheers for Democracy*, 1951.

C393 THE VIGILANTES. *News Chronicle*, 19 July 1945, p. 2. Letter.

1946

C394 INDIA AFTER TWENTY-FIVE YEARS. *Listener*, 31 January
and 7 February 1946, pp. 133–134, 171–172. Broadcast talks in
the Home Service.
Reprinted as: India Again, *Two Cheers for Democracy*, 1951.

C395 THE CHALLENGE OF OUR TIME: THE VIEW OF THE CREATIVE
ARTIST. *Listener*, 11 April 1946, pp. 451–452. Fourth in a
series of broadcast talks in the Home Service, the other speakers
being Arthur Koestler, E. L. Woodward, J. D. Bernal, Benjamin
Farrington, Michael Polanyi, J. B. S. Haldane, V. A. Demant,
C. H. Waddington, A. D. Ritchie, and Lord Lindsay.

Reprinted as: The Point of View of the Creative Artist, *The Challenge of Our Time*, 1948. *See* B22. The Challenge of Our Time, *Two Cheers for Democracy*, 1951.

C396 A GREAT INDIAN POET-PHILOSOPHER. *Listener*, 23 May 1946, p. 686. Broadcast talk in the Home Service.
Reprinted as: Mohammed Iqbal, *Two Cheers for Democracy*, 1951.

C397 BLACK LIST FOR AUTHORS? *Listener*, 8 August 1946, p. 174. Extract from a broadcast talk in the Indian Service on recent events in the literary world and in particular the Congress of the International PEN at Stockholm.

1947

C398 FORREST REID: 1876–1947. *Listener*, 16 January 1947, p. 120. Personal tribute.
Reprinted as: Forrest Reid, *Two Cheers for Democracy*, 1951.

C399 ON CRITICISM IN THE ARTS, ESPECIALLY MUSIC. *Harper's Magazine*, July 1947, Vol. 195 [European edition, Vol. 134], pp. 9–17. Address delivered at the Harvard University Symposium on Music.
Reprinted as: The Raison d'Être of Criticism, *Horizon*, December 1948, Vol. 18, pp. 397–411. Reprinted (omitting the last paragraph) as: The Raison d'Être of Criticism in the Arts, *Two Cheers for Democracy*, 1951.
Broadcast by the author in the Third Programme on 4 November 1948.

C400 THE EDINBURGH FESTIVAL. *Sunday Times*, 31 August 1947, p. 4.

C401 IMPRESSIONS OF THE UNITED STATES. *Listener*, 4 September 1947, pp. 387–388. Broadcast talk in the Home Service.
Reprinted as: The United States, *Two Cheers for Democracy*, 1951.

C402 LITERATURE IN INDIA. *London Calling*, 11 September 1947, No. 416, p. 2. Short extract from broadcast talk in the Eastern Service.

C403 THE P.E.N. AND THE SWORD. *Listener*, 11 December 1947, pp. 1029–1030. Review of *Shuttle*, by Hermon Ould.

1948

C404 THE N.C.C.L. *New Statesman and Nation*, N.S., 15 May 1948, p. 396. Letter on his resignation from the National Council for Civil Liberties. *See also* C405.

C405 CIVIL LIBERTIES. *New Statesman and Nation*, N.S., 5 June 1948, p. 460. Letter in reply to one by L. C. White, Chairman of the National Council for Civil Liberties in the issue of 29 May, p. 436, who had commented on E. M. Forster's previous letter. *See* C404.

C406 LOOKING BACK ON THE ALDEBURGH FESTIVAL. *Listener*, 24 June 1948, pp. 1011, 1013. Broadcast talk in the Third Programme. *See also* C407.

C407 THE ALDEBURGH FESTIVAL. *Listener*, 8 July 1948, p. 61. Letter in reply to one from Scott Goddard in the issue of 1 July, p. 22, in connection with E. M. Forster's talk. *See* C406.

C408 BUTLER APPROACHED. *Spectator*, 12 November 1948, p. 634. Review of *Samuel Butler*, by P. N. Furbank.

C409 ENTRANCE TO AN UNWRITTEN NOVEL. *Listener*, 23 December 1948, pp. 975–976. Opening chapters of an abandoned novel; for other unfinished novels *see also* B12, 40, C426, 438. Reprinted as: Cocoanut & Co.: Entrance to an Abandoned Novel, *New York Times Book Review*, 6 February 1949, pp. 3, 31. A note accompanying this reprint erroneously records: 'It is known that there reposes in the British Museum the manuscript of a completed Forster novel, but the impression is general that he will never consent to its publication.' This statement is repeated in *The Art of E. M. Forster*, by H. J. Oliver, Melbourne University Press, 1960, p. 5.

1949

C410 THE THREE T. S. ELIOTS. *Listener*, 20 January 1949, p. 111. Review of *Notes Towards the Definition of Culture*, by T. S. Eliot.
Reprinted as: Two Books by T. S. Eliot, 1: Notes Towards the Definition of Culture, *Two Cheers for Democracy*, 1951.

C411 AN OUTSIDER ON POETRY. *Listener*, 28 April 1949, p. 728. Review of *Poetry of the Present*, compiled and introduced by Geoffrey Grigson.
Reprinted: *Two Cheers for Democracy*, 1951.

C412 BOOKSHELVES OF A LOVER OF WORDS. *London Calling*, 26 May 1949, No. 505, p. 18. Broadcast talk in the Overseas Service; the third in a series entitled 'In My Library', the earlier contributors being Desmond MacCarthy and Harold Nicolson. Reprinted as: In My Library, *Listener*, 7 July 1949, p. 24. On the Meaning of a Man's Books: E. M. Forster, Looking Over his Library, finds Old Friends and Some Strangers, *New York Times Book Review*, 11 September 1949, pp. 1, 14. In My Library, *Two Cheers for Democracy*, 1951.

C413 ART FOR ART'S SAKE. *Harper's Magazine*, New York, August 1949, Vol. 199 [European edition, Vol. 138], pp. 31–34. '. . . slightly emended version of an address delivered before a combined meeting of the American Academy and the National Institute of Art and Letters.' Incorporates to a large extent 'The New Disorder'. See A27, B14, C373.
Reprinted: *Two Cheers for Democracy*, 1951.

C414 [REVIEW OF] *The Veiled Wanderer*, by Princess Marthe Bibesco. *Listener*, 27 October 1949, p. 725. Unsigned.

1950

C415 MR. ELIOT'S 'COMEDY'. *Listener*, 23 March 1950, p. 533. Review of *The Cocktail Party*, by T. S. Eliot.
Reprinted as: Two Books by T. S. Eliot, 2: The Cocktail Party, A Comedy, *Two Cheers for Democracy*, 1951.

C416 BIKANER. *Listener*, 22 June 1950, p. 1065. Review of *The Art and Architecture of Bikaner State*, by Hermann Goetz.

C417 MAURICE O'SULLIVAN. *Listener*, 13 July 1950, p. 59. Letter on the occasion of O'Sullivan's death by drowning.

C418 [REVIEW OF] *Suffolk*, by William Addison. *Listener*, 21 September 1950, p. 391. Unsigned.

C419 GEORGE ORWELL. *Listener*, 2 November 1950, p. 471. Review of *Shooting an Elephant and Other Essays*, by George Orwell.
Reprinted: *Two Cheers for Democracy*, 1951.

C420 THE CAMBRIDGE CHANCELLORSHIP. *Spectator*, 10 November 1950, p. 468. Letter.

C421 NOMINATING THE CHANCELLOR. *Cambridge Review*, 18 November 1950, p. 146. Letter.

1951

C422 LETTER FROM E. M. FORSTER. *Griffin*, 1951, Vol. 1, pp. 4–6. On *Billy Budd*. *See also* A29, E10*h*.

C423 ANDRÉ GIDE: A PERSONAL TRIBUTE. *Listener*, 1 March 1951, p. 343. Letter.
Reprinted as: Gide's Death, *Two Cheers for Democracy*, 1951.

C424 THE UNBUILT CITY. *Listener*, 26 April 1951, p. 673. Review of *The Enchafèd Flood*, by W. H. Auden.
Reprinted as: The Enchafèd Flood, *Two Cheers for Democracy*, 1951.

C425 MOUNT LEBANON. *Listener*, 24 May 1951, p. 845. On the Shaker sect.
Reprinted: *Two Cheers for Democracy*, 1951.

C426 A NOVEL THAT "WENT WRONG": AUTHOR GIVES FIRST —AND ONLY—PUBLIC READING AT ALDEBURGH FESTIVAL. *Manchester Guardian*, 13 June 1951, p. 3. Report on E. M. Forster's reading from an unfinished novel, *Arctic Summer*, from which a few sentences are quoted. *See also* B40, C438, and for other unfinished novels, B12, C409.

C427 'IN THE RUE LEPSIUS'. *Listener*, 5 July 1951, pp. 28–29. Broadcast talk on *The Poems of C. P. Cavafy*, translated by John Mavrogordato, with an introduction by Rex Warner.
Reprinted as: The Complete Poems of C. P. Cavafy, *Two Cheers for Democracy*, 1951.

C428 FIFTH ANNIVERSARY OF THE THIRD PROGRAMME. *Listener*, 4 October 1951, pp. 539–541. Broadcast talk in the Third Programme. *See also* C429.

C429 AUDIENCE RESEARCH. *Listener*, 18 October and 1 November 1951, pp. 655, 742. Letters in reply to two from R. J. E. Silvey, Head of Audience Research, in the issues of 11 and 25 October, pp. 607, 705, in connection with E. M. Forster's talk on the fifth anniversary of the Third Programme. *See* C428.

1952

C430 VOYAGE OF DISCOVERY. *Times Literary Supplement*, 8 February 1952, p. 103. Review of *Venture to the Interior*, by Laurens van der Post. Unsigned.

C431 THE CHAPEL OF KINGS [*sic*]. *Listener*, 29 May 1952, pp. 885, 887. Review of *The Windows of King's College Chapel*, by Kenneth Harrison.

C432 ALDEBURGH. *Adam International Review*, March/May 1952, Year 20, Nos. 224/226, pp. 12–13.

C433 THE LEGACY OF SAMUEL BUTLER. *Listener*, 12 June 1952, pp. 955–956. Broadcast talk in the Third Programme.

C434 TRIBUTES TO SIR DESMOND MACCARTHY, 2. *Listener*, 26 June 1952, p. 1031. 'From talks in the Home Service', the other contributors being Sir Max Beerbohm, V. S. Pritchett, Philip Hope-Wallace, and C. V. Wedgwood.
Reprinted as: *Desmond MacCarthy*, Mill House Press, 1952. *See* A30.

C435 PORTRAITS FROM MEMORY. *Listener*, 24 July 1952, p. 142. Letter defending Lytton Strachey against an attack by Bertrand Russell in the issue of 17 July, pp. 97–98.

C436 THE POSSESSED. *Listener*, 9 October 1952, pp. 595, 597. Review of *The Devils of Loudun*, by Aldous Huxley.

1953

C437 TOWARD A DEFINITION OF TOLERANCE. *New York Times Magazine*, Section 6, 22 February 1953, p. 13.
The holograph manuscript entitled 'A Definition of Tolerance' was presented by the author and sold for £105 on behalf of the Aldeburgh Festival of Music and the Arts at the sale at Christie, Manson & Woods on 23 March 1961. It is now in the Academic Center, University of Texas.

C438 THE ART OF FICTION, I: E. M. FORSTER. *Paris Review*, Spring 1953, Vol. I, pp. 28–41. Interview of E. M. Forster by P. N. Furbank and F. J. H. Haskell including a facsimile reproduction, p. 28, of the first page of an unfinished novel, *Arctic Summer. See also* B40, C426, and for other unfinished novels B12, C409.

C439 LEAR IN INDIA. *Listener*, 26 March 1953, p. 519. Review of *Edward Lear's Indian Journal: Water-colours and Extracts*, edited by Ray Murphy.

C440 'LÉLIA: THE LIFE OF GEORGE SAND'. *Listener*, 18 June 1953, p. 1015. Letter on the review of *Lélia: The Life of George Sand*, by André Maurois, in the issue of 11 June, p. 979.

C441 THE ART AND ARCHITECTURE OF INDIA. *Listener*, 10 September 1953, pp. 419–421. Broadcast talk in the Third Programme on *The Art and Architecture of India: Buddhist, Hindu, Jain*, by Benjamin Rowland.

C. CONTRIBUTIONS TO PERIODICALS

C442 THE BIRTH OF KRISHNA. *Observer*, 11 October 1953, p. 9.
Letter written on 28 August 1921.
Reprinted: *The Hill of Devi*, 1953, pp. 108–113.

C443 SOCIETY AND THE HOMOSEXUAL: A MAGISTRATE'S
FIGURES. *New Statesman and Nation*, N.S., 31 October 1953,
pp. 508–509. One of two articles, the other, by Kingsley Martin,
with the sub-title: The Abominable Crime, was published on
p. 508.

1954

C444 DR TREVELYAN'S LOVE OF LETTERS. *Cambridge Review*,
13 February 1954, Vol. 75, p. 292. Review of *A Layman's Love
of Letters*, by G. M. Trevelyan.

C445 EAST AND WEST. *Observer*, 21 February 1954, p. 9. Review of
Asia and Western Dominance, by K. M. Panikkar; and *The Men
Who Ruled India, Vol. 1: The Founders*, by Philip Woodruff.

C446 TIDYING INDIA. *Listener*, 11 March 1954, pp. 435–436.
Review of *My Public Life*, by Sir Mirza Ismail.

C447 A VISIT TO AMERICA. *Listener*, 13 May 1954, p. 831. Letter
defending a talk by Dylan Thomas.

C448 [REVIEW OF] *India: Paintings from Ajanta Caves*. *Listener*,
12 August 1954, p. 253. Unsigned.

C449 REVOLUTION AT BAYREUTH. *Listener*, 4 November 1954,
pp. 755–757. Broadcast talk given on 29 October.
Reprinted: *Center*, February 1955, Vol. 2, pp. 2–6.

C450 THE LAW AND OBSCENITY. *Listener*, 11 November and 23
December 1954, pp. 813, 1117. Letters.

C451 THE WORLD MOUNTAIN. *Listener*, 2 December 1954, pp.
977–978. Review of *The Art of India*, by Stella Kramrisch.

C452 BOOKS OF 1954: A SYMPOSIUM. *Observer*, 26 December 1954,
p. 7. Includes a contribution by E. M. Forster.

1955

C453 A LETTER. *Twentieth Century*, February 1955, Vol. 157, pp.
99–101.
Reprinted as: '*I Assert That There is an Alternative in Humanism*',
Ethical Union, 1955. *See* A32. *See also* C456.

C454 [REVIEW OF] *Cambridgeshire*, by Nikolaus Pevsner. *Listener*,
10 February 1955, p. 257. Unsigned.

C455 'THE MINT' BY T. E. LAWRENCE. *Listener*, 17 February 1955, pp. 279–280. Broadcast talk in the Third Programme on the book.

C456 [LETTER]. *Twentieth Century*, May 1955, Vol. 157, p. 453. In reply to an article entitled 'Lilies that Fester' by C. S. Lewis in the issue of April, pp. 330–341, containing comments on E. M. Forster's 'A Letter'. *See* C453.

C457 SIDLING AFTER CRABBE. *Listener*, 9 June 1955, pp. 1039, 1041. Review of *The Poetry of Crabbe*, by Lillian Haddakin.

C458 A SHRINE FOR DIAGHILEV. *Observer*, 25 December 1955, p. 4. Review of *In Search of Diaghilev*, by Richard Buckle.

1956

C459 [REVIEW OF] *Indian Painting for the British: 1770–1880*, by Mildred and W. G. Archer. *Listener*, 19 January 1956, p. 111. Unsigned.

C460 [REVIEW OF] *Letters from Madame de Sévigné*, selected and translated by Violet Hammersley. *Listener*, 16 February 1956, p. 257. Unsigned.

C461 THE SWINDON CLASSICS. *Observer*, 11 March 1956, p. 17. Review of *Obscenity and the Law*, by Norman St John-Stevas.

C462 DAUGHTER DEAR. *London Magazine*, April 1956, Vol. 3, pp. 15–19.
Reprinted: *Marianne Thornton*, 1956, Chapter 1. *See* A34; *see also* A33.

C463 CATS AND KING'S. *Listener*, 12 April 1956, p. 417. Review of *Letters to a Friend*, by M. R. James, edited by Gwendolen McBryde.

C464 MONEY FOR THE ARTS. *Times Literary Supplement*, 17 August 1956, p. 487. Letter. *See also* a letter in reply by Norman MacDermott in the issue of 31 August, p. 511.

C465 A GREAT HUMANIST: E. M. FORSTER ON GOLDSWORTHY LOWES DICKINSON. *Listener*, 11 October 1956, pp. 545–547. Broadcast talk in the Third Programme given on 5 October as an introduction to a shortened version of Dickinson's *A Modern Symposium* broadcast on 6 October.

C466 HENRY JAMES AS ART CRITIC. *Listener*, 11 October 1956, p. 572. Review of *The Painter's Eye*, by Henry James, edited by John L. Sweeney.

Reprinted as: Henry James in the Galleries, *New Republic*, 17 December 1956, Vol. 135, pp. 24–25.

C467 BLOOMSBURY, AN EARLY NOTE: FEBRUARY, 1929. *Pawn*, November 1956, No. 3, p. [10].

C468 "PYGMALION". *The Times*, 7 December 1956, p. 11. Letter on *Pygmalion* and *My Fair Lady*.

C469 BOOKS OF THE YEAR, I: CHOSEN BY EMINENT CONTEMPORARIES. *Sunday Times*, 23 December 1956, pp. 6, 8. Includes a contribution by E. M. Forster.

1957

C470 TOURISM V. THUGGISM. *Listener*, 17 January 1957, p. 124 Review of *Portrait of Greece*, by Lord Kinross. Also issued separately as an offprint. *See* A35.

C471 DULL OPIATE. *Observer*, 24 February 1957, p. 12. Review of *A Drug-taker's Notes*, by R. H. Ward.

C472 THE BLUE BOY. *Listener*, 14 March 1957, p. 444. Review of *The Loves of Krishna*, by W. G. Archer.

C473 THE CHARM AND STRENGTH OF MRS. GASKELL. *Sunday Times*, 7 April 1957, pp. 10–11. First in a series of articles by various authors entitled 'Great Writers Rediscovered'.

C474 NEGLECTED SPINSTER. *Observer*, 25 August 1957, p. 12. Review of *The Life and Work of Harriet Martineau*, by Vera Wheatley.

C475 PROF. EDWARD DENT. *The Times*, 26 August 1957, p. 10. Personal tribute.

C476 ON REMAINING AN AGNOSTIC. *Listener*, 31 October 1957, p. 701. Letter supporting the BBC for their decision to broadcast Professor Stephen Toulmin's talk.

C477 DE SENECTUTE. *London Magazine*, November 1957, Vol. 4, pp. 15–18.

C478 [REVIEW OF] *The Magic Flute: English Version of the Libretto*, by W. H. Auden and Chester Kallman. *Listener*, 21 November 1957, pp. 850, 853. Unsigned.

C479 LIGHT ON DEOLI. *Listener*, 5 December 1957, p. 951. Review of *The Twice Born*, by G. Morris Carstairs.

1958

C480 FROM PARIS TO PAREE. *Listener*, 16 January 1958, p. 123.
Review of *Paris in the Past* and *Paris in Our Time*, by Pierre
Courthion; *Paris*, by André George; *Paris Sketchbook*, by
Ronald Searle and Kaye Webb; *Paris à la Mode*, by Célia
Bertin; and *Paris*, Michelin Tyre Co.

C481 VICE PROSECUTIONS. *Spectator*, 17 January 1958, p. 73.
Letter supporting one by R. D. Reid in the issue of 3 January,
p. 18. *See also* letters in the issues of 24 January, p. 103, 31
January, p. 133, and 7 February, p. 171.

C482 MOVING THE STATUE. *The Times*, 13 March 1958, p. 11.
Letter supporting the retention of James II's statue in Trafalgar
Square.

C483 HIGH PRINCIPLES AND LOW SPIRITS. *Spectator*, 28 March
1958, p. 398. Review of *John Venn and the Clapham Sect*, by
Michael Hennell.

C484 WOLFENDEN REPORT. *The Times*, 9 May 1958, p. 13. Letter.

C485 THIS WORRYING WORLD. *Listener*, 22 May 1958, p. 865.
Review of *The American Earthquake*, by Edmund Wilson;
Man's Western Quest, by Denis de Rougemont; and *The
Question*, by Henri Alleg.

C486 [REVIEW OF] *Authors at Work: An Address delivered by Robert
H. Taylor at the Opening of an Exhibition of Literary Manuscripts
at the Grolier Club*. *Library*, June 1958, Series 5, Vol. 13, pp.
142–143.

C487 [REVIEW OF] *The Thrones of Earth and Heaven: Photographs*,
by Roloff Beny. *Listener*, 19 June 1958, p. 1027. Unsigned.

C488 A VIEW WITHOUT A ROOM. *Observer*, 27 July 1958, p. 15.
A Room with a View brought up to date. *See* A3.
Reprinted as: A View Without a Room: Old Friends Fifty
Years Later, *New York Times Book Review*, 27 July 1958, p. 4.

C489 C. P. CAVAFY 1883–1933. *Umbrella*, October 1958, Vol. 1,
pp. 5–7.

C490 E. K. BENNETT (FRANCIS) (1887–1958). *Caian*, Michaelmas
Term 1958, Vol. 55, pp. 123–127. Personal tribute. Also issued
separately as an offprint. *See* A36.

C491 UNCLE AND NIECE. *Listener*, 4 December 1958, p. 949.
Review of *The Love Letters of Voltaire to his Niece*, edited and
translated by Theodore Besterman.

C492 FOG OVER FERNEY: A FANTASY. *Listener*, 18 December 1958, pp. 1029–1030. On Voltaire.

1959

C493 RECOLLECTIONS OF NASSENHEIDE. *Listener*, 1 January 1959, pp. 12–14. Reminiscences, broadcast in the Third Programme, arising out of *Elizabeth of the German Garden*, by Leslie de Charms [pseud.]. *See also* B34.

C494 EROTIC INDIAN SCULPTURE. *Listener*, 12 March 1959, pp. 469, 471. Review of *Kama Kala*, by Mulk Raj Anand.

C495 ART TREASURES OF CAMBRIDGE. *Listener*, 26 March 1959, p. 551. On the exhibition at the Goldsmiths' Hall, London.

C496 MR. C. H. COLLINS BAKER. *The Times*, 14 July 1959, p. 9. Personal tribute.

C497 HENRY JAMES AND THE YOUNG MEN. *Listener*, 16 July 1959, p. 103. Letter arising out of Leonard Woolf's recollections in the issue of 9 July, pp. 53–54.

C498 A KNOWN INDIAN. *Observer*, 16 August 1959, p. 14. Review of *A Passage to England*, by Nirad C. Chaudhuri.

C499 NUISANCE VALUE. *Spectator*, 2 October 1959, p. 431. Contribution to a symposium entitled 'Marks the Spot: Election Comments by Kingsley Amis, E. M. Forster, Lord Beveridge, Christopher Hollis, Wolf Mankowitz, Angus Wilson, Evelyn Waugh, Trog'.

C500 THE CONSETT CASE. *The Times*, 11 December 1959, p. 13. Letter.

1960

C501 THE PRINCE'S TALE. *Spectator*, 13 May 1960, p. 702. Review of *The Leopard*, by Giuseppe di Lampedusa, translated by Archibald Colquhoun.

C502 DESCENT TO THE PLAINS. *Observer*, 14 August 1960, p. 20. Review of *Gone Away*, by Dom Moraes.

C503 [REVIEW OF] *Discovering Rome*, by Alec Randall. *Listener*, 18 August 1960, p. 269.

1961

C504 THE SAHIB FROM BLOOMSBURY. *Observer*, 5 November 1961, p. 29. Review of *Growing: An Autobiography of the Years 1904 to 1911*, by Leonard Woolf.

C. CONTRIBUTIONS TO PERIODICALS

C505 LETTER FROM THE COLLEGE (11). *Fleur-de-Lys*, December 1961, p. 9. Letter.

C506 BOOKS OF THE YEAR: CONTRIBUTORS TO THE OBSERVER NAME SOME OF THE OUTSTANDING BOOKS THEY HAVE READ IN THE PAST YEAR. *Observer*, 17 December 1961, p. 22. Includes a contribution by E. M. Forster.

1962

C507 INDIAN ENTRIES. *Encounter*, January 1962, Vol. 18, pp. 20–27. Extracts from E. M. Forster's diary from 8 October 1912 to 2 April 1913.
Reprinted as: Indian Entries from a Diary, *Harper's Magazine*, February 1962, Vol. 224, pp. 46–52, 55–56, with an introduction by Santha Rama Rau, pp. 46–47.

C508 GOING INTO EUROPE: A SYMPOSIUM. *Encounter*, December 1962, Vol. 19, p. 64. Includes a contribution by E. M. Forster.

C509 A COMMERCIALISED FESTIVAL. *Guardian*, 29 December 1962, p. 6. Letter on the leading article 'The Festival' in the issue of 24 December, p. 6.

1963

C510 A PRESIDENTIAL ADDRESS TO THE CAMBRIDGE HUMANISTS—SUMMER 1959. *University Humanist Federation Bulletin*, Spring 1963, No. 11, pp. 2–8. Also issued separately as an offprint. *See* A37.

C511 MY FIRST OPERA. *Opera*, June 1963, Vol. 14, pp. 373–374.

C512 "WHERE ANGELS FEAR TO TREAD". *The Times*, 12 July 1963, p. 11. Letter arising out of the review of the dramatic version in the issue of 7 June, p. 15. *See also* A1a.

C513 BOOKS OF THE YEAR: A PERSONAL CHOICE. *Observer*, 22 December 1963, p. 15. Includes a contribution by E. M. Forster.

1964

C514 E. M. FORSTER POINTS OUT—VICE VERSA. *Cambridge News*, 22 February 1964, p. 4. Letter signed E. M. Forster (President, Cambridge Humanists), on the report 'Humanism Without God is not Enough' in the issue of 19 February, p. 10.

C515 MOONSTRUCK. *Guardian*, 7 August 1964, p. 8. Letter on the leading article 'Towards Two Men on the Moon' in the issue of 3 August, p. 6.

C. CONTRIBUTIONS TO PERIODICALS

C516 PYLONS ON THE MARCH: PROFITS THAT WILL BE MADE.
  The Times, 5 September 1964, p. 9. Letter on articles in the
  issues of 1 September, p. 11 and 2 September, p. 11.

C. CONTRIBUTIONS TO PERIODICALS

ADDENDA

D. TRANSLATIONS INTO FOREIGN LANGUAGES

ARABIC

BOOKS:

D1   RIHLAT ELA AL HIND. AL- QĀHIRAH, MAKTABAT AL NAH-
DAT AL MISRIAH*
488 pp.
A translation by Ezz Eldin Ismail of *A Passage to India*;
published 1959.

D2   ARKĀN AL- QIṢṢAH. AL- QĀHIRAH, DĀR AL- KARNAK
LIL-NASHR WAL-TAB' WAL-TAWIZĪ'*
210 pp.
A translation by Kamāl 'ayyād Jād of *Aspects of the Novel*;
published 1960.

D3   MAJMŪ 'AT AL -QIṢAṢ AL -QAṢĪRAH. AL -QĀHIRAH, DĀR
AL- FIKR AL- 'ARABĪ*
280 pp.
A translation by Majdi Ḥifnī Nāṣif of *The Collected Tales*;
published ?1960.

CZECH

BOOK:

D4   E. M. FORSTER | CESTA DO INDIE | ROMÁN | 1926 | [*rule*]
| ČIN · PRAHA
Large crown 8vo. 396 pp. 7¾ × 5½ in.
A translation by Karel Kraus of *A Passage to India*.

DANISH

BOOKS:

D5a. E. M. FORSTER | INDISKE DAGE | *ROMAN* | [*publisher's device*]
| KØBENHAVN | BERLINGSKE FORLAG | 1935
Medium 8vo. 288 pp. 8¼ × 6 in.
A translation by Paul Laessøe Müller of *A Passage to India*.

  b. E. M. FORSTER | INDISKE DAGE | [*ornament*] | STJERNE-
BØGERNE | VINTENS FORLAG
Small crown 8vo. 280 pp. 7½ × 4⅜ in.
A translation by Paul Laessøe Müller of *A Passage to India*;
published in Copenhagen, 1963.

D. TRANSLATIONS

D6   E. M. FORSTER | [*short rule*] | VAERELSE MED UDSIGT | PÅ
DANSK VED | AASE HANSEN | KØBENHAVN | GYLDENDAL
| 1954
Crown 8vo. 256 pp. 7⅝ × 4⅝ in.
A translation by Aase Hansen of *A Room with a View*; published
as *Gyldendals Nye Serie*, Vol. 12.

D7   E. M. FORSTER | HIMMELBUSSEN | OG ANDEN PROSA |
»*Min Skov*« *er oversat af* | BENDIX BECH-THOSTRUP | *det
øvrige Udvalg af* | JØRGEN ANDERSEN | [*publisher's device*]
| KØBENHAVN | STEEN HASSELBALCHS FORLAG|MCMLXIII
Small crown 8vo. 62 pp. 7 × 4¾ in.
Translations by Bendix Bech-Thostrup of 'My Wood', and by
Jørgen Andersen of 'The Celestial Omnibus', 'Notes on the
English Character' and 'The Nine Gems of Ujjain'; published
as *Hasselbalchs Kultur-Bibliotek*, Vol. 220.

DUTCH
BOOK:

D8   E. M. FORSTER | [*within an oval frame:*] DE ECHO | VAN DE
MARABAR | [*outside frame:*] [*monogram*] | UIT HET ENGELS
VERTAALD DOOR JEROEN FRANKE | AMSTERDAM · N.V.
DE ARBEIDERSPERS · 1950
Crown 8vo. 304 pp. 7½ × 5 in.
A translation by Jeroen Franke of *A Passage to India*.

ESTONIAN
BOOK:

D9   TEINE KUNINGRIIK. TALLINN, GAZ. -ŽURN. IZD. 1961*
Large crown 8vo. 86 pp. 8 × 5¼ in.
A translation by E. Roks of 'The Road from Colonus', 'The
Celestial Omnibus', 'The Eternal Moment', and 'Other King-
dom'; published as the *Looming Library*, Vol. 177.

FINNISH
BOOKS:

D10   [*within a rule, within a frame:*] E. M. FORSTER | MATKA
INDIAAN | ESIPUHEEN KIRJOITTANUT | ANDERS ÖSTERL-
ING | SUOMENTANUT | VÄINÖ NYMAN | [*ornament*] | KUS-
TANNUSOSAKEYHTIÖ KIRJA | HELSINKI
Small crown 8vo. 440 pp. 7½ × 4¾ in.
A translation by Väinö Nyman of *A Passage to India*, with an
introduction by Anders Österling; published 1928.

D. TRANSLATIONS

DII E. M. FORSTER | TALO JALAVAN | VARJOSSA | SUOMENTAN-
UT | EILA PENNANEN | [*publisher's device*] | PORVOO · HEL-
SINKI | WERNER SÖDERSTRÖM OSAKEYHTIÖ
Crown 8vo. 374 pp. 7½ × 5 in.
A translation by Eila Pennanen of *Howards End*; published 1953.

FRENCH

BOOKS:

DI2*a*. E. M. FORSTER | [*rule*] | ROUTE DES INDES | (A PASSAGE TO
INDIA) | *TRADUIT DE L'ANGLAIS PAR C. MAURON* [*quota-*
| *tion*] | [*publisher's device*] | PARIS | LIBRAIRIE PLON | *LES*
PETITS-FILS DE PLON ET NOURRIT | IMPRIMEURS-
ÉDITEURS—8, RUE GARANCIÈRE, 6ᵉ | [*short rule*] | *Tous*
droits réservés
Crown 8vo. [viii], 396 pp. 7⅞ × 5⅛ in.
A translation by Charles Mauron of *A Passage to India*; published 1927.

   b. [*across two pages with coloured illustration:*] PASSAGE TO
INDIA | route des Indes | E. M. FORSTER TRADUIT DE
L'ANGLAIS PAR C. MAURON | CLUB DU LIVRE SÉLEC-
TIONNÉ
Large crown 8vo. 348 pp. illus. 7¾ × 5¼ in.
Published in Paris, 1956.

DI3 E. M. FORSTER | AVEC VUE | SUR L'ARNO | A Room with a
View | *roman traduit de l'anglais* | *par Charles Mauron* | [*pub-
lisher's device*] | ROBERT LAFFONT | MCMXLVII
Small crown 8vo. 328 pp. 7⅞ × 4¾ in.
A translation by Charles Mauron of *A Room with a View*;
published in Paris.

DI4 FEUX CROISÉS | AMES ET TERRES ÉTRANGÈRES | [*short rule*]
| E. M. FORSTER | LE LEGS | DE | MRS. WILCOX | *Traduit de*
l'anglais par | CH. MAURON | [*publisher's device*] | PARIS
| LIBRAIRIE PLON | LES PETITS-FILS DE PLON ET NOURRIT
| Imprimeurs-Éditeurs, 8, rue Garancière, 6ᵉ
Small crown 8vo. 384 pp. 7⅞ × 4¾ in.
A translation by Charles Mauron of *Howards End*; published
1950.

DI5 FEUX CROISÉS | AMES ET TERRES ÉTRANGÈRES | [*short rule*]
| E. M. FORSTER | LE PLUS LONG | DES | VOYAGES | *Traduit*
de l'anglais par | CH. MAURON | [*publisher's device*] | *Paris* |
LIBRAIRIE PLON | LES PETITS-FILS DE PLON ET NOURRIT
| Imprimeurs-Éditeurs—8, rue Garancière, 6ᵉ

Small crown 8vo. 328 pp. 7⅜ × 4⅝ in.
A translation by Charles Mauron of *The Longest Journey*;
published 1952.

D16 FEUX CROISÉS | AMES ET TERRES ÉTRANGÈRES | [*short
rule*] | E. M. FORSTER | MONTERIANO | ROMAN | *Traduit de
l'anglais par* | CHARLES MAURON | [*publisher's device*] | PARIS
| LIBRAIRIE PLON | LES PETITS-FILS DE PLON ET NOURRIT
| Imprimeurs-Éditeurs—8, rue Garancière, 6ᵉ
Small crown 8vo. 256 pp. 7½× 4⅝ in.
A translation by Charles Mauron of *Where Angels Fear to Tread*;
published 1954.

PERIODICALS:

D17 MON AMI EST ANGLAIS. *Revue du Monde libre*, July 1943,
No. 7, pp. 17–18.
A translation of 'Mon Camarade est Anglais.'

D18 LE DÉSORDRE NOUVEAU. *Revue du Monde libre*, September
1943, No. 9, pp. 7–9.
A translation of 'The New Disorder', Part 1.

D19 VINGT ANS DE LITTÉRATURE ANGLAISE (1918–1939).
Revue du Monde libre, December 1943, No. 12, pp. 29–30.
A translation of *The Development of English Prose between 1918
and 1939*, pp. 5–11.

D20 MARCEL PROUST ET SON OEUVRE. *Revue du Monde libre*,
January 1944, No. 13, pp. 30–32.
A translation of 'The Second Greatest Novel?.'

D21 VINGT ANS DE LITTÉRATURE ANGLAISE. *Fontaine*, 1944,
Nos. 37/40, pp. 9–13.
A translation of *The Development of English Prose between 1918
and 1939*, pp. 1–11 with some omissions, by Mary Kesteven.
This special number of *Fontaine* is entitled *Aspects de la Littéra-
ture anglaise de 1918 à 1940*.

D22 CE QUE JE CROIS (ÉCRIT EN 1939). *Mercure de France*, July
1953, Vol. 318, pp. 385–395.
A translation by Charles Mauron of 'Two Cheers for Democracy'.

GERMAN
BOOKS:

D23*a*. E. M. FORSTER | INDIEN | ROMAN | 1932 | PAUL NEFF
VERLAG · BERLIN

Large crown 8vo. 436 pp. 7⅞ × 5 in.
A translation by Paul Fohr of *A Passage to India*.

b. E. M. FORSTER | Auf der Suche nach Indien | ROMAN |
FISCHER BÜCHEREI
Small crown 8vo. 328 pp. 7⅞ × 4¼ in.
A translation by Wolfgang von Einsiedel of *A Passage to India*;
published in Frankfurt-am-Main and Hamburg, 1960.

D24 E. M. Forster | Die Maschine versagt | Wien 1947 | [*rule*] |
Amandus-Edition
Large crown 8vo. 48 pp. 7⅞ × 4¾ in.
A translation by Hermen von Kleeborn of 'The Machine
Stops.'

D25 E. M. FORSTER | ENGEL UND NARREN | Roman | 1948 |
[*long rule*] | CHRISTIAN WEGNER VERLAG | HAMBURG
Small crown 8vo. 276 pp. 7 × 4¼ in.
A translation by Irma Tiedtge of *Where Angels Fear to
Tread*.

D26*a.* E. M. FORSTER | ANSICHTEN DES ROMANS | 1949 | SUHR-
KAMP VERLAG VORM. S. FISCHER
Small crown 8vo. 212 pp. 7⅜ × 4½ in.
A translation by Walter Schürenberg of *Aspects of the Novel*;
published in Frankfurt-am-Main.

b. E. M. Forster | Ansichten des Romans | Suhrkamp Verlag
Small crown 8vo. 184 pp. 7⅞ × 4⅜ in.
A translation by Walter Schürenberg of *Aspects of the Novel*;
published in Frankfurt-am-Main, 1962.

D27*a.* E. M. FORSTER | HOWARDS | END | Roman | CLAASSEN &
GOVERTS | HAMBURG UND BADEN-BADEN
Large crown 8vo. 428 pp. 8 × 4¾ in.
A translation by W. E. Süskind of *Howards End*; published
1949.

b. E. M. FORSTER | HOWARDS END | Roman | FISCHER
BÜCHEREI
Small crown 8vo. 336 pp. 7¼ × 4¼ in.
A translation by W. E. Süskind; published 1958.

D28 Edward Morgan Forster | DER | EWIGE AUGENBLICK |
Erzählung | Übersetzung von Ernst Sander | Nachwort von Hans
Hennecke | Reclam-Verlag Stuttgart
Foolscap 8vo. 64 pp. 6 × 3⅝ in.
A translation by Ernst Sander of 'The Eternal Moment'; fore
word by Hans Hennecke; published 1953.

D. TRANSLATIONS

D29 E. M. FORSTER | DER HÜGEL | DEVI | [*publisher's monogram*]
| CLAASSEN VERLAG | HAMBURG
Large crown 8vo. 240 pp. 7⅞ × 4¾ in.
A translation by Wolfgang von Einsiedel of *The Hill of Devi*;
published 1955.

D30 "BILLY BUDD" | [*rule*] | Oper in 4 Akten | Musik von |
BENJAMIN BRITTEN | [*rule*] | Libretto von | E. M. FORSTER
und ERIC CROZIER | (nach dem Roman von Herman Melville)
| [*rule*] | Deutscher Text von | ALFRED H. UNGER | [*rule*]
Demy 4to. [ii], 53 leaves. (mimeographed). 11⅜ × 8¼ in.
A translation by Alfred H. Unger of *Billy Budd*; published *c.*
1955.

PERIODICALS:

D31 FORMEN DES ROMANS.* *Wissen und Leben*, 1929, Jahrgang
18, pp. 406–416.
A translation of an extract from *Aspects of the Novel*.

D32 ZUR KUNSTKRITIK.* *Amerikanische Rundschau*, 1948, Jahrgang
3, No. 15, pp. 64–78.
A translation of 'On Criticism in the Arts.'

D33 DIE ANTWORT DES SCHÖPFERISCHEN KÜNSTLERS AUF
DIE FORDERUNG DER ZEIT.* *Thema*, 1949, No. 5, pp. 4–5.
A translation by Fritz Volquard Arnold of 'The Challenge of
our Time.'

D34 KLEINES HIMMELREICH. *Neue Rundschau*, 1961, Jahrgang
72, pp. 315–339.
A translation by Ruth von Marcard of 'Other Kingdom.'

GREEK
PERIODICALS:

D35 TO OYRANIO LEŌPHOREIO. *Néa Hestia*, 1948, Vol. 44, pp.
878–885.
A translation by Demetres Stayroy of 'The Celestial Omnibus.'

D36 MĒCHANĒ STAMATĒSE.* *Eklogē*, 1951–1952, 1954, Vols. 7–8,
10, pp. 93–107, 87–96, 87–96.
A translation by George Patsadelis of 'The Machine Stops.'

D37 EMADA N' AKONŌ MOUSIKĒ.* *Eklogē*, 1952, Vol. 8, pp. 41–43.
A translation of 'How I Listen to Music.'

D38 GEORGE GEMISTO-PLETHOU.* *Anglo-Helliniki Epitheorisis*,
1953, Series 2, Vol. 6, No. 1, pp. 40–47.
A translation by G. P. Savides of 'Gemistus Pletho'.

D. TRANSLATIONS

HUNGARIAN

BOOK:

D39 A KOLONOSZI UT. AZ EREDETI TELJES SZÖVEG ÉS HÖ
MAGYAR FORDITÁSA. FORD. E. MÁTHÉ. BUDAPEST,
TERRA, 1958*
Royal 16mo. 40 pp. 6⅝ × 4¾ in.
A translation by E. Máthé of 'The Road from Colonus' with
English text.

ITALIAN

BOOKS:

D40 *a.* PASSAGGIO | ALL'INDIA | *romanzo di* | E. M. FORSTER |
PERRELLA—ROMA
Small royal 8vo. 360 pp. 8⅜ × 6 in.
A translation by Augusto Guidi of *A Passage to India*, with a
preface by the translator; published 1945.

  b. Edward M. Forster | [*in pale blue:*] PASSAGGIO IN INDIA | [*in
black:*] *Traduzione di Adriana Motti* | *Einaudi*
Small demy 8vo. 360 pp. plate (port.). 8¾ × 5⅝ in.
A translation by Adriana Motti of *A Passage to India*; published
in Turin, 1962.

D41 *a.* [*within a double rule in orange:*] LA FINESTRA | SULL'ARNO
| di | *E. M. Forster* | S.A.I.E.—TORINO
Large crown 8vo. 264 pp. 8⅛ × 5½ in.
A translation by Arjo of *A Room with a View*; published 1954.
This translation is unauthorized but in accordance with the
copyright laws at that time.

  b. E. M. FORSTER | CAMERA | CON VISTA | *Rizzoli* ~*Editore*
Foolscap 8vo. 280 pp. 6¼ × 4⅛ in.
A translation by Giuliana Aldi Pompili of *A Room with a View*;
published in Milan, 1958. This translation is unauthorized but
in accordance with the copyright laws at that time.

D42 *E. M. Forster* | Casa Howard | "Solo connettere . . ." | [*pub-
lisher's device*] | Feltrinelli Editore Milano
Large crown 8vo. 444 pp. 7¾ × 4⅞ in.
A translation by Luisa Chiarelli of *Howards End*, with a preface
by Agostino Lombardo; published 1959.

D43 *E. M. Forster* | Monteriano | [*publisher's device*] | Feltrinelli
Editore Milano
Large crown 8vo. 232 pp. 7⅞ × 4⅞ in.

D. TRANSLATIONS

A translation by Luisa Chiarelli of *Where Angels Fear to Tread*; published 1961.

D44 [*within a right angle in orange-brown:*] [*in orange-brown:*] E. [*in black:*] M. Forster | *Aspetti* | *del romanzo* | Traduzione di Corrado Pavolini | [*outside angle in orange-brown:*] Il Saggiatore

Small crown 8vo. 224 pp. 7⅜ × 4¾ in.

A translation by Corrado Pavolini of *Aspects of the Novel*; published in Milan, 1963.

D45 E. M. Forster | Il cammino | piú lungo | romanzo | [*publisher's device*] Feltrinelli

Large crown 8vo. 380 pp. 7¾ × 4⅞ in.

A translation by Luisa Chiarelli of *The Longest Journey*, with a preface by Agostino Lombardo; published in Milan, 1964.

JAPANESE

BOOKS:

D46 [*within a rule rounded at angles:*] SHINCHŌ BUNKO | INDO E NO MICHI | FŌSUTĀ | TANAKA SEIJIRŌ YAKU | [*publisher's device*] | [*rule*] | SHINCHŌSHA HAN | 299

Demy 16mo. 438 pp. 5⅞ × 4⅛ in.

A translation by Seijirō Tanaka of *A Passage to India*; published in Tokyo, 1952.

D47 *a.* SHÔSETSU TO WA NANI KA? FŌSUTĀ. TOKYO, DABIDDO-SHA 1954*

Crown 8vo. 206 pp. 7½ × 5¼ in.

A translation by Kazuhiko Yoneda of *Aspects of the Novel*.

b. [*within a rule rounded at angles:*] SHINCHŌ BUNKO | SHŌSETSU NO SHOSŌ | FŌSUTĀ | TANAKA SEIJIRŌ YAKU | [*publisher's device*] | [*rule*] | SHINCHŌSHA HAN | 1126

Demy 16mo. 232 pp. 6 × 4¼ in.

A translation by Seijirō Tanaka of *Aspects of the Novel*; published in Tokyo, 1958.

D48 *a.* TENGOKU YUKI BASHA; EIEN NO SHUNKAN. TOKYO, NAN'UNDÔ 1957*

Foolscap 8vo. 152 pp. 7¼ × 4 in.

Translations by Minoru Ôsawa of 'The Other Side of the Hedge', 'The Celestial Omnibus', 'Other Kingdom', 'Mr Andrews', 'The Story of the Siren', and 'The Eternal Moment'.

b. TENGOKU YUKI NO NORIAI-BASHA; EIEN NO SHUNKAN. TOKYO, EIHÔSHA, 1957*

Small crown 8vo. 226 pp. 7¼ × 4⅜ in.

D. TRANSLATIONS

Translations by Shikô Murakami of 'The Other Side of the Hedge', 'The Celestial Omnibus', and 'The Machine Stops', and by Kazuhiko Yoneda of 'The Road from Colonus', 'The Story of the Siren', and 'The Eternal Moment'.

NORWEGIAN

BOOK:

D49 H. [sic] M. FORSTER | [rule] | EN REISE TIL INDIA | OVERSATT AV | PETER MAGNUS | GYLDENDAL | NORSK FORLAG | [rule] | OSLO 1959
Small demy 8vo. 312 pp. 8⅝ × 5½ in.
A translation by Peter Magnus of *A Passage to India*.

POLISH

BOOK:

D50 E. M. FORSTER | W SŁOŃCU INDYJ | WARSZAWA [rule] 1938 | [rule] | TOWARZYSTWO WYDAWNICZE ,,RÓJ''
Crown 8vo. 348 pp. 7½ × 5 in.
A translation by H. Mysłakowska of *A Passage to India*.

PORTUGUESE

BOOK:

D51 O MORRO DOS CINCO DEDOS. SÃO PAULO, INSTITUTO PROGRESSO EDITORIAL, 1949*
Demy 8vo. 301 pp. 8¾ in.
A translation of *A Passage to India*; published as *Coleção oceano*, Vol. 2.

RUSSIAN

BOOKS:

D52 *a.* E. FORSTER | POEZDKA V INDIYU | (ISTORIYAODNO GO PRESTUPLENIYA) | ROMAN | PEREVOD S ANGLIYSKOGO | L. I. NEKRASOVOY | IZDANIE M. I S. SABSHINKOVYKH | 1926
Small crown 8vo. 368 pp. 7⅛ × 5⅜ in.
A translation by L. I. Nekrasov of *A Passage to India*; published in Moscow.

b. POEZDKA V INDIJU. LENINGRAD, GOSLITIZDAT 1937*
[xx],312 pp. illus.
A translation by V. P. Isakov of *A Passage to India*.

D. TRANSLATIONS

SERBO-CROAT

BOOKS:

D53*a*. EDWARD MORGAN FORSTER | KROZ INDIJU | ROMAN U
TRI DIJELA | [*publisher's device*] | [*rule*] | KULTURA · ZAGREB
Large crown 8vo. 308 pp. 7⅝ × 5⅜ in.
A translation by Jakša Sedmak of *A Passage to India*; published
1947.

b. E. M. FORSTER | JEDNO PUTOVANJE U INDIJU | ROMAN |
PROSVETA | IZDAVACHKO PREDUZEĆE SRBIJE | BEOGRAD
1947
Large crown 8vo. 348 pp. 8 × 5⅝ in.
A translation by Mikhailo Djordjevič of *A Passage to India*;
published January 1948.

SLOVENE

BOOKS:

D54*a*. E. M. Forster | CESTA DO INDIE | (A Passage to India) | [*rule*]
| [*publisher's monogram*] | Z anglického originálu preložil
Dr. Ján Mihál
Large crown 8vo. 336 pp. 7⅛ × 5⅜ in.
A translation by Ján Mihál of *A Passage to India*; published by
Matica Slovenska in Turč. Sv. Martin, 1949.

b. EDVARD MORGAN FORSTER | POPOTOVANJE V INDIJO |
ROMAN | CANKARJEVA ZALOŽBA | *Ljubljana* | *1953*
Small crown 8vo. 376 pp. 7 × 4¾ in.
A translation by Janez Gradišnik of *A Passage to India*.

SPANISH

BOOKS:

D55 [*in black*]: E. M. FORSTER | [*in pink:*] EL PASO | A LA INDIA |
[*in black:*] *Traducción de* | J. R. WILCOCK | [*across an arrow in
pink:*] SUR | BUENOS AIRES
Large crown 8vo. 304 pp. 8 × 5¾ in.
A translation by J. R. Wilcock of *A Passage to India*; published
1955.

D56 [*in black:*] E. M. FORSTER | [*in pale golden-brown:*] DONDE
LOS ÁNGELES | NO SE AVENTURAN | [*in black:*] *Traducción de* |
CARLOS PERALTA | [*across an arrow in pale golden-brown:*]
SUR | BUENOS AIRES
Large crown 8vo. 160 pp. 8 × 5¾ in.

D. TRANSLATIONS

A translation by Carlos Peralta of *Where Angels Fear to Tread*; published 1955.

D57   *E. M. Forster* | Aspectos de la Novela | Cuadernos de la Facultad de Filosofía y Letras | Universidad Veracruzana | Xalapa México | 1961
Crown 8vo. 216 pp. 7 × 4¾ in.
A translation by Francisco González Aramburu of *Aspects of the Novel*; published as *Cuadernos de la Facultad de Filosofía y Letras*, Vol. 7.

SWEDISH
BOOKS:

D58   EN FÄRD | TILL INDIEN | AV | *E. M. FORSTER* | MED FÖRETAL AV | *ANDERS ÖSTERLING* | ÖVERSÄTTNING AV | *TORA RAMM-ERICSON* | [*publisher's monogram*] | STOCKHOLM | ALBERT BONNIERS FÖRLAG
Crown 8vo. 376 pp. 7⅝ × 4⅞ in.
A translation by Tora Ramm-Ericson of *A Passage to India*, with a foreword by Anders Österling; published 1925.

D59   CREDO | AV | E. M. FORSTER | FRAN ENGELSKAN AV | SONJA BERGVALL | [*publisher's monogram*] | STOCKHOLM | ALBERT BONNIERS FÖRLAG
Crown 8vo. 128 pp. 7¾ × 5 in.
A translation by Sonja Bergvall of 'Two Cheers for Democracy'; published 1939.

D60   DÄR ÄNGLAR VÄGRA GÅ | *E. M. Forster* | [*illustration*] | ENGELSKA KLASSIKER | TIDENS FÖRLAG STOCKHOLM
Small crown 8vo. 180 pp. 7 × 4½ in.
A translation by Karin Alin of *Where Angels Fear to Tread*; published 1956.

TURKISH
BOOK:

D61   HINDISTANDA BIR GEÇIT. ROMAN. İSTANBUL, VARLIK YAYINEVI, 1961*
Royal 16mo. 272 pp. 6½ × 4¾ in.
A translation by Filiz Karabey of *A Passage to India*; published as *Varlik Yayinlari*, Vol. 822.

D. TRANSLATIONS

ADDENDA

E. SYLLABUSES—INTERVIEWS—PLAYS

SYLLABUSES

E. M. Forster was responsible for these syllabuses

a. [*title on upper wrapper:*] [*in black letter:*] Cambridge University Local Lectures. | [*rule*] | SYLLABUS | OF | A SHORT COURSE OF SIX LECTURES | ON | THE REPUBLIC OF FLORENCE | BY | E. M. FORSTER, B.A. | KING'S COLLEGE, CAMBRIDGE. | [*device of the arms of the University of Cambridge*] | [*in black letter:*] Cambridge: | PRINTED AT THE UNIVERSITY PRESS. | 1903 | (150.9.03)
Crown 8vo. 12 pp. $7\frac{1}{4} \times 5$ in.

b. [*title on upper wrapper:*] UNIVERSITY OF LONDON. | (University Extension Lectures.) | [*device of the arms of the University of London*] | [*double rule*] | SYLLABUS | OF A | COURSE OF TEN LECTURES | ON THE | REPUBLIC OF FLORENCE. | BY | E. M. FORSTER, B.A., | *King's College, Cambridge.* | [*double rule*] | [*in black letter:*] London: | PRINTED BY HAMPTON & CO., 12–13, CURSITOR STREET, E.C. | 1907. | [*short rule*] | *Published Price, Sixpence.*
Crown 8vo. 20 pp. $7\frac{3}{8} \times 4\frac{7}{8}$ in.
This syllabus is an enlarged and revised version of E1*a.*

c. [*title on upper wrapper:*] UNIVERSITY OF LONDON. | (University Extension Lectures.) | [*double rule*] | SYLLABUS | OF A | COURSE OF TEN LECTURES | ON | THE RENAISSANCE AT ROME | (1350–1550). | BY | E. M. FORSTER, B.A., | *King's College, Cambridge.* | [*double rule*] | [*in black letter:*] London: | PRINTED BY HAMPTON & CO., 12–13, CURSITOR STREET, E.C. | 1909. | [*short rule*] | *Published Price, Sixpence.*
Crown 8vo. 16 pp. $7\frac{3}{8} \times 5$ in.

E2   QUOTED LETTERS IN BOOKS AND PERIODICALS

a. Hart-Davis, Rupert. *Hugh Walpole: A Biography.* London Macmillan, 1952. P. 59.

b. Woolf, Virginia. *A Writer's Diary: Being Extracts from the Diary of Virginia Woolf; edited by Leonard Woolf.* London, Hogarth Press, 1953. Pp. 20, 101, 176, 243 (including quotations from conversations with E. M. Forster).

c. Lehmann, John. *The Whispering Gallery: Autobiography I.* London, [etc.], Longmans, Green, [1955]. P. 243.

d. Spence, Jonathan. 'E.M. Forster at Eighty.' *New Republic*, 5 October 1959, pp. 17–18, 21 (including quotations from conversations with E. M. Forster).

e. Lehmann, John. *I Am my Brother: Autobiography II.* [London, etc.], Longmans, [Green, 1960]. Pp. 101–102 (*see also* pp. 179–180).

f. Woolf, Leonard. *Sowing: An Autobiography of the Years 1880–1904.* London, Hogarth Press, 1960. P. 172.

g. Heilbrun, Carolyn G. *The Garnett Family.* London, George Allen & Unwin, [1961]. Pp. 139–140, 186 (to Edward Garnett).

h. Häusermann, H. W. 'Begegnung mit E. M. Forster.' *Neue Zürcher Zeitung*, 2 Dezember 1961, Blatt 19 (extracts from letters to W. J. Turner).

i. Crews, Frederick C. *E. M. Forster: The Perils of Humanism.* Princeton, N.J., Princeton University Press, 1962. P. 23, footnote.

j. Lawrence, T. E. *Letters to T. E. Lawrence; edited by A. W. Lawrence.* London, Jonathan Cape, [1962]. Pp. 58–75 (extracts were printed in the *Observer*, 15 July 1962, p. 18 by David Garnett in his review of the book 'Top People's Views of a Hero.' *See also The Letters of T. E. Lawrence; edited by David Garnett.* London, Jonathan Cape, [1938], p. 555.

E3   ENGLISH EDITIONS

a. GUILD BOOKS No. G 16 | [*short rule*] | A ROOM WITH | A VIEW | By | E. M. FORSTER | Guild [*publisher's device*] Books | *Published for* | The British Publishers Guild
Small crown 8vo. 192 pp. $7\frac{3}{8} \times 4\frac{3}{4}$ in.
Printed in Düsseldorf, 1944.

b. GUILD BOOKS | [*rule*] | WHERE ANGELS | FEAR TO TREAD | E. M. FORSTER | [*publisher's device*] | Published for | THE BRITISH PUBLISHERS GUILD | *by Australasian Publishing Co. Pty. Ltd.,* | *55 York St., Sydney.*
Small crown 8vo. [iv], 140 pp. $7\frac{1}{8} \times 4\frac{1}{2}$ in.
Published 1944.

c. GUILD BOOKS No. C 10 | [*swelled rule*] | WHERE ANGELS FEAR | TO TREAD | By | E. M. FORSTER | [*publisher's device*] | *Published for* | THE BRITISH PUBLISHERS GUILD | *by AB Ljus Förlag, Stockholm*
Small crown 8vo. 156 pp. $7\frac{1}{8} \times 4\frac{3}{8}$ in.
Published 1945.

d. [*within a rule, within a frame, within a double rule:*] A PASSAGE | TO INDIA | *by* | E. M. FORSTER | [*wavy rule*] | *published by* | THE ALBATROSS | MCMXLVII
Small crown 8vo. 304 pp. 7¼ × 4½ in.
Published in Verona as the *Modern Continental Library*, Vol. 96.

e. HOWARDS END BY E. M. FORSTER. STOCKHOLM, THE CONTINENTAL BOOK COMPANY AB, 1949*
Small crown 8vo. 330 pp. 7⅜ × 4¾ in.
Published as *Zephyr Books*, Vol. 133.

f. Nan'un-do's Contemporary Library | [*rule*] | E. M. FORSTER | THE CELESTIAL OMNIBUS | AND OTHER STORIES | *Edited with Notes* | *by* | Atsuo Kobayashi | Katsuzō Sakata | [*publisher's device*] | TOKYO | NAN'UN-DO
Crown 8vo. [vi], 92 pp. front. (port.). 7 × 5 in.
Published 1953.
Contents: The Celestial Omnibus—The Other Side of the Hedge—Other Kingdom.

g. SILVA-SCHULAUSGABEN | ENGLISCHE REIHE | Band 14 | [*long rule*] | E. M. FORSTER | SHORT STORIES | [*long rule*] | SILVA-VERLAG ISERLOHN
Foolscap 8vo. 40 pp. 6⅝ × 4¾ in.
Published 1955.
Contents: The Road from Colonus—The Other Side of the Hedge—The Curate's Friend.

h. TWO CHEERS | FOR | DEMOCRACY | BY | E. M. FORSTER | EDITED AND ANNOTATED | BY | KAZUHIKO YONEDA | *Professor of English* | *in Kobe University* | [*rule*] | KINSEIDO LTD | TOKYO
Crown 8vo. viii, 152 pp. 7⅛ × 5 in.
Published 1955.
Contents: Culture and Freedom—Tolerance—The Challenge of our Time—What I Believe—Anonymity: An Enquiry—Art for Art's Sake—The Duty of Society to the Artist—Does Culture Matter?—The Raison d'Être of Criticism in the Arts—A Book that Influenced Me—In my Library.

i. NEUSPRACHLICHE TEXTAUSGABEN | Englische Reihe | [*one line*] | HEFT 53 | [*long rule*] | THREE FANTASIES | by | E. M. FORSTER | Herausgegeben von | Oswald Stein | 1961 | HIRSCH-GRABEN-VERLAG · FRANKFURT AM MAIN | Bestell-Nr. 1673
Small demy 8vo. 64 pp. 8⅜ × 5⅞ in.
Contents: The Celestial Omnibus—Other Kingdom—The Eternal Moment.

E4   EVIDENCE

a. REPORT | FROM THE | SELECT COMMITTEE | ON | OBSCENE
PUBLICATIONS | TOGETHER WITH THE PROCEEDINGS | OF
THE COMMITTEE, MINUTES OF | EVIDENCE AND APPENDICES
| [*rule*] | *Ordered by* The House of Commons *to be Printed* | *20th*
March 1958 | [*rule*] | LONDON | HER MAJESTY'S STATIONERY
OFFICE | PRICE 3*s.* 6*d.* NET | 123–I
Small royal 8vo. xx, 28 pp. 9¾ × 6 in.
Pp. 14–21 evidence by T. S. Eliot and E. M. Forster.

b. THE TRIAL OF | LADY CHATTERLEY | REGINA *v.* PENGUIN
BOOKS LIMITED | *The Transcript of the Trial edited by* | C. H
ROLPH | PENGUIN BOOKS | [*illustration carried over from p.* [*ii*]]
Small crown 8vo. [vi], 250 pp. illus. 7⅛ × 4⅜ in.
Published 1961 as *Penguin Special*, Vol. 192.
Pp. 112–113 evidence by E. M. Forster; a summary of the evidence
was published in *The Times*, 29 October 1960, p. 10.

E5   FILM SCRIPT

A DIARY FOR TIMOTHY MADE IN THE YEARS 1944/45 BY THE
CROWN FILM UNIT AND PRESENTED BY THE MINISTRY OF
INFORMATION. COMMENTARY WRITTEN BY E. M. FORSTER
AND SPOKEN BY MICHAEL REDGRAVE. PRODUCED BY BASIL
WRIGHT. DIRECTED BY HUMPHREY JENNINGS
Length 3100 ft. Certificate "U".
Distributed November 1945 in the United Kingdom by Film
Traders Limited.

E6   GRAMOPHONE RECORD

THE ROAD FROM COLONUS. WHAT I BELIEVE. London, Argo
Ltd, 1959.
12-inch long playing record. RG153. £1 19*s.* 9*d.*
Published 'to coincide with Mr. Forster's eightieth year.'
This reading of 'The Road from Colonus' was broadcast in the
Third Programme on 29 July 1964.

E7   INTERVIEWS

a. THE ART OF FICTION: I, E. M. FORSTER, by P. N. Furbank and
F. J. H. Haskell. *Paris Review*, Spring 1953, Vol. 1, No. 1, pp.
28–41; portrait.

P. [28] facsimile of E. M. Forster's unfinished novel, *Arctic Summer*, p. 1.

b. A VISIT WITH E. M. FORSTER, by William van O'Connor. *Western Review*, Spring 1955, Vol. 19, pp. 215–219.

c. A CONVERSATION WITH E. M. FORSTER, by Angus Wilson. *Encounter*, November 1957, Vol. 9, No. 5, pp. 52–57.

d. E. M. FORSTER AT EIGHTY, by Philip Toynbee. *Observer*, 28 December 1958, pp. 8, 10; portrait.

e. E. M. FORSTER ON HIS LIFE AND HIS BOOKS: AN INTERVIEW RECORDED FOR TELEVISION, by David Jones. *Listener*, 1 January 1959, pp. 11–12; portrait.

f. MR FORSTER AT THE PLAY, by J. W. Lambert. *Sunday Times*, 4 August 1963, p. 20; portrait.

E8   LETTERS TO THE PRESS SIGNED BY
E. M. FORSTER

Apart from his own Letters to the Press, listed in Section C, E. M. Forster signed the following communications to the Press:

a. COUNCIL FOR CIVIL LIBERTIES: APPEAL FOR FUNDS. *Manchester Guardian*, 24 July 1934, p. 18. Signed E. M. Forster (President), Ruth Fry, Hewlett Johnson, Henry W. Nevinson, A. P. Herbert, and Ronald Kidd (Secretary), The Council for Civil Liberties.

b. PROSECUTIONS OF PUBLISHERS. *Spectator*, 26 April 1935, p. 696. Signed E. M. Forster (President), A. P. Herbert, A. A. Milne, J. B. Priestley, and H. G. Wells (Vice-Presidents), The National Council for Civil Liberties.
Reprinted as: The Prosecution of "Boy", *New Statesman and Nation*, N.S., 27 April 1935, p. 583. *Time and Tide*, 27 April 1935, p. 620. Forster made reference to this letter in his evidence before the Select Committee on Obscene Publications, *see* the *Report* (E4*a*), p. 18. Further reference is made in 'Liberty in England'. *See* c286.

c. INTERNING ALIENS. *The Times*, 23 July 1940, p. 5. Signed E. M. Forster, H. H. Gordon Clark, Wilfrid Greene, Newcastle, and Ralph Vaughan Williams.

d. THE NATIONAL COUNCIL FOR CIVIL LIBERTIES. *Time and Tide*, 21 June 1941, p. 520. Signed Henry W. Nevinson (President), Faringdon (Hon. Treasurer), E. M. Forster (ex-President and Vice-President), W. H. Thompson (Chairman of Executive), and

Ronald Kidd (General Secretary), The National Council for Civil Liberties. *See also* editorial comment on pp. 520–521. *See also* C367.

e. THIRD PROGRAMME. *The Times*, 4 October 1957, p. 11. Signed Beveridge, Adrian C. Boult, George Cicestr., E. M. Forster, and others.

f. HUNGARIAN WRITERS ON TRIAL. *The Times*, 29 October 1957, p. 11. Signed Phyllis Bentley, Richard Church, T. S. Eliot, E. M. Forster, and others on behalf of the PEN.

g. B.B.C. PROGRAMMES. *The Times*, 19 February 1958, p. 9. Signed A. J. Ayer, Arthur Bliss, Adrian C. Boult, T. S. Eliot, E. M. Forster, and others.

h. PROCTORS AND "VARSITY". *Cambridge Review*, 16 May 1959, Vol. 80, p. 519. Signed H. B. Barlow, James Cargill Thompson, and others including E. M. Forster. Letter on the suppression of the correspondence on homosexuality in *Varsity*.

i. SOUTH AFRICA'S PLACE: EXCLUSION NEED NOT BE FOR EVER. *The Times*, 13 March 1961, p. 15. Signed Richard Stone, R. B. Braithwaite, J. E. Meade, Alec R. Vidler, W. B. Reddaway, Ruth Cohen, Horace Barlow, J. E. Raven, and E. M. Forster.

j. THE DEATH PENALTY. *The Times*, 2 January 1962, p. 9. Signed Harewood (Chairman of the Committee of Honour), N. G. Annan, Anthony Asquith, and other members of the Committee of Honour of the National Campaign for the Abolition of Capital Punishment, including E. M. Forster.

k. THE DJILAS CASE. *Encounter*, July 1962, Vol. 19, p. 94. Signed Mark Abrams, and others including E. M. Forster. Letter protesting at the re-arrest of Milovan Djilas.

l. BACK INDIA APPEAL. *Spectator*, 30 November 1962, p. 856. Signed E. M. Forster, Olaf Caroe, Barbara Ward, and Guy Wint on behalf of the United India Defence Fund.

m. A COUNCIL'S ACTION. *The Times*, 21 June 1963, p. 13. Signed Barbara Carter, Will Carter, and others including E. M. Forster. Letter on Cambridge's midsummer fair.

E9   PLAYS

a. A ROOM WITH A | VIEW | *A play by* | STEPHEN TAIT | *and* | KENNETH ALLOTT | *adapted from the novel by* | E. M. FORSTER | [*publisher's device*] | LONDON | EDWARD ARNOLD & CO.
Small crown 8vo. [ii], 126 pp. $7\frac{1}{4} \times 4\frac{3}{4}$ in.

Published 19 July 1951.
The play was first performed at the Arts Theatre, Cambridge on 6 February 1950; it was presented on television by Associated-Rediffusion on 2 July 1958.

b. A PASSAGE TO | INDIA | A Play in Three Acts | by | SANTHA RAMA RAU | From the novel | by | E. M. FORSTER | SAMUEL [*publisher's device*] FRENCH | LONDON
Demy 8vo. [vi], 82 pp. 4 plates, 4 illus. $8\frac{5}{8} \times 5\frac{1}{2}$ in.
Published 1960 as *French's Acting Edition*.
The play was first performed at the Playhouse, Oxford on 19 January 1960.

c. A PASSAGE TO | INDIA | *a play by* | SANTHA RAMA RAU | *from the novel by* | E. M. FORSTER | [*publisher's device*] | LONDON | EDWARD ARNOLD
Small crown 8vo. 112 pp. $7\frac{1}{4} \times 4\frac{7}{8}$ in.
Published 27 October 1960.

d. *A Passage to India* | *a play by Santha Rama Rau* | *from the novel by E. M. Forster* | *Harcourt, Brace & World, Inc.* | *New York* | [*illustration*]
Crown 8vo. 112 pp. $7\frac{3}{8} \times 5$ in.
Issued 27 October 1960; a reprint of the second edition. *See* E9c.

E10   UNPUBLISHED BBC BROADCASTS
AND INTERVIEWS

a. 15 February 1929   The Great Frost. 12-minute talk.

b. 20 February 1932   On the 9.20. Discussion between E. M. Forster and Police Constable R. J. Buckingham in the series 'Conversations in the Train'. 21-minute discussion.

c. 24 September 1937   Talk for Sixth Forms, 1: Introductory Talk. School Broadcast. 20-minute talk.

d. 3 July 1942   Books and the Writer: Review of Some Outstanding Books Published during the Second Quarter of 1942. 15-minute talk.

e. 16 November 1944   Text and Context: E. M. Forster on Matthew Arnold. Speakers: E. M. Forster, Gerald Cooper, and Gladys Young. 15-minute discussion.

f. 11 March 1949   I Speak for Myself. Originally broadcast as an introduction to a series of autobiographical talks in the Far Eastern Service. Third Programme. 15-minute talk.

g. 19 February 1959   First Meeting: Sir John Wolfenden, Vice-Chancellor of Reading University meets the Writer, E. M. Forster. General Overseas Service. 15-minute interview.

h. 12 November 1960   Billy Budd. Discussion between Benjamin Britten, E. M. Forster, and Eric Crozier on 'how they made an opera from Melville's story'. Third Programme. 40-minute discussion. *See also* A29.

E. M. Forster also broadcast at regular intervals from 1941 to 1945 in the Far Eastern Service. Most of the broadcasts, over 70, were entitled 'Some Books' and surveyed new books; 23 were published in whole or in part.

E11   BOOK ANNOUNCED BUT
                  NOT PUBLISHED

ESSAYS & POEMS, by Peter Burra with an introduction by E. M. Forster. Announced in a prospectus circulated on 24 July 1939 by Oxford University Press 'who will issue the volume privately to subscribers at the price of 10*s.* 6*d.*'

INDEX

Books reviewed by E. M. Forster have been included under the author of the work in addition to the title of the review.

INDEX

INDEX

Culture and Freedom, *see* Two Cultures: The Quick and the Dead

Curate's Friend, The, A5, 26; C26; E3*g*

D.O.R.A., C254

Dabiddosha, Tokyo, publisher, D47*a*

Daily Herald, The, London, C88, 90–91, 103, 110, 115, 119, 127, 137–138, 142, 145–147, 298

Daily News, The, London, *see* Daily News and Leader, The, London

Daily News and Leader, The, London, C49–50, 52–55, 78, 80, 82, 84–85, 89, 94–96, 104, 108, 111, 117, 120, 125, 129–130, 143, 165, 174

Daily Telegraph and Morning Post, The, London, C346

Dante, C28

Dār al- Fikr al- 'Arabī, Cairo, publisher, D3

Dār al- Karnak lil- Nashr wal-Ṭab' wal-Tawzi', Cairo, publisher, D2

Darling, Sir Malcolm, A31*a*

Daughter Dear, C462

Day Off, A, C16

De Senectute, C477

Death of a Poet: Birth of a Critic, C227

Death Penalty, The, E8*j*

Dedlock Papers, The, C156

Definition of Tolerance, A, *see* Toward a Definition of Tolerance

Den, The, p. 12; A9; C64

Dent, Prof. Edward, C475

Dent, J. M., & Co., publisher, A10*d*; B1*a, c,* 11

Desani, G. V., *Hali*, B23

Descent to the Plains, C502

DESMOND MACCARTHY, A30

DEVELOPMENT OF ENGLISH PROSE, THE, A25, 28; D19, 21

Dey, S. M. C., *My Pilgrimages to Ajanta and Bagh*, review, C187

Dial, The, Scranton, Pennsylvania, C180

Diana's Dilemma, C58

Diary for Timothy, A, E5

Dickinson, Goldsworthy Lowes, A16; B21, 32; C248–249, 255, 258, 465

—— The Greek View of Life, B32

—— Letters from John Chinaman, B21

—— The Magic Flute, review, C165

—— Points of View, review, C218

Djilas Case, The, E8*k*

Djordjević, Mikhailo, trans., D53*b*

Dodwell, H., editor, *The Diary of Ananda Ranga Pillai*, review, C159

Does Culture Matter?, A28; C287, 355; E3*h*

Doll Souse, The, *see* Bad Fairies, The

Dorking and Leith Hill District Preservation Society, A19

Dostoevsky, F., *An Honest Thief and Other Stories*, review, C117

Doubleday & Co., Inc., publisher, A8*c*; B10*b*, 34*b*

Doughty, C. M., *Mansoul*, review, C130

Douglas, Norman, *Looking Back: An Autobiographical Excursion*, review, C266

Downing, Clement, *A History of the Indian Wars*, review, C182

Dual Control, C85

Ducal Reminiscences, *later* A Duke Remembers, A28; C308

Duhamel, Georges, *Civilisation*, review, C127

Duke Remembers, A, *see* Ducal Reminiscences

Dull Opiate, C471

Dust Jackets, C138

Duty of an Editor, The, C320

Duty of Society to the Artist, The, A28; C374; E3*h*

E. K. BENNETT, A36

E. M. Forster Points Out—Vice Versa, C514

Early Novels of Virginia Woolf, The, *see* Novels of Virginia Woolf, The

East and West, C445

Eccentric Englishwomen, C302

Ede, H. S., *A Life of Gaudier-Brzeska*, review, C223

Edinburgh Festival, The, C400

Edward VII, C185

EDWARD CARPENTER, B5

Edy-Legrand, E. L. L., *Macao et Cosmage*, review, C128

Efficiency and Liberty—Great Britain, C312

EGYPT, A7

Egyptian Labour Corps, The, C118

Egyptian Mail, The, Cairo, pp. 11–12; C58–76

Eight Snakes, C88

Eighteenth-Century Sailor, An, C182

Eihôsha, Tokyo, publisher, D48*b*

Einaudi, Turin, publisher, D40*b*

Einsiedel, Wolfgang von, trans., D23*b*, 29

Eklogē, Athens, D36–37

Elder Tagore, The, C49

Elgood, P. G., *Bonaparte's Adventure in Egypt*, review, C235

INDEX

Ganguli, T. N., *Svarnalata*, review, C50

Garnett, David, *No Love*, review, C213

Garnett, Edward, *The Trial of Jeanne d'Arc and Other Plays*, review, C232

Gaskell, Mrs., The Charm and Strength of, C473

Gathorne-Hardy, Robert, A30

Gatliff, The Rev. James, *Stations, Gentlemen: The Autobiography of James Gatliff*, review, C313

Gauguin, Paul, *Lettres . . . à G. -D. de Monfreid*, review, C98

Gaz. -Zurn. Izd., Tallinn, publisher, D9

Gemistus Pletho, A18; C22; D38

General Knowledge, C311

George, André, *Paris*, review, C480

George, Stefan, C382

Ghosts Ancient and Modern, C231

Gibbon, Edward, A18, 28; C225, 376

Gide, André, A28; C423

—— *Back from the U.S.S.R.*, review, C301

—— *Prometheus Ill-bound*, review, C96

Gide and George, *see* Humanist and Authoritarian

Gippo English, C63

Gishford, Anthony, editor, *Tribute to Benjamin Britten*, B40

Givry, Grillot de, *Witchcraft, Magic and Alchemy*, review, C231

Glasgow University Publications, A25

Glyn, Elinor, *The Price of Things*, review, C88

God Abandons Antony, The, A9; C83

Gods of India, The, C43

Goetz, Hermann, *The Art and Architecture of Bikaner State*, C416

Going into Europe, C508

Golden Hynde, The, London, C37

Golden Library, B7a

Golden Peak, The, C140

Golding, William, *Lord of the Flies*, B38

GOLDSWORTHY LOWES DICKINSON, A16

Gollancz, Victor, Ltd, publisher, B33

Good Society, C273

Goslitizdat,Leningrad, publisher, D52b

Gow, A. S. F., *A. E. Housman*, review, C293

Gradišnik, Janez, trans., D54b

Granta, Cambridge, B29; C34

GRANTA AND THE PROCTORS, B29

Great Anglo-Indian, A, C52

Great Frost, The, E10a

Great History, A, C148

Great Humanist, A, C465

Great Indian Poet-Philosopher, A, *later* Mohammed Iqbal, A28; C396

GREEK VIEW OF LIFE, THE, B32

Green Pastures and Piccadilly, C109

Greene, Graham, editor, *The Old School*, review, C276

Grey of Fallodon, Viscount, *Recreation*, review, C149

Griffin, The, New York, C422

Grigson, Geoffrey, compiler, *Poetry of the Present*, review, C411

Grip, C112

Grosset & Dunlap, publisher, A10b

Grundy at the Parkers', Mrs., A18; C252

Guardian, The, Manchester, *see Manchester Guardian, The*

Guidi, Augusto, trans., D40a

Guild Books, A3f; E3a–c

Gyldendal Forlag, Copenhagen, publisher, D6

Gyldendal Norsk Forlag, Oslo, publisher, D49

Hackney Marshes, C290

Haddakin, Lillian, *The Poetry of Crabbe*, review, C457

Haeusermann, H. W., 'Begegnung mit E. M. Forster', E2h

Hakluyt's Voyages, review, C204

HALI, B23

Halifax's Broadcast, Lord, C352

Hall, H. Fielding, *Love's Legend*, review, C48

Hall, Radclyffe, *The Well of Loneliness*, C208–209

Hall School, Weybridge, C102, 161

Hamilton, Clayton, *Materials and Methods of Fiction*, C82

Handel in Egypt, C65

Hansen, Aase, trans., D6

Happiness!, *see* Expérience du Bonheur, L'

Happy Ending, *later* Ferney, A28; C358

Harbrace Modern Classics, A10b, 12b

Harcourt, Brace & Co., publisher, A10b, 12b, d, 13b, 14b, 16b, 18b, 24b, 28b, 31b, 33, 34b; B3b, 4b, 12b; E9d

Harper's Magazine, New York, C399, 413, 507

Harris, Frank, *Oscar Wilde*, review, C317

INDEX

INDEX

Tragic Interior, A, C7, 11
Transatlantic Book Service Ltd, A8c
Travellers' Library, B4c
Trees—and Peace, C315
Trevelyan, G. M., *A Layman's Love of Letters*, review, C444
Trevelyan, R. C., *The Bride of Dionysus*, review, C243
Tribune, London, C387
TRIBUTE TO BENJAMIN BRITTEN, B40
Trigger, The, *later*, Gerald Heard, A28; C337
Trooper Silas Tomkyn Comberbacke, *see* Incongruities: 'Comberbacke'
Trotsky, Leon, *History of the Russian Revolution*, review, C261
Trouble in Egypt, The, C79
Troublesome Molluscs, *see* Incongruities: Voltaire's Slugs
True Joan of Arc: Shaw's or France's?, The, C186
Tukoji Rao Puar III, His Highness Sir, A10d, 31; C309
Turner, W. J., E2h
Twentieth Century, The, London, *see Nineteenth Century and After, The*, London
XXth Century Alexandria, C62
TWENTY YEARS A-GROWING, B7
Two Books by Tagore, A18; C44, 105
TWO CHEERS FOR DEMOCRACY, A28
Two Cheers for Democracy, *later* Credo, *later* What I Believe, A20, 28; C316; D22, 59; E3h
Two Cultures: The Quick and the Dead, *later* Three anti-Nazi Broadcasts, 1: Culture and Freedom, A28; C353; E3h
Two Egypts, C92
TWO STORIES AND A MEMORY, B39
Tyndale-Biscoe, C. E., *Character Building in Kashmir*, review, C155

Umbrella, Coventry, C489
Unbuilt City, The, *later* The Enchafèd Flood, A28; C424
Uncle and Niece, C491
Unger, Alfred H., trans., D30
United India Defence Fund, E8*l*
United States, The, *see* Impressions of the United States
University and the Universe, The, C264
University Humanist Federation Bulletin, Cambridge, C510
University of Michigan Press, B32b
University Paperbacks, B32c

Unsung Virtue of Tolerance, The, *later* Tolerance, A28; C369
Untidy Gentleman, The, C160
UNTOUCHABLE, B8
Urdu, The, Aurangabad, Deccan, C306

Valassopoulo, G., C83, 86
Varlik Yayinevi, Istanbul, publisher, D61
Varsity, Cambridge, E8h
Veracruzana, Universidad, Facultad de Filosofía y Letras, D57
Vice Prosecutions, C481
Victorian Writers, C164
View Without a Room, A, C488
Vigilantes, The, C393
Viking Press, The, publisher, B7b
Villard, Léonie, *Jane Austen*, review, C178
Vintage Books, A1e, 2g, 3j, 4i
Virgil, *The Aeneid*, B1
Virgil and Tommy, C201
VIRGINIA WOOLF, A24
Virginia Woolf's "Enlightened Greediness", A24a
Visions, C104
Visit to America, A, C447
Vital Speeches of the Day, New York, C353, 369
Voltaire, A28; C226, 228, 358, 491–492
—— *The Love Letters . . . to his Niece*, review, C491
Voltaire and Frederick the Great, *see* 'But . . .'
Voltaire's Laboratory, *see* Incongruities: Weighing Fire
Voter's Dilemma, A, A18; C177
Voyage of Discovery, C430

W. P. Ker Memorial Lecture, A25
Wadia, A. S., *Reflections on the Problems of India*, review, C39
Waley, Arthur, *Japanese Poetry*, review, C129
—— *More Translations from the Chinese*, review, C129
Walpole, Hugh, E2a
Walsh, J. H., *A Manual of Domestic Economy*, review, C32
Walsh's Secret History of the Victorian Movement, Mr., C32
Walton, John, *Green Pastures*, dramatic review, C109
Ward, R. H., *A Drug-taker's Notes*, review, C471
WARM COUNTRY, THE, B37